WESTERN NORTH AMERICA

ALL ABOUT
BACKYARD
BIRDS

Cornell Lab of Ornithology

Illustrations by **Pedro Fernandes**

PRINCETON

WESTERN NORTH AMERICA

ALL ABOUT
BACKYARD
BIRDS

The**Cornell**Lab of Ornithology

Red-shouldered Hawk
Photo by Bruce Parsons

Editors: Hugh Powell, Brian Scott Sockin, and Laura Erickson
Designer: Patricia Mitter
Assistant editors: Kathi Borgmann, Diane Tessaglia-Hymes,
and Francesca Chu
Illustrator: Pedro Fernandes
Cover photo: Western Bluebird and Black-headed Grosbeak
by Ken Phenicie, Jr.; Northern Flicker by Stephen Parsons;
Woodhouse's Scrub-Jay by Laura Hughes/Macaulay Library.

ISBN: 978-1-943645-06-0

Printed in China

Library of Congress Cataloging-in-Publication Data
available.

10 9 8 7 6 5 4 3 2

PRINCETON
press.princeton.edu

FSC MARK FPO

By buying products with the FSC label you are
supporting the growth of responsible forest
management worldwide.

CONTENTS

Introduction   8

How to Use This Book
Getting Started   12
Bird QR   14

Birding 101
Bird Identification   16
Use Merlin® App to See the Possibilities   30
The Right Stuff   31
Listening to Birds   34
Photographing Birds   36

Attracting Birds to Your Backyard
Birdscaping   42
Bird Feeders   44
Bird Food   47
Water Sources   51
Nest Boxes   52

Getting Involved
Citizen Science   56
eBird   57
Great Backyard Bird Count   59
Project FeederWatch   61
NestWatch   63
Celebrate Urban Birds   64
Habitat Network   65

Guide to Western Species
Canada Goose   68   Geese • Ducks
Wood Duck   69
Mallard   70
California Quail   71   Grouse • Quail
Gambel's Quail   72
Ring-necked Pheasant   73
Wild Turkey   74
Pied-billed Grebe   75   Grebes
Double-crested Cormorant   76   Cormorants
Great Blue Heron   77   Herons
Great Egret   78
Turkey Vulture   79   Vultures
Northern Harrier   80   Ospreys • Eagles • Hawks
Sharp-shinned Hawk   81
Cooper's Hawk   82
Red-shouldered Hawk   83
Red-tailed Hawk   84
American Coot   85   Coots
Killdeer   86   Plovers
Ring-billed Gull   87   Gulls
California Gull   88
Rock Pigeon   89   Pigeons • Doves
Band-tailed Pigeon   90
Eurasian Collared-Dove   91
White-winged Dove   92
Mourning Dove   93

CONTENTS

Great Horned Owl	94	Owls
Common Nighthawk	95	Nightjars
Black-chinned Hummingbird	96	Hummingbirds
Anna's Hummingbird	97	
Broad-tailed Hummingbird	98	
Rufous Hummingbird	99	
Belted Kingfisher	100	Kingfishers
Acorn Woodpecker	101	Woodpeckers
Red-naped Sapsucker	102	
Nuttall's Woodpecker	103	
Downy Woodpecker	104	
Hairy Woodpecker	105	
Northern Flicker	106	
American Kestrel	107	Falcons
Western Wood-Pewee	108	Tyrant Flycatchers
Black Phoebe	109	
Say's Phoebe	110	
Ash-throated Flycatcher	111	
Western Kingbird	112	
Gray Jay	113	Jays • Crows
Steller's Jay	114	
Woodhouse's Scrub-Jay	115	
Black-billed Magpie	116	
American Crow	117	
Common Raven	118	
Horned Lark	119	Larks
Tree Swallow	120	Swallows
Violet-green Swallow	121	
Cliff Swallow	122	
Barn Swallow	123	
Black-capped Chickadee	124	Chickadees • Titmice
Mountain Chickadee	125	
Chestnut-backed Chickadee	126	
Oak Titmouse	127	
Bushtit	128	Bushtits
Red-breasted Nuthatch	129	Nuthatches
White-breasted Nuthatch	130	
Pygmy Nuthatch	131	
Brown Creeper	132	Creepers
House Wren	133	Wrens
Pacific Wren	134	
Bewick's Wren	135	
Cactus Wren	136	
Ruby-crowned Kinglet	137	Kinglets
Wrentit	138	Wrentits
Western Bluebird	139	Thrushes
Mountain Bluebird	140	
Townsend's Solitaire	141	
Hermit Thrush	142	
American Robin	143	
Varied Thrush	144	
Northern Mockingbird	145	Mockingbirds
European Starling	146	Starlings

Belted
Kingfisher

Cedar Waxwing 147 Waxwings
Orange-crowned Warbler 148 Wood-Warblers
Common Yellowthroat 149
Yellow Warbler 150
Yellow-rumped Warbler 151
Townsend's Warbler 152
Wilson's Warbler 153
Spotted Towhee 154 Towhees • Sparrows
Canyon Towhee 155
California Towhee 156
Chipping Sparrow 157
Savannah Sparrow 158
Fox Sparrow 159
Song Sparrow 160
Lincoln's Sparrow 161
Harris's Sparrow 162
White-crowned Sparrow 163
Golden-crowned Sparrow 164
Dark-eyed Junco 165
Western Tanager 166 Cardinals • Grosbeaks • Buntings
Northern Cardinal 167
Black-headed Grosbeak 168
Blue Grosbeak 169
Lazuli Bunting 170
Red-winged Blackbird 171 Blackbirds • Grackles • Orioles
Western Meadowlark 172
Yellow-headed Blackbird 173
Brewer's Blackbird 174
Common Grackle 175
Great-tailed Grackle 176
Brown-headed Cowbird 177
Hooded Oriole 178
Bullock's Oriole 179
House Finch 180 Finches
Purple Finch 181
Cassin's Finch 182
Pine Siskin 183
Lesser Goldfinch 184
American Goldfinch 185
Evening Grosbeak 186
House Sparrow 187 Old World Sparrows

About the Cornell Lab 188
The All About Backyard Birds Team 189
Acknowledgments 191
Photo Credits 192
More to Explore 194
Index 195

Common Grackle

Of all this planet's living creatures, birds are the ones that draw our attention most insistently, year-round, with vivid plumage and myriad sounds. Their flight stirs our imagination; their song inspires our music. Birds are depicted on national emblems, postage stamps, and coins. In our imaginings, Pegasus and angels bear the feathered wings of birds.

Of all wildlife, birds are the most easily seen and heard, in wilderness, on farms, and in the heart of large cities. Birds are accessible everywhere and to almost everyone, a portal to the natural world. When we start paying attention, look and listen, we develop a familiarity with nature that enriches our time outdoors, whether in wild spaces or urban and suburban settings. Think of your home as your own personal "great outdoors" and start exploring the rich tapestry of visual and auditory wonder that surrounds you every day.

Of the roughly 10,000 bird species worldwide, some are iconic and easily recognizable, such as the Bald Eagle, the national symbol of the United States. Other species have inspired names of sports teams, such as the Northern Cardinal, the Common Raven, the Blue Jay, and the Baltimore Oriole. But many birds that surround us are less familiar, their songs woven into the background soundtrack of our everyday lives and the movies and TV shows we watch.

But how exactly do you go about identifying an unfamiliar wild creature likely to fly away before you can figure out what it is? When you notice any bird, pay attention to its size and shape, color pattern, behavior, and the habitat where you saw it. If you have a camera, take pictures, but make sure you're also noticing these features on the living, breathing bird. When you encounter a bird you already know, keep watching to improve your familiarity (e.g., many more people recognize robins hopping on lawns than flying overhead).

Great Blue Heron

All About Backyard Birds is based on the #1 birding website, *AllAboutBirds.org* from the Cornell Lab, used by more than 14 million people each year. In this book, you will find a treasure trove of information, best practices, and advice about backyard birding, whether you're just starting out or are a seasoned birder. You will also discover information about the Cornell Lab's vast online resources and learn about our free **Merlin®** Bird ID app, downloaded by more than one million people.

We've also included a special section about the Cornell Lab's "citizen science" projects—scientific studies driven by contributions from bird watchers just like you—including the Cornell Lab's Project FeederWatch, NestWatch, and Great Backyard Bird Count. Our largest citizen-science initiative is called **eBird**, which provides a free portal for you to create and keep your own bird lists. eBird is the preeminent bird recording tool, with which citizen scientists record more than 100 million bird sightings each year. These projects empower you to participate and contribute to important science while having fun.

Following these primers are pages for each of our 120 common western North American backyard birds, replete with gorgeous illustrations created for this book by science illustrator Pedro Fernandes.

All About Backyard Birds is the first Cornell Lab Publishing Group book to use our dedicated book companion app, **Bird QR**, which you can tap to scan symbols on each bird page to hear the sounds and calls of that species. You can also use Bird QR with other symbols throughout the book to directly link your smartphone browser to deeper content to learn more on *AllAboutBirds.org*, giving you an optional multimedia experience when you use this guide.

So, let's get started and have fun!

Brian Scott Sockin
CEO/Publisher
Cornell Lab Publishing Group

HOW TO USE THIS BOOK

GETTING STARTED

All About Backyard Birds is an interactive field guide for new and developing birders, based on *allaboutbirds.org*, the #1 North American birding website from the Cornell Lab of Ornithology. The content you will find in this book was curated by some of the world's leading bird experts and is presented in a friendly, easy-to-understand manner, just like the All About Birds website.

The **first** section of this book is presented as "Birding 101," a primer for beginning and novice birders, but also a refresher for more advanced birders. You will learn how to identify birds with best practices, how to find, watch, and listen to birds, how to choose equipment, and how to take photos of birds (including how to "digiscope" with your smartphone).

The **second** section, "Attracting Birds to Your Backyard," shares some of our best advice and tools to help you "birdscape" or create bird-friendly habitat outside your home. We begin with the three essential elements that all birds need to thrive—food, water, and shelter—followed by descriptions of different types of bird feeders and information on bird food options and what to look for when buying or building nest boxes. We also equip you with the things you need to know to attract the birds you want to see at home, and how you can protect and keep them safe while enjoying them.

The **third** section, "Getting Involved," shares information about citizen science and how you can participate and contribute to important scientific studies at the Cornell Lab.

The **fourth** section is the bird field guide, covering 120 species of common backyard birds in western North America. Each species page features easy-to-use sections with graphics, cool facts, backyard tips, and more. The diagram on the following page will show you how to navigate the species field guide pages, including where you will use the **Bird QR** app to listen to bird sounds with your smartphone or tablet (you can also use Bird QR on other pages to connect you with content from All About Birds).

Instructions on how to download Bird QR free from Apple and Android stores can be found on page 14.

Group

Common and scientific names

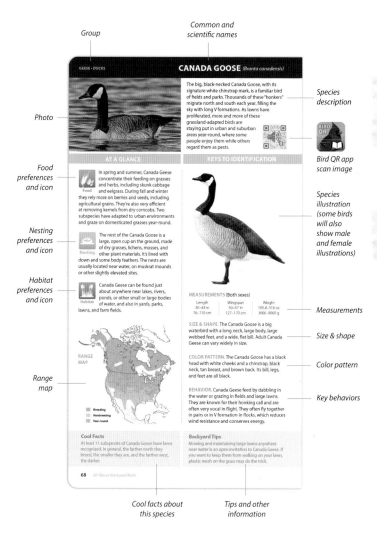

CANADA GOOSE *(Branta canadensis)*

Photo

The big, black-necked Canada Goose, with its signature white chinstrap mark, is a familiar bird of fields and parks. Thousands of these "honkers" migrate north and south each year, filling the sky with long V formations. As lawns have proliferated, more and more of these grassland-adapted birds are staying put in urban and suburban areas year-round, where some people enjoy them while others regard them as pests.

Species description

Bird QR app scan image

AT A GLANCE

Food preferences and icon

Food
In spring and summer, Canada Geese concentrate their feeding on grasses and herbs, including skunk cabbage and eelgrass. During fall and winter they rely more on berries and seeds, including agricultural grains. They're also very efficient at removing kernels from dry corncobs. Two subspecies have adapted to urban environments and graze on domesticated grasses year-round.

Nesting preferences and icon

Nesting
The nest of the Canada Goose is a large, open cup on the ground, made of dry grasses, lichens, mosses, and other plant materials. It's lined with down and some body feathers. The nests are usually located near water, on muskrat mounds or other slightly elevated sites.

Habitat preferences and icon

Habitat
Canada Geese can be found just about anywhere near lakes, rivers, ponds, or other small or large bodies of water, and also in yards, parks, lawns, and farm fields.

Range map

RANGE MAP

Breeding
Nonbreeding
Year-round

KEYS TO IDENTIFICATION

Species illustration (some birds will also show male and female illustrations)

MEASUREMENTS (Both sexes)

Length	Wingspan	Weight
30–43 in	50–67 in	105.8–318 oz
76–110 cm	127–170 cm	3000–9000 g

Measurements

SIZE & SHAPE. The Canada Goose is a big waterbird with a long neck, large body, large webbed feet, and a wide, flat bill. Adult Canada Geese can vary widely in size.

Size & shape

COLOR PATTERN. The Canada Goose has a black head with white cheeks and a chinstrap, black neck, tan breast, and brown back. Its bill, legs, and feet are all black.

Color pattern

BEHAVIOR. Canada Geese feed by dabbling in the water or grazing in fields and large lawns. They are known for their honking call and are often very vocal in flight. They often fly together in pairs or in V formation in flocks, which reduces wind resistance and conserves energy.

Key behaviors

Cool Facts
At least 11 subspecies of Canada Goose have been recognized. In general, the farther north they breed, the smaller they are, and the farther west, the darker.

Cool facts about this species

Backyard Tips
Mowing and maintaining large lawns anywhere near water is an open invitation to Canada Geese. If you want to keep them from walking on your lawn, plastic mesh on the grass may do the trick.

Tips and other information

BIRD QR

BIRD QR is a dedicated book companion app that helps to bring *All About Backyard Birds* to life, created especially for this and other books from the Cornell Lab Publishing Group.

Visit the Apple or Android store to search "Bird QR" and download the app for free. Once downloaded, open the app and touch "Tap To Start," which will bring you to the main menu screen (shown bottom right). From there, you can start scanning symbols in the book by touching the "Scan Book QR Now" button or navigate to another page.

All About Backyard Birds features two kinds of color-coded scannable symbols for use with Bird QR:

 Listen to Bird Sounds. Each bird species page in this book has this symbol to listen to bird sounds on that page with Bird QR. Simply scan the symbol and choose the sounds you want to hear. They are also stored in "Scan History" for you to quickly pull up later on your smartphone.

 Open Website URL. When you see this symbol on a page in this book and scan with Bird QR, it will open your browser and take you to a specific URL page to learn more.

In Bird QR, you can also learn how to get the free Merlin® Bird ID app from the Cornell Lab, new Cornell Lab Publishing Group books that also work with Bird QR, and resources available from the Cornell Lab's All About Birds website (*AllAboutBirds.org*), from which this book was created.

 Look for new capabilities and functions of the Bird QR app such as video streaming in future updates.

BIRDING
101

BIRD IDENTIFICATION

**KEYS TO BIRD
IDENTIFICATION:**
To identify an unfamiliar
bird, focus first on four
keys to identification.

With more than 800 species of
birds in the U.S. and Canada,
it's easy for a beginning bird
watcher to feel overwhelmed
by possibilities. Field guides
often look crammed with
similar birds arranged in
seemingly haphazard order.
We can help you figure out
where to begin.

Western Bluebird

First we share where *not* to start. Many ID tips focus on very
specific details of plumage called field marks, such as the eyering
of a Ruby-crowned Kinglet, or the double breast band of a
Killdeer. While these tips are useful, they assume you've already
narrowed down your search to just a few similar species.

Instead, start by learning how to recognize the group a mystery
bird belongs to. You may still need to look at field marks to clinch
some IDs. But these four keys—**Size and Shape, Color Pattern,
Behavior,** and **Habitat**—will quickly get you to the right group of
species, so you'll know exactly which field marks to look for.

1 SIZE AND SHAPE

*Birds are built for what they do. Every part of the bird you're
looking at is a clue to what it is.*

The combination of size and shape is one of the most powerful
tools to identification. Though you may be drawn to watching
birds because of their wonderful colors or fascinating behavior,
when it comes to making identifications, size and shape are the
first pieces of information you should examine.

With just a little practice and observation, you'll find that
differences in size and shape will jump out at you. The first steps

are to learn typical bird silhouettes, find reliable ways to gauge the size of a bird, and notice differences in telltale parts of a bird such as the bill, wings, and tail.

Soon, you'll know the difference between Red-winged Blackbirds and European Starlings while they're still in flight, and be able to identify a Red-tailed Hawk or Turkey Vulture without taking your eyes off the road.

Become Familiar with Silhouettes

Often you don't need to see any color at all to know what kind of bird you're looking at.

Silhouettes quickly tell you a bird's size, proportions, and posture, and quickly rule out many groups of birds—even ones of nearly identical overall size.

HOUSE FINCH.
A small-bodied finch with a fairly large beak and somewhat long, flat head. The House Finch has a relatively shallow notch in its tail.

Beginning bird watchers often get sidetracked by a bird's bright colors, only to be frustrated when they search through their field guides. Finches, for example, can be red, yellow, blue, brown, or green, but they're still always shaped like finches. Learn silhouettes, and you'll always be close to an ID.

Judge Size Against Birds You Know Well

Size is trickier to judge than shape.

You never know how far away a bird is or how big that nearby rock or tree limb really is. Throw in fluffed-up or hunkered-down birds and it's easy to get fooled. But with a few tricks, you can still use size as an ID key.

Sometimes you need two reference birds for comparison. A crow is bigger than a robin but smaller than a goose.

Compare your mystery bird to a bird you know well. It helps just to know that your bird is larger or smaller than a sparrow, a robin, a crow, or a goose, and it may help you choose between two similar species, such as Downy and Hairy woodpeckers or Sharp-shinned and Cooper's hawks.

Judge Against Birds in the Same Field of View

Your estimate of size gets much more accurate if you can compare one bird directly against another.

When you find groups of different species, you can use the ones you recognize to sort out the ones you don't.

Use size and shape to find the full range of species hiding in a large flock. Amid these orange-billed Royal Terns are some smaller Sandwich Terns. You'll also notice a giant Herring Gull in the background, as well as several smaller Laughing Gulls to its right.

For instance, if you're looking at a gull you don't recognize, you can start by noticing that it's larger than a more familiar bird, such as a Ring-billed Gull, that's standing right next to it. For some groups of birds, including shorebirds, seabirds, and waterfowl, using a known bird as a ruler is a crucial identification technique.

Apply Your Size & Shape Skills to the Parts of a Bird

After you've taken note of a bird's overall size and shape, there's still plenty of room to hone your identification.

Turn your attention to the size and shape of individual body parts. Here you'll find clues to how the bird lives its life: what it eats, how it flies, and where it lives.

Start with the bill—that all-purpose tool that functions as a bird's hands, pliers, knitting needles, knife-and-fork, and bullhorn. A flycatcher's broad, flat, bug-snatching bill looks very different from the thick, conical nut-smasher of a finch. Notice the slightly downcurved bills of the Northern Flickers in your backyard. That's an unusual shape for a woodpecker's bill, but perfect for a bird that digs into the ground after ants, as flickers often do.

Bills are an invaluable clue to identification, but tail shape and wing shape are important, too. Even subtle differences in head shape, neck length, and body shape can all yield useful insights if you study them carefully.

Noticing details like these can help you avoid classic identification mistakes. For example, the Ovenbird is a common eastern warbler that has tricked many a bird watcher into thinking it's a thrush. The field marks are certainly thrushlike—warm brown above, strongly streaked below, even a crisp white eyering. But look at overall shape and size rather than field marks, and you'll see the body plan of a warbler—plump, compact body, short tail and wings, thin, pointed, insect-grabbing bill.

Measure the Bird Against Itself

This is the most powerful way to use a bird's size for identification.

It's hard to judge a lone bird's size, and an unusual posture can make shape hard to interpret. But you can always measure key body parts (e.g., wings, bill, tail, legs) against the bird itself.

Look for details such as how long the bird's bill is relative to the head. That's a great way to tell apart Downy and Hairy woodpeckers as well as Greater and Lesser yellowlegs, but it's useful with other confusing species, too. Judging how big the head is compared to the rest of the body helps separate Cooper's Hawks from Sharp-shinned Hawks in flight. Get in the habit of using the bird itself as a ruler, and you'll be amazed at how much information you can glean from each view. Good places to start include noting how long the legs are; how long the neck is; how far the tail extends past the body; and how far the primary feathers of the wing end compared to the tail.

2 COLOR PATTERN

When identifying a bird, focus on patterns instead of trying to match every feather.

A picture, even a fleeting glimpse, can be worth a thousand words. As soon as you spot a bird, your eyes take in the overall pattern of light and dark. And if the light allows, you'll probably

Lazuli Bunting

glimpse the main colors as well. This is all you need to start your identification.

Use these quick glimpses to build a hunch about what your mystery bird is, even if you just saw it flash across a path and vanish into the underbrush. Then, if the bird is kind enough to hop back into view, you'll know what else to look for to settle the identification.

Imagine that you're on vacation in Yosemite National Park. You see a small, bright-yellow bird flitting into the understory. Yellow immediately suggests a warbler (or the larger Western Tanager). Did you pick up a hint of grayness to the head? Or perhaps some glossy black? Just noticing that much can put you on track to identifying either a MacGillivray's Warbler or a Wilson's Warbler.

Some birds have very fine differences that take practice even to see at all. But don't start looking for those details until you've used overall patterns to let the bird remind you what it is. Read on for a few tips about noticing patches of light and dark, and the boldness or faintness of a bird's markings.

Light and Dark

When you're trying to make an ID, keep in mind that details can change, but overall patterns stay the same.

Remember that birds molt and their feathers wear. Their appearance can vary if the bird is old or young, or by how well it had been eating last time it molted. And of course, the light the bird is sitting in can have a huge effect on the colors you see.

At a distance and in very quick sightings, colors fade and all that's left are light and dark. It helps to familiarize yourself with common patterns. For example, American White Pelicans are large white birds with black trailing edges to their wings. Snow Geese are similarly shaped and colored, but the black in their wings is confined to the wingtips.

Ring-necked Duck

Ring-necked Ducks and scaup are dark ducks with a pale patch on the side; Northern Shovelers are the opposite: light-bodied ducks with a dark patch on the side.

Many birds are dark above and pale below—a widespread pattern in the animal world that helps avoid notice by predators. By reversing this pattern, male Bobolinks, with their dark underparts and light backs, look conspicuous even from all the way across a field.

Other birds seem to be trying to call attention to themselves by wearing bright patches of color in prominent places. Male Red-winged Blackbirds use their vivid shoulder patches to intimidate their rivals (notice how they cover up the patches when sneaking around off their territory). American Redstarts flick bright orange patches in their wings and tail, perhaps to scare insects out of their hiding places.

Many birds, including Dark-eyed Juncos, Spotted and Eastern towhees, American Robins, and several hummingbirds, flash white in the tail when they fly, possibly as a way of confusing predators. White flashes in the wings are common, too: look for them in Northern Mockingbirds; Acorn, Golden-fronted, and Red-bellied woodpeckers; Common and Lesser nighthawks; and Phainopeplas.

Bold and Faint

Notice strong and fine patterns.

There are some confusing bird species that sit side by side in your field guide, wearing what seems like the exact same markings and defying you to identify them. Experienced birders can find clues to these tricky identifications by noticing how boldly or finely patterned their bird is. These differences can take a trained eye to detect, but the good news is that there's a great trial case right outside at your backyard feeder.

House Finch

House Finches are common across most of North America. Much of the continent also gets visits from the very similar Purple Finch. Males of the two species are red on the head and chest and brown and streaky elsewhere. The females are both brown and streaky. So how do you tell them apart? Look at how strongly they're marked.

Male House Finches tend to be boldly streaked down the flanks, whereas male Purple Finches are much paler and more diffusely streaked. Even the red is more distinct, and more confined to the head and breast, in a male House Finch. Male Purple Finches look washed all over, even on the back, in a paler raspberry red.

Purple Finch

The all-brown females of these two species are an even better way to build your skills. The streaks on female House Finches are indistinct, brown on brown, with little actual white showing through. If a female Purple Finch lands next to it, she'll stand out with crisply defined brown streaks against a white background, particularly on the head.

Once you've had some practice, these small differences can be very useful. Similar degrees in marking can be seen between the coarsely marked Song Sparrow and finely painted Lincoln's Sparrow, and between immature Sharp-shinned and Cooper's hawks.

3 BEHAVIOR

There's what birds wear, and then there's how they wear it. A bird's attitude goes a long way in identification.

Bird species don't just look unique, they have unique ways of acting, moving, sitting, and flying. When you learn these habits, you can recognize many birds the same way you notice a friend walking through a crowd of strangers.

Chances are you'll never see a Cedar Waxwing poking through the underbrush for seeds, or a Wood Thrush zigzagging over a summer pond catching insects. But similar-sized birds such as towhees and swallows do this all the time. Behavior is one key way these birds differ.

Because so much of a bird's identity is evident in how it acts, behavior can lead you to an ID in the blink of an eye, in bad light, or from a quarter-mile away. Before you even pick up your binoculars, notice how your bird is sitting, how it's feeding or moving, whether it's in a flock, and if it has any nervous habits such as flicking its wings or bobbing its tail.

And remember that to get good at recognizing birds by their behavior, you must spend time watching them. It's tempting to grab your field guide as soon as you see a field mark. Or, after identifying a common bird, you might feel rushed to move on and find something more unusual. Resist these urges. Relax and watch the bird for as long as it will let you. This is how you learn the way a bird acts, how you discover something new...and let's face it, it's probably why you went out bird watching in the first place.

Posture

The most basic aspect of behavior is posture, or how a bird presents itself.

You can learn to distinguish many similarly proportioned birds just from the poses they assume. It's a skill that includes recognizing a bird's size and shape, and adds in the impression of the bird's habits and attitude.

Warblers and flycatchers can be distinguished by posture.

Warbler
Silhouette

Flycatcher
Silhouette

For example, in the fall season, the small, drab-green Pine Warbler looks similar to the Acadian Flycatcher, right down to the two wingbars and the straight bill. But you're unlikely to confuse the two because their postures are so different. Pine Warblers hold their bodies horizontally and often seem to crouch. Flycatchers sit straight up and down, staying on alert for passing insects.

Horizontal versus vertical posture is the first step. Next, get an impression of the how the bird carries itself. Does it seem inquisitive like a chickadee or placid like a thrush? Does it lean forward, ready for mischief, like a crow? Or is it assertive and stiff, like a robin? Do the bird's eyes dart around after targets, like a flycatcher, or methodically scan the foliage like a vireo? Is the bird constantly on alert, like a finch in the open? Nervous and skittish like a kinglet?

Movement

As soon as a sitting bird starts to move, it gives you a new set of clues about what it is.

You'll not only see different parts of the bird and new postures, you'll sense more of the bird's attitude through the rhythm of its movements. There's a huge difference between the bold way a robin bounces up to a perch, a mockingbird's showy, fluttering arrival, and the meekness of a towhee skulking around.

On the water, some ducks, such as Mallard and Northern Pintail, tip up (or "dabble") to reach submerged vegetation. Others, including scaup and Redhead, disappear from view as they dive for shellfish and other prey. Among the divers, you'll notice that some species, such as eiders, open their wings just before they dive. These ducks flap their wings for propulsion underwater, and they almost always begin a dive this way.

Flight Pattern

Certain birds have flight patterns that give them away.

Almost nothing flaps as slowly as a Great Blue Heron—you can see this from miles away. Learn the long swooping flight of most woodpeckers and you'll be able to pick them out before they've even landed.

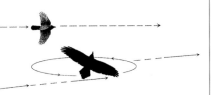

Crows and Ravens
Flight style can be a great way to identify birds at a distance. Although crows and ravens look very similar, they fly quite differently. American Crows flap slowly and methodically, whereas Common Ravens take frequent breaks from flapping to soar or glide.

Many small birds, particularly finches, have bouncy, roller-coaster-like trajectories caused by fluttering their wings and then actually folding them shut for a split second.

Birds of prey have their own distinct styles. Red-tailed Hawks and other buteos fly with deep, regular wingbeats or soar in circles on broad wings. Falcons fly with powerful beats of their sharply pointed wings.

Feeding Style

Much of the time that you watch birds on the move, you'll be watching them feed, so it pays to become familiar with foraging styles.

Some are obvious: the patient stalking of a heron; the continual up-and-back sprints of Sanderlings; the plunge of a kingfisher. But you can develop a surprisingly specific impression of almost any bird just from a few seconds of watching it forage.

For example, swallows, flycatchers, vireos, finches, and thrushes are all roughly the same size, but they feed in totally different manners: swallows eat on the wing; flycatchers dart out from perches and quickly return; vireos creep through leaves; finches sit still and crush seeds; and thrushes hop low to the ground eating insects and fruit.

Flocking

A flock of kingfishers? A single starling all on its own? Some species seem to be born loners, and others are never found solo.

Even among flocking birds, there are those content to travel in threes and fours, and others that gather by the dozens and hundreds. A noisy group of yellow birds in a treetop is much more likely to be a flock of American Goldfinches than a group of Yellow Warblers. A visit to northern coasts in winter might net you several thousand Brant, but you'll probably only see Harlequin Ducks by the handful. Learning the tendencies of birds to flock and their tolerance for crowding is one more aspect of behavior you can use. Just remember that many species get more sociable as summer draws to a close. After nesting is over and young are feeding themselves, adults can relax and stop defending their territories.

You'll often see gulls in flocks, whether standing on a beach, or in a parking lot, or wheeling overhead.

Herring Gulls

4 HABITAT

A habitat is a bird's home, and many birds are choosy. Narrow down your list by keeping in mind where you are.

Identifying birds quickly and correctly is often about probability. By knowing what's likely to be seen you can get a head start on recognizing the birds you run into. And when you see a bird you weren't expecting, you'll know to take an extra look.

Habitat is both the first and last question to ask yourself when identifying a bird. Ask it first, so you know what you're likely to see, and last as a double-check. You can fine-tune your expectations by taking geographic range and time of year into consideration.

Birding by Probability

We think of habitats as collections of plants—grassland, cypress, pine woods, deciduous forest. But they're equally collections of birds. By noting the habitat you're in, you can build a hunch about the kinds of birds you're most likely to see.

Of course, if you only let yourself identify birds you expect to see, you'll have a hard time finding unusual birds. The best way to find rarities is to know your common birds first (the ones left over are the rare ones). Birding by probability just helps you sort through them that much more quickly.

Red-breasted Nuthatch

Use Range Maps

You don't have to give
yourself headaches
trying to keep straight
every last bird in your field
guide. They may all be lined
up next to each other on the
pages, but that doesn't mean
they're all in your backyard or
local park.

Breeding
Migration
Winter
Winter (scarce)
Year-round

Range map of the Yellow-rumped Warbler.

Make it a habit to check the
range maps before you make an
identification. For example, you
can strike off at least half of the
devilishly similar *Empidonax* flycatchers at once, just by taking
into account where you are when you see one. Similarly, North
America has two kinds of small nuthatches with brown heads, but
they don't occur within about 800 miles of each other.

Of course, birds do stray from their home ranges, sometimes
fantastically—that's part of the fun. But remember that you're
birding by probability, so first compare your bird against what's
likely to be present. If nothing matches, then start taking notes.

Check the Time of Year

Range maps hold another clue to
identification—they tell you when a
bird is likely to be around.

Many of summer's birds, including
most of the warblers, flycatchers,
thrushes, hummingbirds, and
shorebirds, are gone by late fall.
Other birds move in to replace them.
This mass exodus and arrival is part
of what makes bird watching during
migration so exciting.

Yellow-rumped Warbler

Use eBird to Help

eBird's online species maps are a great way to explore both
range and season. You can zoom in to see bird records from your

immediate surroundings, and you can filter the map to show you just sightings from a particular month or season.

Another way to focus on the most likely birds near you is to use our free Merlin® Bird ID app for iOS and Android. Merlin takes your location and date, asks you a few simple questions, and gives you a short list of matching possibilities. See page 30 for more on Merlin.

USING FIELD MARKS TO IDENTIFY BIRDS

Once you've looked at Size and Shape, Color Pattern, Behavior, and Habitat to decide what general type of bird you're looking at, you may still have a few similar birds to choose between. To be certain of your identification, you'll need to look at field marks.

Birds display a huge variety of patterns and colors, which they have evolved in part to recognize other members of their own species. Birders can use these features (called "field marks") to help distinguish species. Pay particular attention to the field marks of the head and the field marks of the wing.

Ornithologists divide a bird's body into topographical regions: beak (or bill), head, back, wings, tail, breast, belly, and legs. To help with identification, many of these regions are divided still further. This diagram shows some of the commonly used descriptive terms.

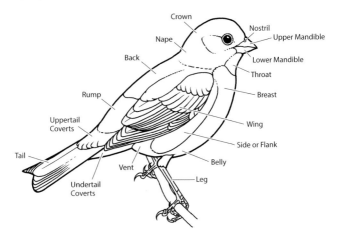

Field Marks of the Head

When identifying an unknown bird, markings on the head are particularly important, as are beak shape and size. Here are head markings visually displayed to help you along.

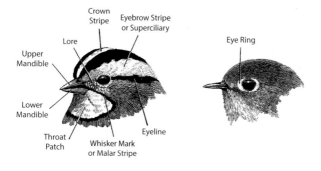

Field Marks of the Wing

A bird's wings are another great place to pick up clues about its identity. In a few groups, notably warblers and vireos, the presence of wingbars and patches of color on the wing can give positive identification even when the bird is in nonbreeding plumage. In other groups, such as flycatchers and sparrows, the absence of wing markings may be important. It also pays to learn the main feather groups, such as primaries, secondaries, tertials, and coverts, and to look for "feather edging"—a different color running along the edges of feathers.

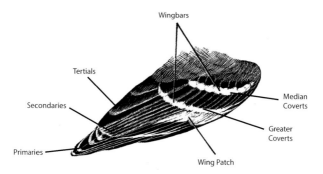

USE MERLIN APP TO SEE THE POSSIBILITIES

Merlin®, an instant bird identification app from the Cornell Lab of Ornithology, can make many identifications simple. It works by narrowing down your choices, prompting you to enter the date, location, and the bird's size, colors, and behavior.

Merlin was designed to be a birding coach for beginning and intermediate bird watchers. Merlin asks you the same questions that an expert birder would ask to help solve a mystery bird sighting. Notice that date and location are Merlin's first and most important questions.

It takes years of experience in the field to know what species are expected at a given location and date. Merlin shares this knowledge with you based on more than 100 million sightings submitted to eBird from birders across the United States and Canada.

Merlin also asks you to describe the color, size, and behavior of the bird you saw. Because no two people describe birds exactly the same way, Merlin presents a shortlist of matching species based on descriptions from Cornell Lab experts as well as thousands of bird enthusiasts who helped "teach" Merlin by participating in online activities.

Much like a modern field guide app, Merlin also provides world-class photos, ID text, sounds, and range maps. You can browse more than 2,000 stunning images taken by top photographers and listen to a selection of songs and calls for each species.

Download Merlin FREE (see page 14 for details).

THE RIGHT STUFF

10 TIPS FOR BEGINNING BIRD WATCHERS

Birding mainly involves patience, careful observation, and a willingness to let the wonder and beauty of the natural world overtake you. But having the right equipment can help too:

1 Binoculars.

Your enjoyment of birds depends hugely on how great they look through your binoculars, so make sure you're getting a big, bright, crisp picture through yours. In recent years excellent binoculars have become available at surprisingly low prices. So while binoculars under $100 may seem tempting, it's truly worth it to spend $250 to $300 for vastly superior images as well as lifetime warranties, waterproof housing, and lighter weight. We suggest getting 7-power or 8-power binoculars—they're a nice mix of magnification while still allowing you a wide enough view that your bird won't be constantly hopping out of your image.

2 Field Guide.

Field guides like this one focus on the most common species in your area and are meant to be portable. Unlike their digital counterparts, they often earn a special place on windowsills, providing a ready resource at home for hours of study and daydreaming.

3 Bird Feeders.

With binoculars for viewing and a guide to help you figure out what's what, the next step is to attract birds to your backyard, where you can get a good look at them. Bird feeders come in all types, but we recommend starting with a black oil sunflower feeder, adding a suet feeder in winter and a hummingbird feeder in summer (or all year in parts of the continent). From there you can diversify to feeders that house millet, thistle seeds, mealworms, and fruit to attract other types of species. In sections that follow, we describe the main types of bird feeders along with images of what they look like, to help you choose the right feeders for your yard and to attract the birds you want to see.

4 Spotting Scope.
By this point in our list, you've got pretty much all the gear you need to be a birder—that is, until you start looking at those ducks on the far side of the pond, or shorebirds in mudflats, or that Golden Eagle perched on a tree limb a quarter-mile away. Though they're not cheap, spotting scopes are indispensable for seeing details at long range—or simply reveling in intricate plumage details that can be brought to life only with a 20x to 60x zoom. And scopes, like binoculars, are coming down in price while going up in quality.

5 Camera.
With the proliferation of digital gadgetry, you can take photos anywhere, anytime. Snapping even a blurry photo of a bird can help you or others clinch its ID. And birds are innately artistic creatures—more and more amateur photographers are connecting with birds through taking gorgeous pictures. There's also the growing practice of digiscoping—pointing your smartphone's camera through a spotting scope or binoculars.

6 Keeping a List.
"Listing" doesn't have to be for hardcore birders only; it's fun to record special moments from your days of birding. Many people save their records online using eBird. A Cornell Lab project, eBird allows you to keep track of every place and day you go bird watching, enter notes, share sightings with friends, and explore the data other eBirders have entered. Learn more about eBird and how to use it for free on pages 57–58.

7 Birding by Ear.
Many people love bird sounds—calls, songs, and other avian utterances that fill the air. You can use these sounds as clues to identify species. Based on the success of our *Backyard Birdsong Guide* series by world-renowned audiologist Donald Kroodsma, we've added audio capabilities to this book with the Bird QR app. See the next section, "Listening to Birds," for more.

8 Visual Bird Identification Skills.

Now that we've covered the physical tools that equip you for bird watching, let's loop back to your mental tools. Once you're outside and surrounded by birds, practice the four-step approach to identification that we shared earlier in Birding 101: Size and Shape; Color Pattern; Behavior; and Habitat.

9 Birding Apps and Digital Field Guides.

If you have a smartphone, you can carry a bookshelf in your pocket. You've already learned about Merlin® Bird ID app, but there are many other resources at your disposal. Download the eBird app to keep track of your bird observations in the field. There are also digital field guides—most of the major printed field guides have an app or eBook version. Some specialized apps cover specific groups of species, such as the Warbler Guide and Raptor ID apps. Others, like LarkWire, focus on helping you learn bird song. Search for them in Apple and Android stores.

And our All About Birds species guide works on mobile devices, giving you access to free ID information and sound recordings straight from your smartphone's Internet browser. With the free Bird QR book companion app, you can scan the QR symbols in this guide to display specific web pages related to what you're reading about right inside the app, so you can learn even more.

10 Connect With Other Birders.

Bird watching can be a relaxing solo pursuit, like a walk in the woods decorated with bird sightings. But birding can also be a social endeavor, and the best way to learn is from other people. A great way to connect with people is to look on *birding.aba.org* and sign up for a listserv for your area. You'll get emails that will tell you what people have been seeing, announce local bird outings, and connect you with members of your local birding club. Many regions also have Facebook groups where people share what they've been seeing and welcome newcomers. There's a decent chance that someone's leading a bird walk near you this weekend—and they'd love to have you come along.

LISTENING TO BIRDS

When a bird sings, it's telling you what it is, where it is, and often what is happening.

You can only see straight ahead, but you can hear in all directions at once. Learning bird songs is a great way to identify birds hidden by dense foliage, birds far away, birds at night, and birds that look identical to each other.

Song Sparrow

And then there's the "dawn chorus," that time as the sun begins to light up the world, when birds join together in a symphony of sound. When you first listen to a dawn chorus in full swing, the sheer onslaught of bird song can be overwhelming. How does anyone begin to pick apart the chirps, whistles, and trills that are echoing out of the woods? The answer, of course, is to concentrate on one bird at a time—and that approach holds true when you're trying to learn individual songs, too. Don't try to memorize each entire song you hear; instead, focus on one quality of the sound at a time. Many birds have a characteristic rhythm, pitch, or tone to their song. Here's how to use them:

Rhythm

Get used to a bird's characteristic tempo as well as the number of distinct sections to its song. Marsh Wrens sing in a hurry, while White-throated Sparrows are much more leisurely.

Repetition

Some birds characteristically repeat syllables or phrases before moving on to a new sound. Northern Mockingbirds do this many times in a row. Though Brown Thrashers sound similar, they typically repeat only twice before changing to a new syllable.

Pitch

Most birds sing in a characteristic range, with smaller birds (such as the Cedar Waxwing) typically having higher voices and larger birds (such as the Common Raven) usually having deeper voices. Many bird songs change pitch, so it helps to pay attention to the overall pitch trend in a song. Some birds are distinctive for having steady voices, such as the Chipping Sparrow's trill.

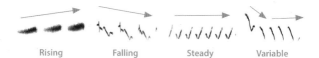

| Rising | Falling | Steady | Variable |

Tone

The tone of a bird's song is sometimes hard to describe, but it can be very distinctive. As a start, pay attention to whether a bird's voice is a clear whistle, harsh or scratchy, liquid and flutelike, or a clear trill. If you can remember the quality of a bird's voice, it can give you a clue to the bird's identity even if the bird doesn't sing the same notes every time.

- **Buzzy**: Like a bee–a good example would be Townsend's Warbler song.

Buzzy

- **Clear**: Something you could whistle. Northern Cardinals have a clear song, as do Yellow Warblers.

Clear

- **Trilled**: A lot of sounds in a row that are too fast to count (technically, more than 11 sounds per second). Chipping Sparrows and Dark-eyed Juncos sing trills.

Trilled

Use Bird QR

Scan the sound QR symbol on each species page to see and listen to different bird sounds. With Bird QR, this book instantly becomes an audio field guide and will also keep track of all your history for future quick access in the app.

SAMPLE

PHOTOGRAPHING BIRDS

5 BASICS OF GOOD BIRD PHOTOGRAPHY

With the explosion in availability and design of digital cameras, it's now possible for hobbyists to take amazingly good photos. Though your photos may not show up on the cover of *National Geographic*, you can up the "wow" factor by paying attention to a few basics.

Beyond the mechanical aspects of shutter speed, aperture, and ISO (which digital cameras increasingly handle automatically), there is an indefinable something that transforms an image into a work of art. Often thought of as talent, just as often it's the result of hours of practice and attention to detail. Here are five basics of good bird photography to bear in mind:

1 **Lighting.** The best times to shoot are morning and late afternoon when the light is angled, warmer, and more subdued. It's harder to take a good picture in the middle of a bright, clear day because images end up with too much contrast, where light areas get washed out and shadows turn inky black. Having the source of light behind and slightly to one side of you creates a more three-dimensional subject. Having your subject backlit rarely works well unless you're deliberately going after a silhouette.

2 **Framing.** Professionals usually avoid placing any subject in the exact center of a photograph. It tends to be more visually stimulating to see the bird off to one side, facing inward. Our own eyes naturally follow the same trajectory. Likewise, avoid placing the horizon line in the middle of a picture, which cuts it in half and divides the image. It's better to frame the horizon in the top or bottom third of your photograph.

3 **Composition.** Non-bird elements in your picture can add or detract from a pleasing composition. Branches, shrubbery, rocks, and flowers can be a distraction—or they can be used artfully to frame the bird within the picture.

Although you want to avoid having a branch right behind the bird, looking like it's growing out of its head, incorporating some part of the bird's habitat often makes a shot better. If the background is too busy, try opening the aperture to blur the background and make your subject stand out.

4 **Angle.** You can shoot from a position that is higher than your subject, lower, at eye level, or somewhere in between. Each situation can be different—but adjusting your height to shoot the bird at eye level is often a

Great Egret

good choice, as it puts the viewer on the same plane as the bird.

To get closer to wary birds, you can wear muted clothing, hide behind vegetation, and move slowly and calmly in a zigzag pattern. It is never a good idea to bait a bird or to approach so closely that you flush it or alter its behavior.

5 **Knowledge of Your Subject.** To be the best bird photographer you can be, you really have to know birds. For example, knowing the habitat and behavior of a species allows you to predict where you're likely to find them and anticipate what they might do next. For example, berry bushes attract Cedar Waxwings; herons haunt the edges of marshes and ponds; waterfowl often rest and preen in the same spot every day. Study your subject and you'll know when and where to get the shot.

What Kind of Camera?

We're in a golden age of camera design and there are great options at every level of interest. Serious enthusiasts tend toward DSLRs (digital single-lens reflex cameras) with interchangeable lenses, but these can be expensive. At the entry level, so-called "superzoom" cameras can produce surprisingly good results while remaining compact and fairly inexpensive.

DIGISCOPING

Placing the lens of a digital camera to the eyepiece of a spotting scope is called "digiscoping." It's an inexpensive way to take decent pictures without a heavy, expensive telephoto lens.

Digiscoped Yellow-bellied Sapsucker.

Both scopes and digital cameras have improved tremendously since the dawn of digiscoping, in 1999. One of the most significant advances has been the advent of smartphones, which are now arguably the best tool for digiscoping and certainly the most convenient. Scopes, too have begun to come down in price.

There can be different goals in digiscoping. It can be practiced slowly and patiently to capture frame-worthy photos, whether detail-rich or artistically blurred. More often, it's a handy way to capture shots to remind yourself of a special moment or to back up a rare bird report. It's even becoming common for people to record video while digiscoping.

Granted, digiscoping does require a spotting scope, which can cost as much as a camera and telephoto lens—but some birders are happy to put their money toward a scope that can do double duty in both bird watching and photography.

Getting a good image when digiscoping comes down to gathering plenty of light, getting the camera lens the correct distance from the scope's eyepiece, and holding everything steady.

Getting Connected

There are a variety of ways to bring the camera lens and scope eyepiece together. For smartphones, the earliest method involved placing a finger between phone and eyepiece both to steady the lens and keep it at the correct distance. Today you can find phone adapters custom-sized to hold a phone in the proper position—greatly cutting down on fiddliness and frustration.

If you don't line up camera and eyepiece perfectly, you may get uneven focus, part of the image cut off, or shadows creeping in as light leaks in between scope and camera lenses.

Remember that the many commercial adapters are not universal, so make sure you get what fits your gear.

Standing Steady

The magnification produced by digiscoping is just what you need to pull your subject in close, but it also magnifies small movements from wind or a shaky trigger finger. Keeping extraneous motion to a minimum is of paramount importance. A quality tripod for your scope will provide stable support and prevent your photos from turning into a blurry mess. You'll find that a rock-steady tripod will be well worth it anyway—even in routine bird watching without attaching a camera.

5 TIPS FOR SUCCESSFUL DIGISCOPING

Digiscoped Northern Cardinal.

1 Let There Be Light.
One cause of blurry photos is low light coming through the scope, which forces a slower shutter speed and increases the effect of motion. Using larger, brighter scopes, such as 85-mm models rather than 65-mm models, results in noticeably better digiscoped photos. If you can change your camera's ISO (a feature becoming more common on smartphones), set it as high as you can and you'll get a faster shutter speed.

2 Resist the Zoom.
For scopes with a zoom, bear in mind that you quickly lose light as you zoom in. The human eye is good at compensating for this; cameras less so. Take advantage of your camera's many megapixels by shooting at a lower, brighter zoom setting and then cropping later.

3 Capture the Motion.
Many cameras and phones have a continuous shooting feature that takes photos one after another. This setting can help you catch birds in just the right pose. As an alternative, consider shooting video of a fast-moving subject—this can be more helpful than still photos when trying to identify a bird later.

4 **Try with Your Binoculars.**
Sometimes called "digibinning," this advanced technique can sometimes produce decent photos. If you don't already have a spotting scope, it's a less expensive way to get into digiscoping. But be warned: it's hard to hold the binocular-phone combination steady. It's a good idea to start with large, stationary birds such as herons.

5 **Practice, Practice, Practice.**
Fortunately, once you've got the equipment, taking digital photos is virtually free. It may seem impossible at first, but you'll quickly improve as you become comfortable with setting up the scope and handling your camera's controls. Don't be afraid to experiment—you never know what you'll come away with.

ATTRACTING
BIRDS TO YOUR
BACKYARD

BIRDSCAPING

You can watch birds anywhere.
Parks, nature preserves, and wildlife refuges provide some of the most diverse species, but the easiest place to watch birds is your own backyard. Enhancing your yard to attract and support birds is called "birdscaping."

Putting up a feeder is an easy way to attract birds. But if you'd prefer a more natural approach or you want to satisfy more than birds' nutritional needs, consider landscaping your yard—even just a part of it—to be more bird friendly. Even a small yard can provide vital habitat.

You'll find a trove of tips, techniques, and local landscaping resources at our Habitat Network project. The core concept is simple—all birds need three basic things from their habitats:

1 Food.
Your birds can get food from feeders that you put up. Landscaping your yard to provide the fruit, seeds, beneficial insects, and other small animals that birds feed on adds natural food sources for birds, too.

2 Water.
All living things need water to survive. Providing this habitat necessity is one of the quickest ways to attract birds to your property. If there is a water source in your yard, such as a pond, creek, birdbath, or even a puddle, you've probably noticed birds using it. If you don't have a water feature yet, a birdbath is an easy way to provide this habitat need.

3 Shelter.
Whether it's protection from the elements, safe places to hide from predators, or secure locations to hide nests, providing shelter is one of the best ways to make your property bird-friendly.

Take a "bird's-eye" look at your backyard. Does it provide those things? If not, there are plants you can grow and many other ways you can enhance your yard to make it safe and inviting for birds.

Here are some tips to help you:

Evaluate Your Yard

First, take stock of what you already have. Draw a map of your property including buildings, sidewalks, fences, trees, shrubs, feeders, and nest boxes. Note sunny or shady sites, low or wet areas, sandy sites, and plants you want to keep. You can do this online with a free tool from the Cornell Lab and The Nature Conservancy, called Habitat Network (learn more in *Getting Involved* starting on page 65).

Purple Coneflowers

Start With a Plan

Before you start digging holes and rearranging your yard, develop a planting plan. Draw each new plant onto a piece of tracing paper, then place that over the map of your yard—or use the point-and-click tools on the Habitat Network site. Once your plants are in, use your map as a reminder about which ones need to be watered and weeded, especially in the first year after planting. Mulch is great for keeping moisture in and weeds out.

Think "Variety!"

Try to include variety and year-round value in your planting plan. Look for places to include grasses, legumes, hummingbird flowers, plants that fruit in summer and fall, winter-persistent plants, and conifers for shelter. Plant native species instead of exotics, and look for places to create shelter with a brush pile or standing dead tree. Habitat Network can give you specific planting recommendations and resources for your zip code.

To learn more about how to improve your backyard habitat, visit *www.Habitat.Network* or scan this symbol with Bird QR.

BIRD FEEDERS

Fifty million people in North America feed birds and it's a great way to attract birds to your backyard. But feeders are not one size fits all—different species are attracted to different designs. Here are the main types of feeders and the types of birds they attract.

Ground

Many species of birds, including sparrows and doves, prefer to feed on large, flat surfaces and may not visit any type of elevated feeder. Song Sparrows and many towhee species, for instance, will rarely land on a feeder, but they will readily eat fallen seed from the ground beneath your feeders. To attract these species, try spreading seed on the ground or on a large surface such as the top of a picnic table. Ground feeders that sit low to the ground with mesh screens for good drainage can also be used. Make sure that there are no predators around, including outdoor cats.

Large and Small Hopper

A hopper feeder is a platform on which walls and a roof are built, forming a "hopper" that protects seed against the weather.

Large hoppers attract most species of feeder birds and will allow larger species, such as doves and grackles, to feed. Small hoppers will attract smaller birds while preventing those larger species from comfortably perching and monopolizing the feeder.

Large and Small Tube

A tube feeder is a hollow cylinder, often made of plastic, with multiple feeding ports and perches. Tube feeders keep seed fairly dry. Feeders with short perches accommodate small birds such as finches but exclude larger birds such as grackles and jays. The size of the feeding ports varies as well, depending on the type of seed to be offered. Note that special smaller feeding ports are required for nyjer (thistle) seed to prevent spillage.

Small tube.   Large tube.

Sugar Water

Sugar-water feeders are specially made to dispense sugar water through small holes. Choose a feeder that is easy to take apart and clean, because the feeder should be washed or run through the dishwasher frequently.

Platform

A platform feeder is any flat, raised surface onto which bird food is spread. The platform should have plenty of drainage holes to prevent water accumulation. A platform with a roof will help keep seeds dry. Trays attract most species of feeder birds. Placed near the ground, they are likely to attract juncos, doves, and sparrows.

Suet Cage

Suet or suet mixes can be placed in a specially made cage, tied to trees, or smeared into knotholes. Cages that are only open at the bottom tend to be starling-resistant but allow woodpeckers, nuthatches, and chickadees to feed by clinging upside down.

Thistle Sock

Thistle "socks" are fine-mesh bags to which birds cling to extract nyjer or thistle seeds. Seed within thistle socks can become quite wet with rain, so only use large ones during periods when you have enough finches to consume the contents in a few days.

Window Feeder

Small plastic feeders affixed to window glass with suction cups, and platform feeders hooked into window frames, attract finches, chickadees, titmice, and some sparrows. They afford wonderful, close-up views of birds, and their placement makes them the safest of all feeder types for preventing window collisions.

FEEDER PLACEMENT & SAFETY

Place feeders in a quiet area where they are easy to see and convenient to refill. Place them close to natural cover, such as trees or shrubs. Evergreens are ideal, as they provide thick foliage that hides birds from predators and buffers winter winds.

Be careful not to place feeders too close to trees with strong branches that can provide jump-off points for squirrels and cats. A distance of about 10 feet is a good compromise.

American Goldfinches and Pine Siskins

Place hummingbird feeders in the shade if possible, as sugar solution spoils quickly in the sun. Don't use honey, artificial sweeteners, or food coloring. If bees or wasps become a problem, try moving the feeder.

Ornithologists estimate that more than 600 million birds are killed by hitting windows in the United States and Canada each year. Placing feeders close to your windows (ideally within 3 feet) can help reduce this problem. When feeders are close, a bird leaving the feeder cannot gain enough momentum to do harm if it strikes the window.

You can prevent more window strikes by breaking up reflections of trees and open space, which birds perceive as a flight path through your home. Techniques include attaching streamers, suction-cup feeders, or decals to windows, crisscrossing branches within the window frames, or installing awnings or screens. Another method is to attach netting to the outside of the window to buffer the impact. Deer netting (the kind used to keep deer from eating plants in your yard) works well.

To learn more about window crashes and how to prevent them, scan this symbol with Bird QR.

BIRD FOOD

Sunflower seeds attract the widest variety of birds and are the mainstay food used in most bird feeders. Other varieties of seed can help attract different types of birds to your feeders and yard and this section highlights many of them. When buying mixtures, note that those that contain red millet, oats, and other fillers are not attractive to most birds and can lead to a lot of waste.

Sunflower

There are two kinds of sunflower—black oil and striped. The black oil seeds ("oilers") have very thin shells, easy for virtually all seed-eating birds to crack open, and the kernels within have a high fat content, which is extremely valuable for most winter birds. Striped sunflower seeds have a thicker shell, much harder for House Sparrows and blackbirds to crack open. So if you're inundated with species you'd rather not subsidize at your feeder, before you do anything else, try switching to striped sunflower. Sunflower in the shell can be offered in a wide variety of feeders, including trays, tube feeders, hoppers, and acrylic window feeders. Sunflower hearts and chips shouldn't be offered in tube feeders where moisture can collect. Since squirrels love sunflower seeds, be prepared to take steps to squirrel-proof your feeder if needed.

Safflower

Safflower has a thick shell, hard for some birds to crack open, but is a favorite among cardinals. Some grosbeaks, chickadees, doves, and native sparrows also eat it. According to some sources, House Sparrows, European Starlings, and squirrels don't like safflower, but in some areas seem to have developed a taste for it. Cardinals and grosbeaks tend to prefer tray and hopper feeders, which makes these feeders a good choice for offering safflower.

Nyjer or Thistle

Small finches including American Goldfinches, Lesser Goldfinches, Indigo Buntings, Pine Siskins, and Common Redpolls often devour these tiny, black, needlelike seeds. As invasive thistle plants became a recognized problem in North America, suppliers shifted to a daisylike plant, known as *Guizotia abyssinica*, that produces

a similar type of small, oily, rich seed. The plant is now known as niger or nyjer, and is imported from overseas. The seeds are heat-sterilized during importation to limit their chance of spreading invasively, while retaining their food value.

White Proso Millet

White millet is a favorite with ground-feeding birds including quails, native sparrows, doves, towhees, juncos, and cardinals. Unfortunately it's also a favorite with cowbirds, other blackbirds, and House Sparrows, which are already subsidized by human activities and supported at unnaturally high population levels by current agricultural practices and habitat changes. When these species are present, it's wisest to not use millet; virtually all the birds that like it are equally attracted to black oil sunflower. Because white millet is so preferred by ground-feeding birds, scatter it on the ground or set low platform feeders with excellent drainage.

Shelled and Cracked Corn

Corn is eaten by grouse, pheasants, turkeys, quail, cardinals, grosbeaks, crows, ravens, jays, doves, ducks, cranes, and other species. Unfortunately, corn has two serious problems. First, it's a favorite of House Sparrows, cowbirds, starlings, geese, bears, raccoons, and deer. Second, corn is the bird food most likely to be contaminated with aflatoxins, which are extremely toxic even at low levels. Never buy corn in plastic bags, never allow it to get wet, never offer it in amounts that can't be consumed in a day during rainy or very humid weather, and be conscientious about raking up old corn. Never offer corn covered in a red dye. Corn should be offered in fairly small amounts at a time on tray feeders. Don't offer it in tube feeders that could harbor moisture.

Peanuts

Peanuts are very popular with jays, crows, chickadees, titmice, woodpeckers, and many other species, but are also favored by squirrels, bears, raccoons, and other animals. Like corn, peanuts have a high likelihood of harboring aflatoxins, so must be kept dry and used up fairly quickly.

Peanuts in the shell can be set out on platform feeders or right on a deck railing or window feeder as a special treat for jays. If peanuts or mixtures of peanuts and other seeds are offered in tube feeders, make sure to change the seed frequently, especially during rainy or humid weather, completely emptying out and cleaning the tube every time.

Milo or Sorghum

Milo is a favorite with many western ground-feeding birds. On Cornell Lab of Ornithology seed preference tests, Steller's Jays, Curve-billed Thrashers, and Gambel's Quails preferred milo to sunflower. In another study, House Sparrows did not eat milo, but cowbirds did. Milo should be scattered on the ground or on low tray feeders.

Golden Millet, Red Millet, Flax, and Others

These seeds are often used as fillers in packaged birdseed mixes, but most birds shun them. Waste seed becomes a breeding ground for bacteria and fungus, contaminating fresh seed more quickly. Make sure to read the ingredients list on birdseed mixtures, avoiding those with these seeds. If a seed mix has a lot of small, red seeds, make sure they're milo or sorghum, not red millet.

Mealworms

Mealworms are the larvae of the mealworm beetle, *Tenebrio molitor*, and they provide a high-protein treat for many birds. Some people provide live mealworms, while others prefer offering dried larvae. Birds such as chickadees, titmice, wrens, and nuthatches relish this food, and mealworms are one of the few food items that reliably attracts bluebirds. Offer mealworms on a flat tray or in a specialized mealworm feeder.

Fruit

Various fruits can prove quite attractive to many species of birds. Oranges cut in half will often attract orioles which will sip the juice and eat the flesh of the orange. Grapes and raisins are a favorite of many fruit-eating birds. Mockingbirds, catbirds, bluebirds, robins, and waxwings are also likely to feed on fruit. Many species are also attracted to the dried seeds of fruits such as pumpkins or apples. Be sure to dispose of any fruit that becomes moldy because some molds create toxins that are harmful to birds.

Sugar Water or Nectar

To make nectar for hummingbirds, add one part table sugar to four parts boiling water and stir. A slightly more diluted mixture can be used for orioles (one part sugar to six parts water). Allow the mixture to cool before filling the feeder.

Store extra sugar water in the refrigerator for up to one week (after that it may become moldy, which is dangerous for birds). Adding red food coloring is unnecessary and possibly harmful to birds. Red portals on the feeder, or even a red ribbon tied on top, will attract the birds just as well.

Grit

Birds "chew" their food in the muscular part of their stomach, called the gizzard. To aid in the grinding, birds swallow small, hard materials such as sand, small pebbles, ground eggshells, and ground oyster shells. Grit, therefore, attracts many birds as a food supplement or even by itself. Oyster shells and eggshells have the added benefit of being a good source of calcium, something birds need during egg laying. If you decide to provide eggshells, be sure to sterilize them first. You can boil them for 10 minutes or heat them in an oven (20 minutes at 250°F). Let the eggshells cool, then crush them into pieces about the size of sunflower seeds. Offer the eggshell in a dish or low platform feeder.

To learn more about bird food, scan this symbol with Bird QR.

WATER SOURCES

Like all animals, birds need water to survive. Though they can extract some moisture from their food, most birds drink water every day. Birds also use water for bathing, to clean their feathers and remove parasites. After splashing around in a bath for a few minutes, a bird usually perches in a sunny spot and fluffs its feathers out to dry. Then it carefully preens each feather, adding a protective coating of oil secreted by a gland at the base of its tail.

Because birds need water for drinking and bathing, they are attracted to water just as they are to feeders. A dependable supply of fresh, clean water is highly attractive. In fact, a birdbath will even bring in birds that don't eat seeds and won't visit your feeders. Providing water for birds can improve the quality of your backyard bird habitat and should provide you with a fantastic opportunity to observe bird behavior.

Birds seem to prefer baths that are at ground level, but these can make birds more vulnerable to predators. Raised baths will attract birds as well, so we recommend them over ground-level baths. Change the water daily to keep it fresh and clean. You can also arrange a few branches or stones in the water so that birds can stand on them and drink without getting wet (this is particularly important in winter).

Birdbaths should be only an inch or two deep with a shallow slope. One of the best ways to make your birdbath more attractive is to provide dripping water. You can buy a dripper or sprayer, or you can recycle an old bucket or plastic container by punching a tiny hole in the bottom, filling it with water, and hanging it above the birdbath so the water drips out. Don't add antifreeze; it is poisonous to all animals including birds.

To learn more about birdbaths, scan this symbol with Bird QR.

NEST BOXES

FEATURES OF A GOOD BIRDHOUSE
BUILD A SAFE AND SUCCESSFUL HOME

IT'S WELL CONSTRUCTED

Untreated Wood. Use untreated, unpainted wood, preferably cedar, pine, cypress, or for larger boxes (owls) non-pressure-treated CDX exterior grade plywood.

Galvanized Screws. Use galvanized screws for the best seal. Nails can loosen over time, allowing rain into the nest box. Screws are also easier to remove for repairs or maintenance. Do not use staples.

IT KEEPS BIRDS DRY

Sloped Roof. A sloped roof that overhangs the front by 2–4" and the sides by 2" will help keep out driving rain, while also thwarting predators. Add 1/4"-deep cuts under the roof on all three edges to serve as gutters that channel rain away from the box.

side view (cutaway)

Recessed Floor. A recessed floor keeps the nest from getting wet and helps the box last longer. Recess the floor at least 1/4" up from the bottom.

bottom view

Drainage Holes. Add at least four drainage holes (3/8" to 1/2" diameter) to the floor to allow any water that enters the box to drain away. Alternatively, you can cut away the corners of the floorboard to create drainage holes.

IT HELPS REGULATE TEMPERATURE

Thick Walls. Walls should be at least 3/4" thick to insulate the nest properly. (Note that boards sold as 1" are actually 3/4" thick.)

Ventilation Holes. For adequate ventilation, there should be two 5/8"-diameter holes on each of the side walls, near the top (four total).

IT KEEPS OUT PREDATORS

No Perches. A perch is unnecessary for the birds and can actually help predators gain access to the box.

Types of Predator Guards. Although predators are a natural part of the environment, birdhouses are typically not as well concealed as natural nests and some predators can make a habit of raiding your boxes. Adding a baffle or guard helps keep nestlings and adults safe from climbing predators. Below are some time-tested options.

 Collar Baffle. A metal collar of about 3 feet in diameter surrounding the pole underneath the nest box.

 Stovepipe Baffle. The most complex, and perhaps the most effective. These baffles are generally 8" in diameter and 24"–36" long.

 Noel Guard. A wire tube attached to the front of the nest box. Use this guard in combination with another, or attach it to boxes installed on trees.

COMMON NEST BOX PREDATORS

 Snakes. Many snakes are excellent climbers and can easily surmount an unguarded pole. Snakes most likely to climb into birdhouses are generally nonvenomous (such as racers and rat snakes) and helpful at controlling rodents. Avoid installing nest boxes next to brush piles.

Raccoons. Raccoons are intelligent and can remember nest box locations from year to year. They can be abundant in populated areas. Mount nest boxes on a metal pole equipped with a baffle; avoid mounting them on trees or fence posts.

 Chipmunks. Chipmunks are both a nest predator and a competitor for nest boxes. To keep chipmunks out, mount boxes away from trees on a metal pole equipped with a baffle.

Cats. Cats are excellent jumpers and can leap to the top of a nest box from a nearby tree or from the ground. Mount your box high enough and far enough from trees so cats cannot spring to the top of the box in a single leap. Keep pet cats indoors for their own safety and for the safety of birds.

IT HAS THE RIGHT ENTRANCE SIZE FOR THE RIGHT BIRD

By providing a properly sized entrance hole, you can attract desirable species to your birdhouses while excluding predators and unwanted occupants. Below are the requirements for entrance-hole size for some common species that nest in boxes.

3"	Screech-owls and American Krestel
2 ½"	Northern Flicker
1 ⁹⁄₁₆"	Ash-throated Flycatcher, Great Crested Flycatcher, Mountain Bluebird
1 ½"	Eastern Bluebird, Western Bluebird, Bewick's Wren, Carolina Wren
1 ⅜"	White-breasted Nuthatch, Tree Swallow, Violet-green Swallow
1 ¼"	Prothonotary Warbler, Red-breasted Nuthatch, Tufted Titmouse
1 ⅛"	House Wren and chickadees

IT HELPS FLEDGLINGS LEAVE THE NEST

Rough Interior Walls. The interior wall below the entrance hole should be rough to help nestlings climb out of the box. For small boxes (wrens and chickadees), plain wood is usually rough enough, but you can roughen smooth boards with coarse sandpaper.

Interior Grooves. A series of shallow horizontal cuts, like a small ladder, works well in medium-sized boxes meant for swallows and bluebirds. Swallows, in particular, need a little help climbing out of boxes.

Duck Boxes. For duck boxes, staple a strip of 1/4"-mesh hardware cloth from floor to hole to help ducklings escape deep boxes.

IT MAKES PLACEMENT AND MAINTENANCE EASY

Extended Back. A few extra inches at the top and bottom of your birdhouse can make it easier to mount on a metal pole. Alternatively, you can predrill mounting holes in the back panel before assembly and use a short-handled screwdriver to install the box.

Hinged Door with a Sturdy Closing Mechanism. A hinged side gives you access for cleaning and monitoring your nest box, both of which are important for a successful nesting season. A latch or nail keeps the box securely closed until you are ready to open it.

Into DIY? Scan this symbol with Bird QR app or visit *nestwatch.org/birdhouses* to get FREE downloadable nest-box plans.

GETTING INVOLVED

Great Blue Heron
Photo by Gerrit Vyn

CITIZEN SCIENCE

Each month, bird watchers report millions of bird observations to citizen-science projects at the Cornell Lab of Ornithology, contributing to the world's most dynamic and powerful source of information on birds.

The Cornell Lab has been at the forefront of citizen science since 1966. Today, the birding community can use our innovative online tools to tap into millions of records and see how their own sightings fit into the continental picture. Scientists can analyze the same data to reveal striking changes in the movements, distributions, and numbers of birds across time, and to determine how birds are affected by habitat loss, pollution, and disease.

If you enjoy watching birds, you can help and contribute to science, whether you are a beginner or a seasoned birder. Participating can take as little or as much time as you want—you decide!

There's a Project for Every Bird Watcher

Our fun and meaningful citizen-science projects enable people to watch birds at their favorite locations and share their sightings:

- eBird is a powerful tool for keeping track of your sightings and for exploring what others have seen—with global coverage and millions of sightings recorded per month.
- Great Backyard Bird Count is possibly the easiest project of all and the best one to start with—a global effort to count birds over one long weekend each February.
- Project FeederWatch is a winter project where you count birds at your feeders to help track bird populations and distributions.
- NestWatch challenges you to monitor the nest success of birds breeding around you—training and best practices are provided.
- Celebrate Urban Birds combines art and science to help communities connect to nature in urban and suburban settings.
- Habitat Network is a growing community of people documenting their landscaping to track the impact of wildlife gardening and green infrastructure around the world.

eBird

Since its inception in 2002, eBird has grown into one of the world's largest data sources about living things—thanks to bird watchers contributing more than 370 million sightings of birds.

eBird works in two ways: It gives bird watchers a convenient, free way to enter, store, and organize their sightings. And it makes those sightings available to others, turning it into a useful resource for studying or finding birds anywhere in the world.

Use eBird to start or maintain your birding lists—or use it to find out where and when to go bird watching. It works all over the world and provides endless ideas about what to do and where to go next. And it's free.

eBird provides easy-to-use online tools for birders and critical data for science. With eBird, you can:

- Record the birds you see
- Keep track of your bird lists
- Learn where to find birds near you
- Share your sightings and join the eBird community
- Contribute to science and conservation

How to Record and Store Sightings in eBird

eBird uses a simple and intuitive interface to allow you to record your bird sightings easily. You simply enter when, where, and how you went birding, then fill out a checklist of all the birds you saw and heard. A free mobile app allows you to track sightings faster than ever. Data-quality filters review all submissions automatically, and local experts review any unusual records before they enter the database.

eBird automatically organizes your checklists into local and national lists, state lists, year lists, and more. eBird also keeps your recordings current with new information that affects nomenclature. For example, when official bird names change, or species are split apart or lumped together, eBird automatically adjusts your lists accordingly. You can also add all of your bird photos to your checklist, letting you share with friends while helping build automatic photo-identification tools that can help you learn more. All these features work in any country in the world and are available in many languages.

How to Explore Data and Learn with eBird

One of eBird's greatest strengths is its ability to show you where and when birds occur, using innovative visualization tools. These free tools are used annually by millions of bird watchers, scientists, and conservationists worldwide. Here are a few:

Range Maps: Choose a species, then explore a map of everywhere it has been reported. Filter the map by date or zoom in to anywhere in the world with pinpoint precision.

Photo and Sound Archive: Each month, eBirders upload thousands of images and sounds. All of them are searchable in the Macaulay Library archive, so you can explore birds both familiar and new.

Bar Charts: Create a customized checklist for any region and season. The list tells you which species to expect when; bars tell you how rare or common each bird is during the year.

Hotspot Explorer: Using an interactive map, explore birding spots in any part of the world and discover which have the most sightings—a great tool for travelers looking for local tips on where to go birding.

Explore a Region: See the full species list, plus recent sightings, best hotspots, and top birders for any county, state, province, or country.

To learn more about eBird and the birds recently seen in your area, visit *ebird.org* or scan this symbol with the Bird QR app.

GREAT BACKYARD BIRD COUNT

The Great Backyard
Bird Count

Art by Charley Harper

Begun in 1998, the four-day Great Backyard Bird Count (GBBC) was the first citizen-science program to collect and display bird observation data online on a large scale. Today, the GBBC is one of the most popular annual events among bird watchers and has expanded to cover the whole world. More than 160,000 people of all ages and walks of life take part. In 2016, more than 162,000 counts flooded in from 130 countries, recording a total of 5,689 species of birds—more than half of all bird species in the world!

Why Count Birds?

Scientists and bird enthusiasts can learn a lot by knowing where the birds are. No single scientist or team of scientists could hope to document and understand the complex distribution and movements of so many species in such a short time. Scientists use information from the GBBC, along with observations from other citizen-science projects, to see the big picture about what is happening to bird populations. You can help scientists investigate far-reaching questions, such as these:

- How do weather and climate change influence bird populations?

- Some birds appear in large numbers during some years but not others. Where are these species from year to year, and what can we learn from these patterns?

- How does the timing of bird migrations compare across years?

- What kinds of differences in bird diversity are apparent in cities versus suburban, rural, and natural areas?

Why Is the GBBC in February?

Originally the GBBC was held in the U.S. and Canada each February to create a snapshot of the distribution of birds just before spring migrations ramped up in March. Scientists at the Cornell Lab of Ornithology, National Audubon Society, Bird Studies Canada, and elsewhere can combine this information with data from surveys conducted at different times of the year. In 2013, the count went global, creating snapshots of birds wherever they are in February, regardless of seasons across the hemispheres.

How to Participate

We invite you to participate! Visit *birdcount.org* to find out when the next GBBC is happening (it falls in February during the U.S. Presidents' Day weekend). If you're new to citizen science, you'll need to register for a free online eBird account to enter your checklist counts. If you have already participated in another Cornell Lab citizen-science project, you can use that login information for GBBC.

Once registered, simply tally the numbers and kinds of birds you see for at least 15 minutes on one or more days of the count every February. You can count from any location, anywhere in the world, for as long as you wish. During the count, you can explore what others are seeing in your area or around the world. You can also participate in an annual photo contest (with great bird-themed prizes), and contribute to a cascade of great images to enjoy as they pour in from across the globe.

To learn more and participate in the GBBC, visit *birdcount.org* or scan this symbol with Bird QR.

The Great Backyard Bird Count is led by the Cornell Lab of Ornithology and National Audubon Society, with Bird Studies Canada and many international partners. The Great Backyard Bird Count is powered by eBird.

PROJECT FEEDERWATCH

Project FeederWatch is a winter-long survey of birds that visit feeders in backyards and at nature centers, community areas, and other locales in North America. Each year, almost 20,000 people participate in Project FeederWatch and count birds at their feeders from November through early April. With more than 1.5 million checklists submitted since 1987, FeederWatchers have contributed valuable data enabling scientists to monitor changes in the distribution and abundance of birds.

Using FeederWatch data, scientists have studied the influence of nonnative species on native bird communities, examined the association between birds and habitats, and tracked unpredictable movements in winter bird populations. Participants gain from the rewarding experience of watching birds at their feeders and contributing their own observations to reveal larger patterns in bird populations across the continent.

Downy Woodpecker

Why Are FeederWatch Data Important?

With each season, FeederWatch increases in importance as a unique monitoring tool for more than 100 bird species that winter in North America.

What sets FeederWatch apart from other monitoring programs is the detailed picture that FeederWatch data provide about weekly changes in bird distribution and abundance across North America. FeederWatch data tell us where birds are as well as where they are not. This crucial information enables scientists to piece together accurate population maps.

Because FeederWatchers count the number of individuals of each species they see several times throughout the winter, FeederWatch data are extremely powerful for detecting and explaining gradual changes in the wintering ranges of many species. In short, FeederWatch data are important because they provide information about bird population biology that cannot be detected by any other available method.

How Are FeederWatch Data Used?

The massive amounts of data collected by FeederWatchers across the continent help scientists understand:

- Long-term trends in bird distribution and abundance
- The timing and extent of winter irruptions of winter finches and other species
- Expansions or contractions in winter ranges of feeder birds
- Kinds of foods and environmental factors that attract birds
- How disease is spread among birds that visit feeders

How to Participate

Anyone interested in birds can participate, including people of all skill levels and backgrounds. FeederWatch is a great project for children, families, individuals, classrooms, retirees, youth groups, nature centers, and bird clubs. You can count birds as often as every week, or as infrequently as you like—the schedule is very flexible. All you need is a bird feeder, birdbath, or plantings that attract birds.

New participants receive a research kit with complete instructions for participating, as well as a bird identification poster and access to the digital version of *Living Bird*, the Cornell Lab's award-winning magazine, plus the year-end report, *Winter Bird Highlights*. As of 2017, there is an $18 annual participation fee for U.S. residents ($15 for Cornell Lab members). Canadians can participate by joining Bird Studies Canada for CAN$35. The participation fee covers materials, staff support, web design, data analysis, and the year-end report. Project FeederWatch is supported almost entirely by participation fees. Without the support of our participants, this project wouldn't be possible.

 To learn more about Project FeederWatch, visit *feederwatch.org* or use your Bird QR app and scan this symbol.

Project FeederWatch is operated by the Cornell Lab of Ornithology and Bird Studies Canada.

NESTWATCH

NestWatch is a nationwide monitoring program designed to track status and trends in the reproductive biology of birds, including when nesting occurs, how many eggs are laid, how many hatch, and how many hatchlings survive. The database is used to study the current condition of breeding bird populations and how they may be changing over time.

By finding and monitoring bird nests, NestWatch participants help scientists track the breeding success of birds across North America. Participants witness fascinating behaviors of birds at the nest, and collect information on the location,

American Robin's nest.

habitat, species, number of eggs, and number of young. Launched in 2007 with funding from the National Science Foundation, NestWatch has collected more than 300,000 nesting records. Combined with historic data, this information will help scientists address how birds are affected by large-scale changes such as global climate change, urbanization, and land conversion.

How to Participate

Participating in NestWatch is free and just about anyone can do it (children should always be accompanied by an adult when observing bird nests). Simply follow the directions on the website to become a certified NestWatcher, find a bird nest using the helpful tips, visit the nest every 3–4 days to record what you see, and then report this information on the website. Your observations will be added to those of thousands of other NestWatchers in a continually growing database used by researchers to understand and study birds. While you contribute extremely valuable information to science, you will also learn firsthand about the breeding behaviors of birds.

To learn more about NestWatch, visit *nestwatch.org* or use your Bird QR app and scan this symbol.

CELEBRATE URBAN BIRDS

Celebrate Urban Birds is a year-round project developed by the Cornell Lab for people in cities, suburbs, and rural areas. It is an easy, fun project for the entire family; no prior knowledge of birds is required, and your data will help scientists understand how birds use green spaces in cities. Since 2007, Celebrate Urban Birds has partnered with 11,000 community organizations and distributed 400,000 educational kits. Educational materials and online trainings are offered in both English and Spanish.

How to Participate

1. Register for free at *CelebrateUrbanBirds.org* and get your educational kit with instructions, ID guides, and sunflower seeds for planting.

2. Learn to identify 16 focal species. You can get additional species lists online at *CelebrateUrbanBirds.org/regional.*

3. Pick a place to watch birds in an area that is 50 feet by 50 feet (the size of half a basketball court).

4. Spend 10 minutes watching birds in the selected area.

5. Repeat observations three times in the same area in one month.

6. Enter data online or send to the Cornell Lab by mail.

Every year Celebrate Urban Birds awards dozens of mini-grants to community organizations, including Alzheimer's support groups, youth clubs, oncology centers, businesses, and rehabilitation centers throughout the Americas to lead community activities focused on birds, greening, and the arts. Anybody can apply for a grant—the application is simple! Visit *CelebrateUrbanBirds.org* to order educational materials, apply for a community grant, or find hundreds of fun, creative activities that involve the arts, greening, and birds for people of all ages.

To learn more, visit *CelebrateUrbanBirds.org* or use your Bird QR app and scan this symbol.

HABITAT NETWORK

Habitat Network is creating a citizen-science movement to explore how our collective efforts to transform yards and urban landscapes into more diverse habitat can support wildlife and connect people to nature in communities around the world.

IT'S A MAP
Habitat Network is a citizen-science mapping tool used to capture, identify, and share the state of private and public lands and other data about ecologically relevant practices in those places.

IT'S A RESOURCE
Habitat Network provides a search tool and local information you need to make informed decisions to plan for and improve a yard, park, school, or other green space.

IT'S EDUCATIONAL
Habitat Network provides informative articles and videos on a wide variety of topics, including native plants, healthy ecosystems, D.I.Y., cover, water, food, birds, pollinators, design advice, and more.

IT'S A COMMUNITY
Habitat Network gives like-minded people the ability to communicate and share their maps by either joining or forming specialized groups.

IT'S ECOLOGICAL
Habitat Network helps you revolutionize and transform your property by expanding native habitat and engaging you as part of the conservation solution to our shared environmental concerns.

How to Participate

Habitat Network is year-round. You can participate from anywhere in the world, although some of its resource tools are specific to North America. To begin mapping habitat, sign up for a free account at *www.Habitat.Network*. You can also browse the project's many gardening and landscaping resources and find tips and tutorials on how to use the mapping tools.

ANATOMY OF A HABITAT MAP

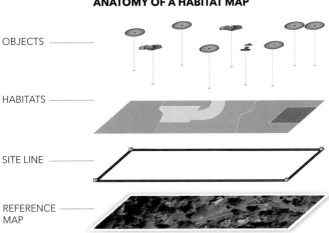

OBJECTS

HABITATS

SITE LINE

REFERENCE
MAP

To learn more about Habitat Network and to create your own habitat map, visit *www.Habitat.Network* or use your Bird QR app and scan this symbol.

*Habitat Network is a partnership between The Nature Conservancy
and the Cornell Lab of Ornithology.*

GUIDE TO WESTERN SPECIES

Violet-green Swallow
Photo by John Fox

The big, black-necked Canada Goose, with its signature white chinstrap mark, is a familiar bird of fields and parks. Thousands of these "honkers" migrate north and south each year, filling the sky with long V formations. As lawns have proliferated, more and more of these grassland-adapted birds are staying put in urban and suburban areas year-round, where some people enjoy them while others regard them as pests.

AT A GLANCE

Food
In spring and summer, Canada Geese concentrate their feeding on grasses and herbs, including skunk cabbage and eelgrass. During fall and winter they rely more on berries and seeds, including agricultural grains. They're also very efficient at removing kernels from dry corncobs. Two subspecies have adapted to urban environments and graze on domesticated grasses year-round.

Nesting
The nest of the Canada Goose is a large, open cup on the ground, made of dry grasses, lichens, mosses, and other plant materials. It's lined with down and some body feathers. The nests are usually located near water, on muskrat mounds or other slightly elevated sites.

Habitat
Canada Geese can be found just about anywhere near lakes, rivers, ponds, or other small or large bodies of water, and also in yards, parks, lawns, and farm fields.

RANGE MAP

- ■ Breeding
- ■ Nonbreeding
- ■ Year-round

KEYS TO IDENTIFICATION

MEASUREMENTS (Both sexes)

Length	Wingspan	Weight
30–43 in	50–67 in	105.8–318 oz
76–110 cm	127–170 cm	3000–9000 g

SIZE & SHAPE. The Canada Goose is a big waterbird with a long neck, large body, large webbed feet, and a wide, flat bill. Adult Canada Geese can vary widely in size.

COLOR PATTERN. The Canada Goose has a black head with white cheeks and a chinstrap, black neck, tan breast, and brown back. Its bill, legs, and feet are all black.

BEHAVIOR. Canada Geese feed by dabbling in the water or grazing in fields and large lawns. They are known for their honking call and are often very vocal in flight. They often fly together in pairs or in V formation in flocks, which reduces wind resistance and conserves energy.

Cool Facts

At least 11 subspecies of Canada Goose have been recognized. In general, the farther north they breed, the smaller they are, and the farther west, the darker.

Backyard Tips

Mowing and maintaining large lawns anywhere near water is an open invitation to Canada Geese. If you want to keep them from walking on your lawn, plastic mesh on the grass may do the trick.

The Wood Duck is one of the most stunningly beautiful of all ducks. The male is iridescent chestnut and green, whereas the elegant female has a distinctive profile and delicate white pattern around the eye. They live in wooded swamps, where they nest in holes in trees, or in nest boxes put up near lakes and ponds. They are one of the few duck species equipped with strong claws that can grip bark and perch on branches.

Food Wood Ducks eat seeds, fruits, acorns, insects, and other arthropods. Some feed heavily on corn and other grains in agricultural fields. Studies indicate that their diets can vary greatly, but plants make up 80% or more of their diet.

Nesting Wood Ducks nest in tree holes with openings that range from 4 inches to a couple of feet across. The cavity depth is variable, averaging about 2 feet deep, but in rotten trees can be as much as 15 feet deep. The young use their clawed feet to climb out. The female lines the nest with down feathers taken from her breast.

Habitat Look for Wood Ducks in wooded swamps, marshes, streams, beaver ponds, and small lakes. They prefer to stick to wet areas with trees or cattails. As cavity nesters, Wood Ducks take readily to nest boxes.

RANGE MAP

- Breeding
- Nonbreeding
- Nonbreeding (scarce)
- Year-round

KEYS TO IDENTIFICATION

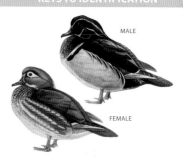

MALE

FEMALE

MEASUREMENTS (Both sexes)

Length	Wingspan	Weight
18.5–21.3 in 47–54 cm	26–28.7 in 66–73 cm	16–30.4 oz 454–862 g

SIZE & SHAPE. The Wood Duck has a unique shape among ducks—boxy, crested head, thin neck, and long, broad tail. In flight, they hold their heads up high, sometimes bobbing them. Overall, their silhouettes show skinny necks, long bodies, thick tails, and short wings.

COLOR PATTERN. In good light, males have a glossy green head with white stripes, a chestnut breast, and buffy sides. In low light, they look dark overall with paler sides. The female is gray-brown with a white-speckled breast. In late summer, males lose their pale sides and bold stripes, but retain their bright eyes and bills.

BEHAVIOR. Unlike most waterfowl species, the Wood Duck perches and nests in trees and often flies through woods. When swimming, its head jerks back and forth, similar to the head movement of a walking pigeon. Wood Ducks often gather in small groups, separate from other waterfowl. Listen for the female's call when these wary birds flush.

Cool Facts

Wood Ducks nest in trees near water. Soon after hatching, ducklings jump down from the nest and go to the water. Ducklings can jump from heights of over 50 feet without injury.

Backyard Tips

Consider putting up a nest box to attract a breeding pair of Wood Ducks—you can find instructions for building one at *nestwatch.org/birdhouses*. Attach a predator guard to protect eggs and young.

The Mallard is perhaps the most familiar of all ducks, occuring throughout North America and Eurasia in ponds and parks, as well as wilder wetlands and estuaries. The male's gleaming green head, black tail-curl, and gray flanks arguably make it the most easily identified duck. Almost all domestic ducks come from this species, and odd-looking hybrid Mallards can be commonly found in parks and towns.

AT A GLANCE

Food Mallards eat a wide variety of food. They don't dive but instead dabble to feed, tipping forward in the water to eat seeds and aquatic vegetation. On the shore, they pick at prey and vegetation on the ground. In city parks, they readily accept handouts from parkgoers.

Nesting Mallards nest on the ground on dry land near water. Nests are generally concealed under overhanging grass or other vegetation, occasionally in agricultural fields. Females construct their nests, which are usually about a foot across, with a bowl for the eggs that is usually 1–6 inches deep and 6–9 inches across.

Habitat Mallards can live in almost any wetland habitat. Look for them on lakes, ponds, marshes, rivers, and coastal habitats, as well as city and suburban parks and residential backyards.

RANGE MAP

■ Breeding
■ Nonbreeding
■ Year-round

KEYS TO IDENTIFICATION

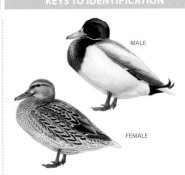

MALE

FEMALE

MEASUREMENTS (Both sexes)

Length	Wingspan	Weight
19.7–25.6 in 50–65 cm	32.3–37.4 in 82–95 cm	35.3–45.9 oz 1000–1300 g

SIZE & SHAPE. Mallards are large ducks with hefty bodies, rounded heads, and wide, flat bills. Like many "dabbling ducks," their bodies are long and their tails ride high out of the water, giving them a blunt shape. In flight, their wings are broad and set back toward the rear.

COLOR PATTERN. Male Mallards have dark, iridescent-green heads and bright yellow bills. Their gray bodies are sandwiched between a brown breast and black rear. Females and juveniles are mottled brown with orange-and-brown bills. Both sexes have a white-bordered, blue "speculum" or bright patch in their wing.

BEHAVIOR. Mallards are "dabbling ducks"—they feed in the water by tipping forward and grazing on underwater plants. They almost never dive. They can be very tame, especially in city ponds, and often group together with other Mallards, other species of dabbling ducks, or even farm ducks.

Cool Facts

The classic quack of a duck comes from the female Mallard. Males don't quack; they make a quieter, rasping sound. Male Mallards don't incubate or care for ducklings after they hatch.

Backyard Tips

If you have a pond or marshy area on your property, Mallards might be attracted to your yard. Mallards sometimes feed on corn and other seeds beneath feeders.

The California Quail is a handsome, round soccer ball of a bird with a curious, forward-drooping head plume. Its stiffly accented *chi-ca-go* call is a common sound of the chaparral and other brushy areas of California and the Northwest. Often seen scratching at the ground in large groups or dashing forward on blurred legs, California Quail are common but unobtrusive and shy. They flush to cover if surprised, so approach them gently.

AT A GLANCE

Food
Mainly a seedeater, this little quail also eats leaves, flowers, catkins, manzanita and poison oak berries, acorns, and invertebrates such as caterpillars, beetles, millipedes, and snails. The diet is about 70% vegetarian.

Nesting
Female California Quail usually hide their nests on the ground amid grasses or at the bases of shrubs or trees, but occasionally up to 10 feet off the ground. The nest is lined with stems and grasses and measures about 5–7 inches across and 1–2 inches deep.

Habitat
You'll find California Quail in chaparral, sagebrush, oak woodlands, and foothill forests of California and the Northwest. They're quite tolerant of people and can be common in city parks, suburban gardens, and agricultural areas.

RANGE MAP

Year-round

KEYS TO IDENTIFICATION

MALE

MEASUREMENTS (Both sexes)

Length	Wingspan	Weight
9.4–10.6 in	12.6–14.6 in	4.9–8.1 oz
24–27 cm	32–37 cm	140–230 g

SIZE & SHAPE. The California Quail is a plump, short-necked game bird with a small head and bill. They fly on short, very broad wings. The tail is square. Both sexes have a comma-shaped topknot of feathers projecting forward from the forehead, longer in males than females.

COLOR PATTERN. Adult males are rich gray and brown, with a black face outlined with bold white stripes. Females are a plainer brown and lack the facial markings. Both sexes have a pattern of white, creamy, and chestnut scales on the belly. Young birds look like females but have a shorter topknot.

BEHAVIOR. California Quail spend most of their time on the ground, walking and scratching in search of food. In morning and evening they forage beneath shrubs or on open ground near cover. They usually travel in groups called coveys. Their flight is explosive but lasts just long enough to reach cover.

Cool Facts

California Quail chicks often mix together after hatching, with the young from several broods being taken care of by all the parents working together.

Backyard Tips

Attract California Quail to your yard by sprinkling grain or birdseed on the ground and providing dense shrubbery nearby for cover. These ground dwellers are very vulnerable to domesticated cats.

Gambel's Quail are gregarious birds of the desert Southwest, where coveys gather along brushy washes and cactus-studded arroyos to feed. Males and females both sport a bobbing black topknot of feathers. The male's prominent black belly patch distinguishes it from the similar California Quail. This ground-hugging desert dweller would rather run than fly— look for one of these tubby birds running between cover or posting a lookout on low shrubs.

AT A GLANCE

Food Gambel's Quail eat mostly seeds of grasses, shrubs, forbs, trees, and cactus. They pick mesquite seeds from cattle and coyote droppings. They also eat leaves and grass blades. Berries and cactus fruit are important when available, as are insects, especially for chicks.

Nesting Female Gambel's Quail choose a concealed nest site on the ground, shielded by protective vegetation. Rarely they nest in trees. The simple, bowl-shaped depression or scrape is 1.5 inches deep, 5–7 inches across, and lined with grass stems, leaves, and feathers.

Habitat Gambel's Quail live in the hot Sonoran, Mohave, and Chihuahuan deserts below about 5,500 feet elevation. They frequent mesquite thickets along river valleys and arroyos, shrub and cactus lands, dry grasslands, and farm fields.

RANGE MAP

■ Year-round

KEYS TO IDENTIFICATION

MALE

MEASUREMENTS (Both sexes)

Length	Wingspan	Weight
9.8 in	13.4–14.2 in	5.6–7.1 oz
25 cm	34–36 cm	160–200 g

SIZE & SHAPE. Like other quail, Gambel's Quail are plump, volleyball-sized birds with short necks, small bills, and square tails. The wings are short and broad. Both sexes have a comma-shaped topknot of feathers atop their small heads, fuller in males than females.

COLOR PATTERN. Gambel's Quail are richly patterned in gray, chestnut, and cream that camouflages them in the desert. Males have a bright rufous shaggy crown, chestnut flanks striped with white, and a creamy belly with a central black patch. Females are grayer and less patterned.

BEHAVIOR. Gambel's Quail walk or run along the ground in groups called coveys that may include a dozen or more birds. They scratch for food under shrubs and cacti, eating grasses and cactus fruits. Flight is explosive, powerful, and brief.

Cool Facts

Hatching chicks cut out a neat round hole in the largest part of the shell, leaving part of the membrane in place to serve as a hinge. Then they can push the little door open to walk out.

Backyard Tips

Offer Gambel's Quail sunflower seeds, cracked corn, millet, milo, and water at ground level or in a sturdy platform feeder.

The Ring-necked Pheasant can be found striding across open fields and weedy roadsides in the U.S. and southern Canada. The male sports iridescent copper-and-gold plumage, a red face, and a crisp white collar. Its crowing can be heard as far as a mile away. Introduced to the U.S. from Asia in the 1880s, pheasants quickly became one of North America's most popular upland game birds. Watch for them along roads or bursting into flight from brushy cover.

AT A GLANCE

Food　In fall and winter, Ring-necked Pheasants eat seeds, grasses, leaves, roots, wild fruits, nuts, and insects. Their spring and summer diet is similar but with a greater emphasis on animal prey and fresh greenery. They forage in grasslands, hayfields, and brushy areas.

Nesting　The Ring-necked Pheasant's nest, built on the ground, is a rudimentary affair—unlined or sparsely lined with vegetation taken from beside the nest depression. The average nest bowl is about 7 inches across and 3 inches deep. Nests are usually surrounded by tall vegetation.

Habitat　Ring-necked Pheasants are birds of agricultural areas intermixed with areas of taller vegetation, which they use for cover. Look for them along rural roadsides, in overgrown or recently harvested fields, and in brushy areas and hedgerows.

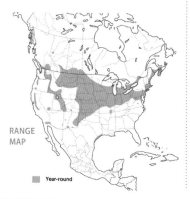

RANGE MAP

■ Year-round

KEYS TO IDENTIFICATION

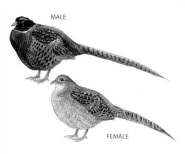

MALE

FEMALE

MEASUREMENTS (Both sexes)

Length	Wingspan	Weight
19.7–27.6 in	22–33.9 in	17.6–105.8 oz
50–70 cm	56–86 cm	500–3000 g

SIZE & SHAPE. The Ring-necked Pheasant is a large, chickenlike bird with a long, pointed tail. It has fairly long legs, a small head, long neck, and plump body.

COLOR PATTERN. The male Ring-necked Pheasant is a gaudy bird with a red face and an iridescent green neck with a bold white ring. The male's very long tail is coppery with thin, black bars. The female is brown with paler scaling on its upperparts, buff or cinnamon on its underparts, black spotting on its sides, and thin, black bars on its tail.

BEHAVIOR. Ring-necked Pheasants forage on the ground in fields, where they eat waste grain, other seeds, and insects when available. They usually walk or run, only occasionally resorting to flying (usually when disturbed at close range by humans or predators). Males give a loud, cackling display that can be heard over long distances.

Cool Facts
Along with most of the grouse family, pheasants have strong breast muscles which create extreme power, allowing them to escape trouble in a hurry when needed.

Backyard Tips
Keep an eye out for Ring-necked Pheasants running between patches of cover as you travel through agricultural areas—particularly along dirt roads where they often forage in weedy areas.

The Wild Turkey is a big, spectacular bird and a common sight throughout the year as flocks stride around woods and clearings. The courting male puffs itself into a feathery ball and fills the air with exuberant gobbling. Many North American kids learn turkey identification by tracing outlines of their hands to make Thanksgiving cards. Reintroductions have made them even more widespread today than historically. They now occur in every state except Alaska.

AT A GLANCE

Food Wild Turkeys forage in flocks, mostly on the ground. Sometimes they climb into shrubs or low trees for fruits. Throughout the year they eat seeds, nuts, berries, buds, and other plant matter, occasionally supplementing their diet with insects and small vertebrates.

Nesting Wild Turkeys nest on the ground in dead leaves at the base of a tree, under a brush pile or shrubbery, or occasionally in an open hayfield. The female scratches a shallow depression in the soil and lines it with only the dead leaves or other plant materials already present at the site.

Habitat Wild Turkeys live in mature forests, particularly with nut trees such as oak, hickory, or beech, interspersed among edges and fields. You may also see them along roads and in woodsy backyards.

RANGE MAP

▨ Year-round

KEYS TO IDENTIFICATION

MALE

MEASUREMENTS (Both sexes)

Length	Wingspan	Weight
43.3–45.3 in	49.2–56.7 in	88–381 oz
110–115 cm	125–144 cm	2500–10800 g

SIZE & SHAPE. The Wild Turkey is a very large, plump bird with long legs, a wide rounded tail, and a small head on a long, slim neck.

COLOR PATTERN. The Wild Turkey is dark overall, with a bronze-green iridescence on most of its plumage. Its wings are dark and boldly barred with white, and its rump and tail feathers are broadly tipped rusty or white. The bare skin of its head and neck varies from red to blue to gray.

BEHAVIOR. Wild Turkeys travel in flocks and search on the ground for nuts, berries, insects, and snails. They use their strong feet to scratch leaf litter out of the way. In early spring, males gather in clearings to perform courtship displays. They puff up their body feathers, flare their tails into a vertical fan, and strut slowly while giving a characteristic gobbling call. At night, Wild Turkeys fly up into trees to roost in groups.

Cool Facts

Newly hatched chicks follow the female, which feeds them for a few days until they learn to find food on their own. As the chicks grow, they band into groups. Male Wild Turkeys don't help out at all.

Backyard Tips

If you have a large yard near woods, you can attract Wild Turkeys by planting nut-bearing or berry trees. Some people attract turkeys by scattering birdseed or corn on their lawns.

Part bird, part submarine, the Pied-billed Grebe is commonly found across much of North America. These expert divers inhabit sluggish rivers, freshwater marshes, lakes, and estuaries. They use their chunky bills to kill and eat large crustaceans along with a great variety of fish, amphibians, insects, and other invertebrates. Rarely seen in flight and often hidden amid vegetation, the Pied-billed Grebe announces its presence with a loud call.

AT A GLANCE

Food
Pied-billed Grebes eat mostly crustaceans (particularly crayfish) and small fish, which they capture and crush with their stout bills and strong jaws. Collecting most of their food underwater during foraging dives, they also eat mussels, snails, beetles, dragonfly nymphs, and other aquatic insects and their larvae.

Nesting
Pied-billed Grebes create an open bowl nest on a platform of floating vegetation, usually situated among tall emergent plants. Its nest bowl is 4–5 inches in diameter and about an inch deep, and may be expanded during the egg-laying period.

Habitat
Look for Pied-billed Grebes on small, quiet ponds and marshes where thick vegetation grows out of the water. In winter, they occur on larger water bodies, occasionally in large groups.

RANGE MAP

- ▨ Breeding
- ▨ Nonbreeding
- ▨ Year-round

KEYS TO IDENTIFICATION

MEASUREMENTS (Both sexes)

Length	Wingspan	Weight
11.8–15 in	17.7–24.4 in	8.9–20 oz
30–38 cm	45–62 cm	253–568 g

SIZE & SHAPE. The Pied-billed Grebe is a small, chunky swimming bird. It has a compact body and a slender neck, with a relatively large, blocky head and short, thick bill. It has virtually no tail.

COLOR PATTERN. These brown birds are slightly darker on their upperparts and more tawny-brown on the underparts. During spring and summer, the crown and nape are dark and the throat is black. While breeding, the bill is whitish with a black band ("pied"), but it's yellow-brown at other times of year. The juvenile has a striped face.

BEHAVIOR. Pied-billed Grebes can adjust their buoyancy and often float with just the upper half of the head above the water. They catch small fish and invertebrates by diving or slowly submerging. After a dive, they may reappear quite a distance from where they went down.

Cool Facts

Pied-billed Grebes create their varying buoyancy by trapping water in their feathers, giving them great control. They can sink deeply or stay just at or below the surface with this ability.

Find This Bird

Look for small-bodied, large-headed Pied-billed Grebes in summer on large ponds and small lakes with emergent vegetation. In winter, look for them in small flocks on larger water bodies.

The gangly Double-crested Cormorant is a prehistoric-looking, matte-black fishing bird with yellow-orange facial skin. Cormorants are a common sight around fresh and salt water across North America—perhaps attracting the most attention when standing in a large group on docks, rocky islands, and channel markers, wings spread out to dry. These solid, heavy-boned birds chase and catch small fish underwater.

AT A GLANCE

Food Double-crested Cormorants eat mostly fish, but may also consume insects, crustaceans, or amphibians. They dive and chase fish underwater with powerful propulsion from webbed feet. The tip of a cormorant's bill is shaped like a hook, helpful for seizing its prey.

Nesting Cormorants often nest in colonies. Nests may be on the ground, on rocks or reefs with no vegetation, or atop trees. They're constructed of small sticks, with some seaweed and flotsam, and lined with grass. The male delivers the material and the female does the building. Nests are 1.5–3 feet in diameter and 4–17 inches high.

Habitat Double-crested Cormorants are the most widespread cormorants in North America, and the ones most often seen in fresh water. They breed on coastlines and along large inland lakes. A colony's stick nests, built high in trees on an island or patch of flooded timber, can be conspicuous.

RANGE MAP

- Breeding
- Migration
- Nonbreeding
- Year-round

KEYS TO IDENTIFICATION

MEASUREMENTS (Both sexes)

Length	Wingspan	Weight
27.6–35.4 in 70–90 cm	44.9–48.4 in 114–123 cm	42.3–88.2 oz 1200–2500 g

SIZE & SHAPE. The Double-crested Cormorant is a large waterbird with a small head on a long, kinked neck. It has a thin, strongly hooked bill, roughly the length of its head. Its heavy body sits low in the water; from a distance or in poor light, it may sometimes be mistaken for a loon.

COLOR PATTERN. Adults are brown-black with a small patch of yellow-orange skin on the face. Immatures are browner overall, palest on the neck and breast. In the breeding season, adults develop a small double crest of stringy black or white feathers.

BEHAVIOR. Double-crested Cormorants float low on the surface of water and dive to catch small fish. After fishing, they stand on docks, rocks, and tree limbs with wings spread open to dry. In flight, they often travel in V-formation flocks that shift and reform as the birds alternate between bursts of choppy flapping and short glides.

Cool Facts

Up close, the all-black Double-crested Cormorant puts lots of bright colors on show, with an orange-yellow throat, sparkling aquamarine eyes, and a mouth that is bright blue on the inside.

Find This Bird

Look near lakes and coastlines for these perched black waterbirds. On the water they sit low, head usually tilted slightly upward. You may also see them holding their wings out to sun themselves.

Whether poised at a river bend or cruising along the coastline with slow, deep wingbeats, the Great Blue Heron is a majestic sight. This widespread heron with subtle blue-gray plumage often stands motionless as it scans for prey, or it may wade belly deep with deliberate steps. It may move slowly, but the Great Blue Heron can strike like lightning to grab a fish or snap up a gopher. In flight, look for its tucked-in neck and long legs trailing out behind.

AT A GLANCE

Food
Great Blue Herons eat nearly any prey within striking distance, including fish, amphibians, reptiles, small mammals, insects, and other birds. They grab small prey in their strong mandibles or use the closed bill to impale larger fish.

Nesting
The male Great Blue Heron gathers the sticks that serve as the bulk of the nest material, presenting them to the female. She builds a platform to support the saucer-shaped nest cup, lining it with smaller materials. The finished nest may be from 20 inches to 4 feet across and nearly 3.5 feet deep.

Habitat
Look for Great Blue Herons in saltwater and freshwater habitats, from open coasts, marshes, sloughs, riverbanks, and lakes to backyard goldfish ponds. They also forage in grasslands and agricultural fields. Breeding birds gather in colonies called "heronries," where they build stick nests high off the ground.

RANGE MAP

Breeding
Nonbreeding
Year-round

KEYS TO IDENTIFICATION

MEASUREMENTS (Both sexes)

Length	Wingspan	Weight
38–54 in	65–79 in	74–88 oz
97–137 cm	167–201 cm	2100–2500 g

SIZE & SHAPE. This largest of North American herons has long legs, a sinuous neck, and a thick, daggerlike bill. Head, chest, and wing plumes give a shaggy appearance. In flight, the Great Blue Heron curls its neck into a tight "S" shape. Its wings are broad and rounded, and the legs trail well beyond the tail.

COLOR PATTERN. The Great Blue Heron appears blue-gray from a distance, with a wide black stripe over the eye. In flight, the upper side of the wings are two-toned, pale on the forewings and darker on the flight feathers.

BEHAVIOR. Hunting Great Blue Herons wade slowly or stand statuelike, stalking fish and other prey in shallow water or open fields. Watch for the lightning-fast thrust of the neck and head as they stab with their strong bills. Their very slow wingbeats, tucked-in neck, and trailing legs create an unmistakable image in flight.

Cool Facts

These birds can hunt day and night thanks to a high percentage of rod-type photoreceptors in their eyes for night vision. Specially shaped vertebrae help them strike prey at a distance.

Backyard Tips

Great Blue Herons sometimes visit yards that feature fish ponds. A length of drain pipe placed in the pond can provide fish with a place to hide from feeding herons.

Great Egrets are a dazzling sight in many North American wetlands. Slightly smaller and more svelte than Great Blue Herons, Great Egrets are still large with an impressive wingspan. They hunt in classic heron fashion, standing immobile or wading through wetlands to capture fish. Great Egrets were hunted nearly to extinction for their plumes in the late nineteenth century, sparking conservation movements and some of the first laws to protect birds.

AT A GLANCE

Food

The Great Egret eats mainly small fish but also takes amphibians, reptiles, birds, small mammals, and invertebrates. It hunts in belly-deep or shallower water, alone or in groups. It wades in search of prey or simply stands still waiting for prey to approach.

Nesting

The male builds the nest platform from long sticks and twigs before pairing up with a female; both members of the pair may collaborate to complete the nest, though the male sometimes finishes it himself. The nest is up to 3 feet across and 1 foot deep.

Habitat

Great Egrets live in freshwater, brackish, and marine wetlands. During the breeding season, they are found in colonies in trees or shrubs with other waterbirds. The colonies are located on lakes, ponds, marshes, estuaries, impoundments, and islands. Great Egrets use similar habitats for migration stopover sites and wintering grounds.

RANGE MAP

- Breeding
- Migration
- Nonbreeding
- Year-round

KEYS TO IDENTIFICATION

MEASUREMENTS (Both sexes)

Length	Wingspan	Weight
37–41 in	51–57 in	35 oz
94–104 cm	131–145 cm	1000 g

SIZE & SHAPE. Great Egrets are tall, long-legged wading birds with long, daggerlike bills and long necks that may be stretched to full length or folded in an S curve. In flight, the long neck is tucked in and the legs extend far beyond the tip of the short tail.

COLOR PATTERN. Every feather on a Great Egret is white. The bill is solid yellowish-orange and the legs and feet are entirely black.

BEHAVIOR. Great Egrets wade in shallow water (both fresh and salt) to hunt fish, frogs, and other small aquatic animals. They typically stand still and watch for unsuspecting prey to pass by, and then, with startling speed, strike with a jab of the long neck and bill.

Cool Facts

During the breeding season, Great Egrets grow long, beautiful plumes on their backs called *aigrettes*. These feathers, once prized for ladies' hats, almost led to the bird's extinction in the late 1800s.

Find This Bird

At any pond, wetland, or coastal marsh within their range, you may see a few kinds of all-white herons. Look for the Great Egret's large size, black legs, and yellow bill.

If you've gone looking for raptors on a clear day, your heart has probably leaped at the sight of a large, soaring bird in the distance. If it's soaring with its wings raised in a V and making wobbly circles, it's probably a Turkey Vulture. These birds ride thermals in the sky and use their keen sense of smell to detect fresh carcasses. They are consummate scavengers, cleaning up the countryside one bite of their sharply hooked bills at a time.

Food

Turkey Vultures eat carrion, which they find largely by their excellent sense of smell. Mostly they eat mammals but also feed on dead reptiles, other birds, amphibians, fish, and even invertebrates. Unlike their Black Vulture relatives, Turkey Vultures almost never attack living prey.

Nesting

Turkey Vultures don't build much of a nest. They may scrape out a spot in the soil or leaf litter, pull aside obstacles, or arrange scraps of vegetation or rotting wood. Some use rotting logs or even old barns. Many nest sites are used repeatedly for a decade or more.

Habitat

Turkey Vultures are common in open areas, along roadsides, and near food sources such as landfills, trash heaps, and construction sites. On sunny days, look for them in the air; in colder weather and at night they roost on poles, towers, and dead trees.

RANGE MAP

- Breeding
- Year-round

MEASUREMENTS (Both sexes)

Length	Wingspan	Weight
25.2–31.9 in	66.9–70.1 in	70.5 oz
64–81 cm	170–178 cm	2000 g

SIZE & SHAPE. Turkey Vultures are large dark birds with long, broad wings. Bigger than most raptors except eagles and condors, they have long "fingers" at their wingtips and long tails that extend past their toe tips in flight. When soaring, Turkey Vultures hold their wings slightly raised, making a V when seen head-on.

COLOR PATTERN. Turkey Vultures appear black from a distance but up close are dark brown with a featherless red head and pale bill. While most of their body and forewing are dark, the undersides of the flight feathers (along the trailing edge and wingtips) are paler, giving a two-toned appearance.

BEHAVIOR. Turkey Vultures are majestic but unsteady soarers. Their teetering flight with very few wingbeats is characteristic. Look for them gliding relatively low to the ground, sniffing for carrion, or riding thermals to higher vantage points. They may soar in small groups and roost in larger numbers. You may see them on the ground in small groups, huddled around roadkill.

Cool Facts

Turkey Vultures have excellent immune systems and can feast on carcasses without contracting botulism, anthrax, cholera, or salmonella.

Find This Bird

Turkey Vultures are accustomed to living near humans and cleaning up messes. Look for them at farm fields or on road edges, as well as in the sky on hot days.

The "marsh hawk" is a slim, long-tailed hawk that glides low over a marshes or grasslands, holding its wings in a V shape and sporting a white patch at the base of its tail. Up close it has an owlish face that helps it hear mice and voles beneath the vegetation. Most of the gray-and-white males have a single mate, but some can attract several females to their territories: those males work extra hard because they provide most of the food for their mates and young.

AT A GLANCE

Food Northern Harriers forage on the wing, coursing low over the ground, relying heavily on their sense of hearing to capture prey hidden in dense vegetation. In the breeding season they eat many vertebrates. During winter, they eat mostly meadow voles and mice.

Nesting Northern Harriers nest on the ground, usually in a dense clump of vegetation. The male may build the nest platform, the female finishing it using nesting material such as grasses, sedges, and rushes. The outside of the nest measures 16–24 inches wide by 1.5–8 inches high.

Habitat Northern Harriers breed in wide-open habitats ranging from Arctic tundra to prairie grasslands to fields and marshes. In migration and winter, they usually move south to open habitats similar to their breeding areas but with little or no snow cover.

RANGE MAP

- Breeding
- Nonbreeding
- Year-round

KEYS TO IDENTIFICATION

MALE

FEMALE

MEASUREMENTS (Both sexes)

Length	Wingspan	Weight
18.1–19.7 in	40.2–46.5 in	10.6–26.5 oz
46–50 cm	102–118 cm	300–750 g

SIZE & SHAPE. Northern Harriers are slender, medium-sized raptors with long, fairly broad wings and a long, rounded tail. They have a flat, owl-like face and a small, sharply hooked bill. Harriers often fly with their wings held in a dihedral or V shape above the horizontal.

COLOR PATTERN. Adult males are gray above and whitish below with black wingtips, a dark trailing edge to the wing, and a black-banded tail. Females and immatures are brown, with black bands on the tail. All Northern Harriers have a white rump patch that is obvious in flight.

BEHAVIOR. Northern Harriers fly low over the ground when hunting, weaving back and forth over fields and marshes as they watch and listen for small animals. They eat on the ground, and they perch on low posts or trees. On the breeding grounds, males perform elaborate flying barrel rolls to court females.

Cool Facts

Northern Harriers are the most owl-like of hawks, relying on hearing as well as vision to capture prey hidden in dense vegetation. The disk-shaped face functions like an owl's, directing sound to the ears.

Find This Bird

Head to your nearest wide-open space, be it grassland, marsh, or field, to look for harriers. They'll be zigzagging low, head down, looking and listening for prey, showing a bright rump patch.

The tiny Sharp-shinned Hawk often appears in a blur of motion and disappears in a flurry of feathers. This smallest hawk in North America is a daring, acrobatic flier. An "accipiter," it has long legs, short wings, and a very long tail, an ideal shape for navigating its deep-woods home at top speed in pursuit of songbirds and occasionally small rodents. The Sharp-shinned Hawk is easiest to spot in fall on its southward migration.

AT A GLANCE

Food

Songbirds make up about 90% of the Sharp-shinned Hawk's diet. Birds the size of American Robins or smaller are the most frequent prey; bigger birds are at less risk but not completely safe. Sharp-shinned Hawks also eat small rodents and an occasional moth or grasshopper.

Nesting

The nest is a broad, flat mass of dead twigs, sometimes lined with flakes of bark. Both members of the pair bring material to the site, but the female does most or all of the construction. The shallow, platformlike nest is usually 1–2 feet in diameter and 4–6 inches deep.

Habitat

Sharp-shinned Hawks breed in deep forests. During migration, look for them in open habitats or high in the sky, migrating along ridgelines. During the nonbreeding season they hunt small birds and mammals along forest edges, and sometimes at backyard bird feeders.

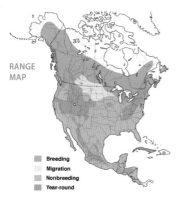

RANGE MAP

- ■ Breeding
- ■ Migration
- ■ Nonbreeding
- ■ Year-round

KEYS TO IDENTIFICATION

MEASUREMENTS (Both sexes)

Length	Wingspan	Weight
9.4–13.4 in 24–34 cm	16.9–22 in 43–56 cm	3.1–7.7 oz 87–218 g

SIZE & SHAPE. Sharp-shinned Hawks are small, long-tailed hawks with short, rounded wings. They have small heads that in flight do not usually project beyond the "wrists" of the wings. The tail tends to be square-tipped and may show a notch at the tip. Females are considerably larger than males.

COLOR PATTERN. Adults are slaty blue-gray above, with narrow red-orange bars on the breast. Immature birds are mostly brown with coarse vertical streaks on white underparts. Adults and young have broad dark bands across their long tails.

BEHAVIOR. Sharp-shinned Hawks are agile fliers that speed through dense woods to surprise their prey, typically songbirds. They may also pounce from low perches. When flying across open areas, they have a distinctive flap-and-glide flight style.

Cool Facts

Sharp-shinned Hawks carry their prey to a stump or low branch to pluck before eating. Unlike owls, they seldom swallow feathers.

Backyard Tips

Bird feeders sometimes attract hawks. If you want to give the small birds a break, take your feeders for a few weeks. The hawk will move on and the songbirds will return when you put your feeders back up.

Among the bird world's most skillful fliers, Cooper's Hawks are common woodland hawks that tear through tree canopies at high speed in pursuit of other birds. You're most likely to see one prowling above a forest edge or field using just a few stiff wingbeats followed by a glide. Their smaller lookalike, the Sharp-shinned Hawk, makes Cooper's Hawks famously tricky to identify.

Food
Cooper's Hawks eat mainly medium-sized birds which they chase. They sometimes rob nests and also eat some rodents and bats.

Nesting
Cooper's Hawks build nests in pines, firs, spruces, oaks, beeches, and other trees, in dense woods or suburban neighborhoods. The male builds the nest over about 2 weeks, with a little help from the female. Nests are piles of sticks roughly 27 inches in diameter and 6–17 inches high. The cup, 8 inches wide and 4 inches deep, is lined with bark flakes and sometimes green twigs.

Habitat
Cooper's Hawks are forest and woodland birds, but they do well in leafy suburbs, too. These lanky hawks are a regular sight in parks, quiet neighborhoods, fields, backyard feeders, and even along busy streets if there are trees around.

RANGE MAP

▇ Breeding
▇ Nonbreeding
▇ Year-round

KEYS TO IDENTIFICATION

MEASUREMENTS

		Length	Wingspan	Weight
Male		14.6–15.4 in 37–39 cm	24.4–35.4 in 62–90 cm	7.8–14.5 oz 220–410 g
Female		16.5–17.7 in 42–45 cm	29.5–35.4 in 75–90 cm	11.6–24 oz 330–680 g

SIZE & SHAPE. This medium-sized hawk has the classic accipiter shape: broad, rounded wings and a long tail. It has a more bull-headed look than the Sharp-shinned, its head often jutting past the bend of the wings, and its tail tip is usually more rounded.

COLOR PATTERN. Adults are steely blue-gray above with warm reddish bars on the underparts and thick dark bands on the tail. Juveniles are brown above and crisply streaked on the upper breast, giving them a cleaner look than the more blurry streaking of young Sharp-shinned Hawks.

BEHAVIOR. Cooper's Hawks fly with the flap-flap-glide pattern typical of accipiters, seldom flapping continuously. One hunting strategy is to fly fast and low to the ground, then up and over an obstruction to surprise prey on the other side.

Cool Facts

A Cooper's Hawk captures a bird with its feet and kills it by squeezing. Falcons tend to kill their prey by biting it, but Cooper's Hawks hold their catch away from the body until it dies.

Find This Bird

During migration, organized hawk watches on ridgetops in both East and West are great places to see lots of Cooper's Hawks.

Whether wheeling over a swamp forest or whistling plaintively from a riverine park, a Red-shouldered Hawk is typically a sign of wet deciduous woodlands. It's one of our most distinctively marked common hawks, with barred reddish-peachy underparts and a strongly banded tail. In flight, translucent crescents near the wingtips help to identify the species at a distance.

AT A GLANCE

Food Red-shouldered Hawks hunt from perches below the forest canopy or at the edge of a pond, sitting silently until they detect prey below. Then they descend swiftly, gliding and snatching a vole, chipmunk, or toad. They also eat frogs, snakes, and crayfish.

Nesting Each year both male and female build a new nest or refurbish a prior year's nest. The stick nest is about 2 feet in diameter, typically placed in a broad-leaved tree (occasionally in a conifer), below the forest canopy but toward the treetop, usually in a crotch of the main trunk.

Habitat Look for Red-shouldered Hawks in deciduous woodlands, often near rivers and swamps. During migration they often move high overhead along ridges or coastlines. They may be abundant at some hawk-watching overlooks.

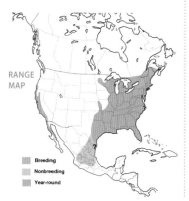

RANGE MAP

Breeding
Nonbreeding
Year-round

KEYS TO IDENTIFICATION

MEASUREMENTS (Both sexes)

Length	Wingspan	Weight
16.9–24 in	37–43.7 in	17.1–27.3 oz
43–61 cm	94–111 cm	486–774 g

SIZE & SHAPE. Red-shouldered Hawks are medium sized, with broad, rounded wings and medium-length tails that they fan out when soaring. In flight, they often glide or soar with their wingtips pushed slightly forward, giving them a distinctive "reaching" posture.

COLOR PATTERN. Adults are colorful hawks with dark-and-white checkered wings and warm reddish barring on the breast. The tail is black with narrow white bands. Immatures are brown above and white below streaked with brown. All ages show narrow, pale crescents near the wingtips in flight.

BEHAVIOR. Red-shouldered Hawks soar over forests or perch on tree branches or utility wires. Their rising, whistled *kee-rah* is a distinctive sound of the forest. They hunt small mammals, amphibians, and reptiles either from perches or while flying.

Cool Facts

American Crows often mob Red-shouldered Hawks, and both species may chase each other to steal food. The two species may also join forces to attack a Great Horned Owl and chase it away.

Find This Bird

A good way to find Red-shouldered Hawks is to learn their distinctive whistle and listen for it in and around wet forests, where you may find them hunting from a perch along a stream or pond.

The Red-tailed Hawk is probably the most common hawk in North America. If you've got sharp eyes, you may see several on almost any long car ride. Red-tailed Hawks soar above open fields, slowly turning circles on their broad, rounded wings. They also perch atop telephone poles, eyes fixed on the ground to catch the movements of a vole or a rabbit, or simply waiting out cold weather before climbing a thermal air current into the sky.

AT A GLANCE

Food
Mammals make up the bulk of most Red-tailed Hawk meals. Frequent prey items include voles, mice, wood rats, rabbits, snowshoe hares, jackrabbits, and ground squirrels. They also take birds, including pheasants, bobwhite, starlings, and blackbirds, as well as snakes and carrion.

Nesting
Both adults build the nest or refurbish one from a previous year. The nest is a tall pile of dry sticks up to 3 feet high, lined with bark strips and fresh green twigs. It's usually placed near the crown of a tall tree where the adults and young have a commanding view of the landscape.

Habitat
Red-tailed Hawks occupy just about every type of open habitat on the continent, including desert, grasslands, roadsides, fields and pastures, parks, broken woodland, and (in Mexico) tropical rainforest. They're also found in many large cities.

RANGE MAP

■ Breeding
■ Year-round

KEYS TO IDENTIFICATION

ADULT

IMMATURE

MEASUREMENTS

	Length	Wingspan	Weight
Male	17.7–22 in 45–56 cm	44.9–52.4 in 114–133 cm	24.3–45.9 oz 690–1300 g
Female	19.7–25.6 in 50–65 cm	44.9–52.4 in 114–133 cm	31.7–51.5 oz 900–1460 g

SIZE & SHAPE. Red-tailed Hawks are large hawks with typical buteo proportions: very broad, rounded wings and a short, wide tail. Large females seen from a distance may deceptively appear as large as an eagle.

COLOR PATTERN. Most Red-tailed Hawks are rich brown above and pale below, with a streaked belly and, on the wing underside, a dark bar between shoulder and wrist. The tail is usually pale below and cinnamon-red above, though in young birds it's brown and banded.

BEHAVIOR. Red-tailed Hawks are most conspicuous when soaring in wide circles high above a field. When flapping, their wingbeats are heavy. They often face into a high wind to hover without flapping, eyes fixed on the ground. They attack in a slow, controlled dive with legs outstretched.

Cool Facts
Whenever a hawk or eagle appears in a TV show or movie, no matter what species, the shrill cry on the soundtrack is almost always that of a Red-tailed Hawk.

Backyard Tips
Red-tailed Hawks eat mostly mammals; they may soar over your house while hunting, but are less likely to be a problem at bird feeders than Cooper's Hawks and Sharp-shinned Hawks.

The waterborne American Coot is a good reminder that not everything that swims is a duck. A close look at the small head, scrawny legs, and funny lobed toes reveals a different kind of bird entirely. The coot's dark body and white bill is a common sight in nearly any open water across the continent. Coots often mix with ducks, but they're actually related to cranes and rails.

Food American Coots eat mainly aquatic plants including duckweed, sedges, water lilies, and cattails. When on land, they pick at terrestrial plants and sometimes grains or leaves. You may also see them eating insects, crustaceans, snails, and small vertebrates.

Nesting Nests are usually built over water on floating platforms and are often associated with dense stands of vegetation such as reeds, sedges, and grasses. The nest material is woven into a shallow basket and lined with finer smooth material to hold the eggs. The average diameter is 12 inches, with an egg cup about 1 inch deep and 6 inches in diameter.

Habitat The American Coot inhabits a wide variety of mainly freshwater wetlands, including prairie potholes, swamps and marshes, suburban parks, sewage ponds, and the edges of large lakes.

RANGE MAP

- **Breeding**
- **Breeding (scarce)**
- **Migration**
- **Nonbreeding**
- **Year-round**

KEYS TO IDENTIFICATION

MEASUREMENTS (Both sexes)

Length	Wingspan	Weight
15.5–16.9 in	23–25 in	21.2–24.7 oz
39.4–42.9 cm	58.4–63.5 cm	600–700 g

SIZE & SHAPE. The American Coot is a plump, chickenlike bird with a rounded head and a sloping bill. Its tiny tail, short wings, and large feet are visible on the rare occasions when it takes flight.

COLOR PATTERN. American Coots are dark-gray to black, with a bright-white bill and forehead. The legs are yellow-green. At close range, you may see a small patch of red on the forehead. American Coots have small, bright-red eyes.

BEHAVIOR. You'll find American Coots eating aquatic plants on almost any body of water. When swimming and diving they look like small ducks, but on land they look more chickenlike, walking rather than waddling. An awkward flier, the American Coot requires a long, noisy running takeoff to get airborne.

Cool Facts

American Coots in the winter can be found in rafts of mixed waterfowl and in groups numbering up to several thousand individuals.

Find This Bird

To find American Coots, scan lakes and ponds for small black birds with bright white bills. You may also see them walking around on land on their long, yellow-green legs.

A shorebird you can see without going to the beach, the Killdeer is a graceful plover common on large lawns, golf courses, athletic fields, and parking lots. This tawny bird runs across the ground in spurts, stopping with a jolt every so often. Its voice, a far-carrying, excited *kill-deer*, is a common sound even after dark, often given in flight as the bird circles overhead on slender wings.

AT A GLANCE

Food Killdeer feed primarily on invertebrates such as earthworms, snails, crayfish, grasshoppers, beetles, and aquatic insect larvae. They follow farmers' plows and take advantage of any unearthed prey; they also eat seeds left on agricultural fields.

Nesting Killdeer nests are simple scrapes, often made on slight rises in open habitats. The nest is a shallow depression scratched into the bare ground, typically 3–3.5 inches across. After egg-laying begins, Killdeer often add rocks, bits of shell, sticks, and trash to the nest.

Habitat Look for Killdeer on open ground with low vegetation (or no vegetation at all), such as on lawns, golf courses, driveways, parking lots, and gravel-covered roofs, as well as pastures, fields, sandbars, and mudflats. It's one of the least water-associated of all shorebirds.

RANGE MAP

Breeding
Nonbreeding
Year-round

KEYS TO IDENTIFICATION

MEASUREMENTS (Both sexes)

Length	Wingspan	Weight
7.9–11 in	18.1–18.9 in	2.6–4.5 oz
20–28 cm	46–48 cm	75–128 g

SIZE & SHAPE. Killdeer have the large, round head, large eyes, and short bill characteristic of other plovers, but are more slender and lanky, with a long, pointed tail and long wings.

COLOR PATTERN. Killdeer are brownish-tan on top and white below. The white chest is barred with two black bands, and the brown face is marked with black and white patches. The bright orange-buff rump is conspicuous in flight.

BEHAVIOR. Killdeer walk along the ground or run ahead a few steps, stopping to look around before running again. When disturbed, they break into flight and circle overhead, calling repeatedly. Their flight is rapid, with stiff, intermittent wingbeats.

Cool Facts

A well-known denizen of dry habitats, the Killdeer is actually a proficient swimmer. Adults swim well in swift-flowing water, and chicks can swim across small streams.

Backyard Tips

Killdeer don't visit feeders, but they do nest in open habitat including driveways and short lawns. Keep an eye out for them in spring and you may find a little Killdeer family at your home.

Adapted to life around humans, Ring-billed Gulls frequent parking lots, garbage dumps, beaches, and fields. They are the gulls you're most likely to see far away from coastal areas—in fact, most Ring-billed Gulls nest in the interior of the continent, near fresh water. A black band encircling the yellow bill helps distinguish adults from other gulls, but some other species have black or red spots on the bill that may look from a distance like this ring.

AT A GLANCE

Food

Able to thrive on almost any source of nutrition, Ring-billed Gulls eat mostly fish, insects, earthworms, rodents, grain, and garbage. In addition to their more common fare, Ring-billed Gulls have been known to eat some fruits as well as French fries and other food discarded—or left unguarded—by people.

Nesting

Ring-billed Gulls nest in colonies numbering from 20 to tens of thousands of pairs. They build their nests on the ground near fresh water, usually on low, sparsely vegetated terrain. The male and female cooperate in constructing the nest—a scrape in the ground lined with plant materials.

Habitat

Ring-billed Gulls are often found in urban, suburban, and agricultural areas. Near coasts, they frequent estuaries, beaches, mudflats, and coastal waters. In winter, they're common around docks, wharves, and harbors.

RANGE MAP

- Breeding
- Migration
- Nonbreeding
- Year-round

KEYS TO IDENTIFICATION

MEASUREMENTS (Both sexes)

Length	Wingspan	Weight
16.9–21.3 in	41.3–46.1 in	10.6–24.7 oz
43–54 cm	105–117 cm	300–700 g

SIZE & SHAPE. The Ring-billed is a medium-sized gull with a fairly short, slim bill. When perched, its long, slender wings extend well past its square-tipped tail. In flight, the birds move lightly on easy flaps of their fairly slender wings.

COLOR PATTERN. Adults are clean gray above with a white head, body, and tail; their black wingtips are spotted with white. They have yellow legs and a yellow bill with a black band around it. Nonbreeding adults have brown-streaked heads. During their first two years, Ring-billed Gulls are mottled brown and gray with a pinkish bill and legs.

BEHAVIOR. These sociable gulls often fly overhead by the hundreds or feed together on golf courses, beaches, and fields. Strong, nimble flyers and opportunistic feeders, Ring-billed Gulls circle and hover acrobatically looking for food; they also forage afloat and on foot.

Cool Facts

Ring-billed Gulls are dedicated parents—maybe too dedicated. They sometimes pull egg-shaped pebbles into their nests and incubate them along with the rest of their clutch.

Find This Bird

Look for these gulls near parking lots, fast food joints, sporting events, sewage ponds, and garbage dumps. They also frequent reservoirs, lakes, marshes, mudflats, and beaches.

Gulls may seem like classic beach birds, but the California Gull spends its summers on lakes, rivers and fields in the West. These medium-sized white-headed gulls nest on islands and feed in farm fields or parking lots. They resemble Ring-billed Gulls but are heftier with a slightly darker back and wings. Like other gulls these are resourceful birds, eating almost anything they can find.

AT A GLANCE

Food
California Gulls are opportunistic foragers that eat fish, insects, earthworms, small mammals, grain, garbage, fruit, and marine invertebrates.

Nesting
California Gulls, like many gulls, nest in colonies. The pair selects the nest site and each makes a few scrapes in sand or dirt before selecting the final spot. They line it with vegetation, feathers, or bones. Pairs may use the same scrape year after year.

Habitat
California Gulls breed on islands in rivers or lakes (including salty or brackish lakes). They forage along lakes, bogs, farm fields, lawns, pastures, sagebrush areas, garbage dumps, feedlots, parking lots, ocean beaches, and open ocean. Most spend winters along the West Coast.

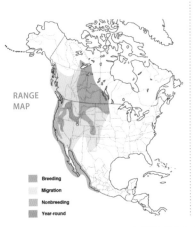

RANGE MAP

- Breeding
- Migration
- Nonbreeding
- Year-round

KEYS TO IDENTIFICATION

MEASUREMENTS (Both sexes)

Length	Wingspan	Weight
18.5–21.3 in	51.2 in	15.2–36.9 oz
47–54 cm	130 cm	430–1045 g

SIZE & SHAPE. This is a medium-sized gull with a round head and somewhat slanted forehead. California Gulls have fairly long wings and a long, slim bill. They are smaller than Herring Gulls but larger than Ring-billed Gulls.

COLOR PATTERN. Adults have a medium gray back, black wingtips, white underparts, and a yellow bill with a red spot and dark band near the tip. In winter, dark streaks mark the back of the neck. Juveniles are mottled brown and white. First-year birds are similar with a flesh-colored bill; second-year birds show some gray on the back. Third-year birds have streaky brown heads and gray backs.

BEHAVIOR. California Gulls feed while on foot (sometimes following plows), as well as by picking food from the surface of water.

Cool Facts
This gull is the state bird of Utah. It once came to the aid of Mormon settlers, helping rid their crops of a plague of grasshoppers. A golden statue in Salt Lake City commemorates the bird and the event.

Find This Bird
California Gulls are one of only a few species you'll find inland. In winter, gull species often form mixed flocks at beaches. Look at size first—California Gulls are rarely the biggest or smallest species in a group.

A common sight in cities around the world, Rock Pigeons crowd streets and public squares, living on discarded food and offerings of birdseed. You'll often see flocks with plain, spotted, pale, or rusty-red varieties in them. Introduced to North America from Europe in the early 1600s, city pigeons nest on buildings and window ledges. In the countryside they also nest on barns and grain towers, under bridges, and on natural cliffs.

AT A GLANCE

Food
Rock Pigeons feed on seeds, fruits, and, more rarely, invertebrates. Pigeons also readily eat food left out by people, including breadcrumbs and litter.

Nesting
Males usually choose the nest site, then sit in place and coo to attract a mate. The site is a nook or ledge on a cliff or structure, often beneath an overhang. The female makes a flimsy platform of straw, stems, and sticks brought to her one at a time by the male. Pigeons reuse their nests and don't carry away the feces of their nestlings. Over time, the nest grows into a sturdy mound, sometimes incorporating unhatched eggs and mummified remains of dead nestlings.

Habitat
Rock Pigeons live in urban areas, on farmlands, and near rocky cliffs. They may gather in large flocks in urban parks where people feed them.

RANGE MAP

Year-round
Year-round (scarce)

KEYS TO IDENTIFICATION

MEASUREMENTS (Both sexes)

Length	Wingspan	Weight
11.8–14.2 in	19.7–26.4 in	9.3–13.4 oz
30–36 cm	50–67 cm	265–380 g

SIZE & SHAPE. Larger and plumper than a Mourning Dove, Rock Pigeons are tubby birds with small heads and short legs. Their wings are broad but pointed and the tail is wide and rounded. In flight they may resemble falcons.

COLOR PATTERN. Rock Pigeons are extremely variable in color, but most are bluish gray with two black bands on each wing and a black tip to the tail. They usually have iridescent throat and neck feathers. Wings may be patterned with two bars or dark spots, or may be plain. The tail is usually dark tipped.

BEHAVIOR. Pigeons often gather in flocks, walking or running on the ground and pecking for food. When alarmed, the flock may suddenly fly into the air and circle several times before coming down again.

Cool Facts

Rock Pigeons carried messages for the U.S. Army Signal Corps during World War I and II, saving lives and providing vital strategic information.

Backyard Tips

Pigeons come to open areas with food on the ground. However, seed on the ground can attract rodents, so provide only as much food as the pigeons will eat during a visit.

The Band-tailed Pigeon is common in forests of the Pacific Coast and Southwest. A sociable bird with a mellow *coo*, it forms large flocks in mountain forests where it feeds on seeds and fruits. As flocks pass overhead, these large, swift-flying pigeons can resemble Rock Pigeons, so look for the long tail with a wide, pale band at the tip. Up close, a distinctive white neck crescent adorns its pastel gray plumage.

AT A GLANCE

Food Band-tailed Pigeons are almost entirely vegetarian, taking grain, fruits (especially raspberries, blackberries, cherries, cascara, madrone, and elderberries), acorns, pine nuts, and flowers of woody plants. They travel long distances every day to feed, often to fields and orchards.

Nesting Band-tailed Pigeons build their nest, a flat or saucer-shaped platform of haphazardly intertwined twigs, on sturdy tree limbs in trees such as Douglas-fir, acacia, lodgepole pine, or live oak.

Habitat Band-tailed Pigeons live in mature coniferous forests in Western mountains, damp forests of the West Coast, and conifer-oak woodlands. They visit forested suburban parks, fields, orchards, and backyard bird feeders to forage.

RANGE MAP

■ Breeding
■ Nonbreeding
■ Year-round

KEYS TO IDENTIFICATION

MEASUREMENTS (Both sexes)

Length	Wingspan	Weight
13–15.7 in	26 in	12.1–12.8 oz
33–40 cm	66 cm	342–364 g

SIZE & SHAPE. Band-tailed Pigeons are large, stocky pigeons with small heads, long, rounded tails, and thick-based, pointed wings.

COLOR PATTERN. These pigeons are soft blue-gray above and purplish-gray below, with a white crescent on the back of the neck. The upper half of the tail is gray, fading to a pale gray band at the tip. The wings are unmarked pale gray with dark wingtips noticeable in flight. The bill and feet are yellow.

BEHAVIOR. These forest pigeons spend much of their time traveling in groups to search for nuts, fruits, and seeds on the ground and in trees. They typically travel and feed in flocks of dozens to hundreds. Their call is a slow one- or two-syllable *coo*, sounding somewhat owl-like.

Cool Facts

Like other doves and pigeons, Band-tailed Pigeons can suck up and swallow water without raising their heads.

Backyard Tips

Band-tailed Pigeons sometimes visit bird feeders to eat a variety of seeds. They are more often attracted to backyard berry bushes and fruit trees.

With a flash of white tail feathers and a flurry of dark-tipped wings, the Eurasian Collared-Dove settles onto a phone wire or fence post to give its rhythmic three-parted coo. This chunky relative of the Mourning Dove gets its name from the black half-collar at the nape of the neck. A few Eurasian Collared-Doves were introduced to the Bahamas in the 1970s. They made their way to Florida by the 1980s and then rapidly colonized most of the continent.

AT A GLANCE

Food Eurasian Collared-Doves eat mainly seed and cereal grain such as millet, sunflower, milo, wheat, and corn. They also eat some berries and green parts of plants, as well as some invertebrates.

Nesting The male brings the female twigs, grasses, roots, and other nesting materials, which he sometimes pushes directly under her. Over 1–3 days, she builds a simple platform nest that may include feathers, wool, string, and wire. A pair often uses the same nest for multiple broods during the year, and may renovate old nests. Nests are usually built 10 or more feet above the ground.

Habitat Eurasian Collared-Doves live in urban and suburban areas throughout much of the U.S. except the Northeast. In rural settings, look for them on farms and in livestock yards where grain is available. In cooler months, flocks may roost together in large trees.

RANGE MAP

■ Year-round
■ Year-round (scarce)

KEYS TO IDENTIFICATION

MEASUREMENTS (Both sexes)

Length	Wingspan	Weight
11.4–11.8 in	13.8 in	4.9–6.3 oz
29–30 cm	35 cm	140–180 g

SIZE & SHAPE. Eurasian Collared-Doves have plump bodies, small heads, and long tails. They're larger than Mourning Doves but slimmer and longer-tailed than Rock Pigeons. The wings are broad and slightly rounded. The broad tail is squared off at the tip rather than pointed like a Mourning Dove's.

COLOR PATTERN. Eurasian Collared-Doves are chalky light brown to gray-buff birds with broad white patches in the tail. The "collar" is a narrow black crescent around the nape of the neck. In flight and when perched, the wingtips are darker than the rest of the wing.

BEHAVIOR. Eurasian Collared-Doves perch on telephone poles, wires, and in large trees while giving incessant three-syllable coos. Their flight pattern features bursts of clipped wingbeats and looping glides. When walking, they bob their heads and flick their tails.

Cool Facts

Bird feeders and trees planted in urban and suburban areas are cited as two of the main factors in the species' colonization of the continent.

Backyard Tips

Eurasian Collared-Doves readily come to backyards for seed and grain, particularly millet. They often nest near houses and other developed areas where food is easily available.

;ED DOVE *(Zenaida asiatica)*

Originally a bird of desert thickets, the White-winged Dove has become a common sight in cities and towns across the southern U.S. When perched, this bird's unspotted brown upperparts and large, neat white crescent along the wing edge distinguish it from the Mourning Dove. In flight, those subdued crescents become flashing white stripes worthy of the bird's name. Look closely to see a remarkably colorful face, bright orange eyes, and blue "eye shadow."

AT A GLANCE

Food

The White-winged Dove eats mostly grains and other agricultural crops, and also takes fruits and large seeds. It seems adapted to large food items because of its large bill and slow eating style (it never pecks quickly, the way Mourning Doves do). White-winged Doves often feed from perches above the ground.

Nesting

The male gathers twigs and brings them to the female; she constructs the nest over a couple of days, arranging twigs and some weeds or grasses into a flimsy bowl about 4 inches across. The nest is usually on a tree branch or crotch under heavy shade.

Habitat

White-winged Doves live in dense, thorny forests, streamside woodlands, deserts full of cactus and palo verde, and, more recently, urban and suburban areas of the southwestern U.S.

RANGE MAP

■ Breeding
■ Nonbreeding
■ Nonbreeding (scarce)
■ Year-round

KEYS TO IDENTIFICATION

MEASUREMENTS (Both sexes)

Length	Wingspan	Weight
11.5 in	19 in	4.4–6.6 oz
29 cm	48 cm	125–187 g

SIZE & SHAPE. White-winged Doves are plump, square-tailed doves with relatively long, thin bills and small heads.

COLOR PATTERN. White-winged Doves are brown overall, with a dark line on the cheek. A white stripe at the edge of the folded wing becomes, as the bird takes flight, a bright flash in the middle of a dark wing. The tail is tipped in white. Their faces are ornately marked with blue skin around the red eyes.

BEHAVIOR. Look for White-winged Doves in deserts of the Southwest and in cities and suburbs of Texas and the coastal Southeast. Individuals travel widely and irregularly across the continent after the breeding season ends.

Cool Facts

In the early 1980s, the singer Stevie Nicks introduced millions of Americans to the White-winged Dove with her song "Edge of Seventeen," which hit #11 on the Billboard charts.

Backyard Tips

White-winged Doves often eat at elevated bird feeders, taking sunflower, milo, corn, and safflower. They may also eat berries from shrubs.

These graceful, slender-tailed, small-headed doves are common across the continent. Mourning Doves perch on telephone wires and forage for seeds on the ground; their flight is fast and bullet straight. Their soft, drawn-out calls sound like laments. When taking off, their wings make a sharp whistling or whinnying sound. Mourning Doves are the most hunted species in North America, but their numbers remain strong throughout their range.

AT A GLANCE

Food
Seeds make up 99% of a Mourning Dove's diet, which includes cultivated grains and peanuts, wild grasses, weeds, herbs, and occasionally berries. Mourning Doves eat roughly 12% to 20% of their body weight per day, averaging about 71 calories.

Nesting
The nest is a flimsy, unlined assembly of pine needles, twigs, and grass stems. The male carries twigs to the female, passing them to her while standing on her back; the female weaves them into a nest 8 inches across. The nest is typically set amid dense foliage on the branch of an evergreen, orchard tree, mesquite, or cottonwood, or on the ground.

Habitat
Mourning Doves are primarily birds of open fields, areas with scattered trees, and woodland edges, but large numbers roost in woodlots during winter. They feed on the ground in grasslands, agricultural fields, backyards, and roadsides.

RANGE MAP

- ■ Breeding
- ■ Year-round
- ■ Nonbreeding

KEYS TO IDENTIFICATION

MEASUREMENTS (Both sexes)

Length	Wingspan	Weight
9.1-13 in	17.7 in	3.0-6.0 oz
23-34 cm	45 cm	86-170 g

SIZE & SHAPE. Mourning Doves are plump-bodied and long-tailed, with short legs, a small bill, and a head that looks tiny in comparison to the body. The long, pointed tail is unique among North American doves.

COLOR PATTERN. Mourning Doves often match their open-country surroundings in color. They're delicate brown to buffy-tan overall, with black spots on the wings and black-bordered white tips to the tail feathers.

BEHAVIOR. Mourning Doves fly fast on powerful wingbeats, sometimes making sudden ascents, descents, and dodges, their pointed tails stretching behind them.

Cool Facts

In spring you might see three Mourning Doves flying in formation. It's a display: the first two are males in a chase. The third is a female paired with the first, and apparently just along for the ride.

Backyard Tips

Scatter seeds, particularly millet, on the ground or on platform feeders. Plant dense shrubs or evergreen trees in your yard to provide nesting sites.

GREAT HORNED OWL (*Bubo virginianus*)

The Great Horned Owl is the quintessential owl of storybooks. This powerful predator can grab birds and mammals even larger than itself, but it also dines on daintier fare such as tiny scorpions, mice, and frogs. It's one of the most common owls in North America, equally at home in deserts, wetlands, forests, grasslands, backyards, cities, and almost any other semiopen habitat between the Arctic and the tropics.

AT A GLANCE

Food Great Horned Owls have the most diverse diet of all North American raptors. Their prey range in size from rodents and scorpions to skunks, geese, and raptors. They eat mostly mammals and birds. Although they are usually nocturnal hunters, Great Horned Owls sometimes hunt in broad daylight.

Nesting Great Horned Owls typically nest in trees such as cottonwood, juniper, beech, and pine. They usually use a nest built by another species, such as a Red-tailed Hawk, but also use tree cavities, deserted buildings, cliff ledges, and human-made platforms.

Habitat Look for this widespread owl in young woods interspersed with fields or other open areas. The broad range of habitats they use includes deciduous and evergreen forests, swamps, desert, tundra edges, and tropical rainforest, as well as cities, orchards, suburbs, and parks.

RANGE MAP

■ Year-round
■ Year-round (scarce)

KEYS TO IDENTIFICATION

MEASUREMENTS (Both sexes)

Length	Wingspan	Weight
18.1–24.8 in 46–63 cm	39.8–57.1 in 101–145 cm	32.1–88.2 oz 910–2500 g

SIZE & SHAPE. These large, thick-bodied owls have a catlike silhouette thanks to two prominent feathered tufts on the head. The wings are broad and rounded. In flight, the rounded face and short bill combine to create a blunt-headed appearance.

COLOR PATTERN. Great Horned Owls are mottled gray-brown, with reddish-brown faces and a neat white patch on the throat. Their overall color tone varies regionally from sooty to pale.

BEHAVIOR. Great Horned Owls are usually nocturnal. You may see them at dusk sitting on fence posts or tree limbs at the edges of open areas, or flying across roads or fields with stiff, deep beats of their rounded wings. Their call is a deep, stuttering series of four or five mellow hoots.

Cool Facts

When clenched, a Great Horned Owl's strong talons require a force of 28 pounds to open. The owls use this deadly grip to sever the spine of large prey.

Find This Bird

It's a thrill to stay up late around wooded areas and listen for owls. The Great Horned is one of the most widespread: listen for its deep, four- or five-noted, stuttering series of hoots.

On warm summer evenings, Common Nighthawks roam the skies over treetops, grasslands, and cities. Their sharp, electric *peent* call is often the first clue they're overhead. In the dim half-light, these long-winged birds fly in graceful loops, flashing a white crescent patch just past the bend of each wing as they chase insects. These fairly common but declining birds build no nest.

Food Common Nighthawks eat flying insects almost exclusively. They hunt on the wing at dawn and dusk, opening their tiny beaks to reveal a cavernous mouth well suited for devouring flying insects. They often take advantage of clouds of insects attracted to streetlamps, stadium lights, and other bright lights.

Nesting Common Nighthawks typically lay eggs right on the bare ground, usually on material such as gravel, sand, bare rock, wood chips, leaves, needles, tar paper (on flat roofs), cinders, or occasionally living vegetation.

Habitat Common Nighthawks are most visible when they forage on the wing over cities and open areas near woods or wetlands. They migrate over fields, river valleys, marshes, woodlands, towns, and suburbs.

RANGE MAP

Breeding
Migration

KEYS TO IDENTIFICATION

MALE

MEASUREMENTS (Both sexes)

Length	Wingspan	Weight
8.7–9.4 in	20.9–22.4 in	2.3–3.5 oz
22–24 cm	53–57 cm	65–98 g

SIZE & SHAPE. Common Nighthawks are medium-sized, slender birds with very long, pointed wings and medium-long tails. The tiny bill, large eyes, and short neck give the bird a big-headed, somewhat owl-like appearance.

COLOR PATTERN. Common Nighthawks are well camouflaged in gray, white, buff, and black. The long, dark wings have a striking white blaze about two-thirds of the way out to the tip. In flight, the male's V-shaped white throat patch contrasts with the rest of his mottled plumage.

BEHAVIOR. Look for Common Nighthawks flying about in early morning and evening. During the day, they roost motionless on tree branches, fence posts, or the ground, and can be very difficult to see. When migrating or feeding over insect-rich areas such as lakes or well-lit billboards, nighthawks may gather in large flocks. Their buzzy, American Woodcock–like *peent* call is distinctive.

Cool Facts

The Common Nighthawk's impressive booming sounds during courtship dives, in combination with its erratic, batlike flight, have earned it the colloquial name "bullbat."

Find This Bird

Common Nighthawks are easiest to see in flight at dawn and dusk as they forage for aerial insects. In towns, look for nighthawks over brightly lit areas.

BLACK-CHINNED HUMMINGBIRD (Archilochus alexandri)

Black-chinned Hummingbirds are small green-backed hummingbirds of the West, with no brilliant colors on their throat except a thin strip of iridescent purple bordering the black chin, visible when light hits it just right. Black-chinned Hummingbirds are exceptionally widespread, found from deserts to mountain forests. Many winter along the Gulf Coast. Their wings produce a low-pitched humming sound.

AT A GLANCE

Food

Black-chinned Hummingbirds feed on flower nectar, tiny insects, spiders, and sugar water at feeders.

Nesting

When newly built, the nest is a compact, deep cup constructed of soft plant matter, spider silk, and cocoon fibers. The female builds it on an exposed, horizontal dead branch well below the canopy. As the nestlings grow, the nest stretches into a wider, shallower cup. Nests in cool areas have thicker walls than nests in warmer areas.

Habitat

This bird is most often seen at feeders or perched on dead branches in tall trees. It may be found anywhere, from lowland deserts to mountainous forests, natural habitats to very urbanized areas. Its only requirements are a few tall trees, and shrubs and vines with nectar-bearing flowers.

RANGE MAP

- ■ Breeding
- ■ Migration
- ■ Nonbreeding
- ■ Year-round

KEYS TO IDENTIFICATION

MALE

FEMALE

MEASUREMENTS (Both sexes)

Length	Wingspan	Weight
3.5 in	4.3 in	0.1–0.2 oz
9 cm	11 cm	2–5 g

SIZE & SHAPE. The Black-chinned Hummingbird is a dainty hummingbird with a fairly straight bill, quite similar in shape to a Ruby-throated Hummingbird.

COLOR PATTERN. The Black-chinned Hummingbird is dull metallic green above and dull grayish-white below. Males have a velvety black throat with a thin, iridescent purple base. Females have a pale throat. In both sexes, the flanks are glossed with dull metallic green. The female's three outer tail feathers on each side have broad white tips. The bill is black.

BEHAVIOR. Black-chinned Hummingbirds hover at flowers and feeders, dart erratically to take tiny swarming insects, and perch atop snags to survey their territory, watching for competitors to chase off and for flying insects to eat. During courtship and territorial defense, males do high-speed display dives from as high as 100 feet.

Cool Facts

A Black-chinned Hummingbird egg is about the size of a coffee bean. The nest, made of plant down and spider silk, expands as the babies grow.

Backyard Tips

It's fairly easy to attract hummingbirds to feeding stations. Mix about one-quarter cup of table sugar to one cup of water. Food coloring is unnecessary.

Anna's Hummingbirds are among the most common hummingbirds of the Pacific Coast. With their iridescent emerald feathers and sparkling rose-pink throats, they are more like flying jewelry than birds. They're no larger than a ping-pong ball and no heavier than a nickel. For his courtship display, the tiny male climbs up to 130 feet in the air and then swoops back to the ground, making a curious buzz with his tail feathers.

AT A GLANCE

Food Anna's Hummingbirds eat nectar from many flowering plants, plus a wide array of insects plucked from understory leaves, flowers, crevices, streambanks, or spider webs, or caught in the air. They also feed on sap and insects at holes made by sapsuckers.

Nesting Female Anna's Hummingbirds build the nest on a horizontal tree branch or other structure, using small fibers such as plant down, lichens, and mosses held together with spider silk. A new nest is about 1 inch tall by 1.5 inches in diameter, but it stretches as the nestlings grow.

Habitat Anna's Hummingbirds are common in yards, parks, residential streets, eucalyptus groves, riverside woods, savannahs, and coastal scrub. They readily come to hummingbird feeders and flowering plants, including cultivated species in gardens.

RANGE MAP

- Breeding
- Nonbreeding
- Nonbreeding (scarce)
- Year-round

KEYS TO IDENTIFICATION

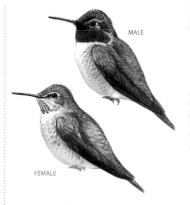

MALE

FEMALE

MEASUREMENTS (Both sexes)

Length	Wingspan	Weight
3.9 in	4.7 in	0.1–0.2 oz
10 cm	12 cm	3–6 g

SIZE & SHAPE. Tiny among birds, Anna's are medium-sized and stocky for hummingbirds. They have a straight, shortish bill and a fairly broad tail. When perched, wingtips nearly meet the tip of the short tail.

COLOR PATTERN. Anna's Hummingbirds are mostly green and gray, without any rufous or orange markings on the body. The male's head and throat are covered in iridescent reddish-pink feathers that can look dull brown or gray without direct sunlight.

BEHAVIOR. Anna's Hummingbirds are a blur of motion as they hover before flowers looking for nectar and insects. Listen for the male's scratchy metallic song and look for him perched above head level in trees and shrubs.

Cool Facts

Hummingbirds are strictly New World creatures. They fascinated early explorers, who wondered if they were a cross between a bird and an insect.

Backyard Tips

Anna's Hummingbirds are easy to attract to feeders filled with a mixture of one part table sugar to four parts water. Don't use honey or food coloring.

IINGBIRD *(Selasphorus platycercus)*

The Broad-tailed Hummingbird of subalpine meadows ranges across the south-central Rockies in summer, with most returning to Mexico and Central America during winter. Males make a loud trilling noise with their wingtips and perform spectacular aerial displays that make them hard to miss. To survive the cold nights in their high-elevation habitats, they can enter torpor, slowing their heart rate and dropping their body temperature until morning.

AT A GLANCE

Food Broad-tailed Hummingbirds drink nectar from red, tubular flowers. During spring migration, they also feed from pussy willow, currant, and glacier lilies. They glean small insects from leaves and snatch them from midair. Sometimes they feed from sapsucker sap wells.

Nesting The female makes a thick inner cup out of spider silk, camouflaging the outside with lichens, moss, and bark fragments. The nest is well insulated and often placed under overhanging branches, keeping it warmer than surrounding areas.

Habitat Broad-tailed Hummingbirds breed in high elevations of the southern and central Rockies and Sierra Nevada, in pinyon-juniper and pine-oak woodlands, montane scrub, and thickets. In migration and winter they are also found in lowlands.

RANGE MAP

- Breeding
- Migration
- Nonbreeding
- Year-round

KEYS TO IDENTIFICATION

MALE

FEMALE

MEASUREMENTS (Both sexes)

Length	Wingspan	Weight
3.1–3.5 in	5.1 in	0.1–0.2 oz
8–9 cm	13 cm	2.8–4.5 g

SIZE & SHAPE. The Broad-tailed is a medium-sized hummingbird with a fairly short, straight bill.

COLOR PATTERN. Broad-tailed Hummingbirds have shiny green upperparts and pale undersides with greenish or greenish-bronzy flanks. Males have glittering rose-red throats. Adult females and all young have white throats speckled with iridescent green or bronze.

BEHAVIOR. Most of the year, Broad-tailed Hummingbirds are easy to find thanks to the loud trilling sound males produce with their wingtips. These sounds get softer as the feather tips wear, and can be impossible to hear by midwinter.

Cool Facts

Breeding males dive and chase intruding males, and the better the territory the more chases occur. A feeder-rich area guarded by a male may result in over 40 chases an hour.

Backyard Tips

Broad-tailed Hummingbirds are attracted to feeders. A sugar-to-water ratio of 1:4 or 1:3 is best; there's no need to use food coloring. Change the mixture every few days to prevent spoilage and fermentation.

The brilliant orange Rufous Hummingbird is the feistiest hummingbird in North America. Relentless attackers at flowers and feeders, they chase (if not always defeat) even the large hummingbirds of the Southwest, which may be double their weight. Rufous Hummingbirds are wide ranging and breed farther north than any other hummingbird. Though they breed in the West, they frequently show up in the East in fall and winter.

AT A GLANCE

Food Rufous Hummingbirds feed primarily on nectar from colorful, tubular flowers including columbine, scarlet gilia, penstemon, Indian paintbrush, mints, lilies, fireweeds, larkspurs, currants, and heaths. They get protein and fat from eating insects, particularly gnats, midges, flies, and aphids.

Nesting The female builds the nest alone, using soft plant down held together with spiderweb. She builds it anywhere from eye level up to about 30 feet high in a tree. The finished nest is about 2 inches across on the outside.

Habitat Rufous Hummingbirds breed in open areas, yards, parks, and forests up to the treeline. On migration, they pass through mountain meadows as high as 12,600 feet where nectar-rich, tubular flowers bloom. Winter habitat in Mexico includes shrubby openings and oak-pine forests.

RANGE MAP

■ Breeding
■ Migration
■ Nonbreeding

KEYS TO IDENTIFICATION

MALE

FEMALE

MEASUREMENTS (Both sexes)

Length	Wingspan	Weight
2.8–3.5 in	4.3 in	0.1–0.2 oz
7–9 cm	11 cm	2–5 g

SIZE & SHAPE. The Rufous Hummingbird is a fairly small hummingbird with a slender, nearly straight bill, a tail that tapers to a point when folded, and fairly short wings that don't reach the end of the tail when the bird is perched.

COLOR PATTERN. In good light, male Rufous Hummingbirds glow like coals: bright orange on the back and belly, with a vivid iridescent-red throat. Females are green above with rufous-washed flanks, rufous patches in the green tail, and often a spot of orange on the throat.

BEHAVIOR. Rufous Hummingbirds have the characteristic hummingbird flight: fast and darting with pinpoint maneuverability. They are pugnacious, tirelessly chasing away other hummingbirds, even in places they're only visiting on migration. Like other hummers, they eat insects as well as nectar, taking them from spiderwebs or catching them in midair.

Cool Facts

Rufous Hummingbirds, like most other hummingbirds, beat their wings extremely fast to hover in place. The wingbeat frequency has been recorded at 52–62 wingbeats per second.

Backyard Tips

Rufous hummers may claim your yard if you have hummingbird flowers or feeders. They'll probably try to chase off any other hummingbirds that visit.

With its top-heavy physique, energetic flight, and piercing rattle, the Belted Kingfisher seems to have an air of self-importance as it patrols up and down rivers and shorelines. It nests in burrows along earthen banks and feeds almost entirely on aquatic prey, diving to catch fish and crayfish with its heavy, straight bill. These ragged-crested birds are a powdery blue-gray. Males have one blue band across the white breast; females have a blue and a chestnut band.

AT A GLANCE

Food Belted Kingfishers eat mostly fish, as well as crustaceans, mollusks, insects, amphibians, reptiles, young birds, small mammals, and berries. They watch for prey from a perch overhanging water, such as a bare branch, telephone wire, or pier piling, or while hovering.

Nesting Belted Kingfishers excavate a nest burrow in an earthen bank, usually one without vegetation. They generally choose a bank near water, but may use a ditch, road cut, or gravel pit. The male and the female take turns digging the burrow 3–6 feet into the bank.

Habitat Kingfishers live near streams, rivers, ponds, lakes, and estuaries. They spend winter in areas where the water doesn't freeze so that they have continual access to their aquatic foods.

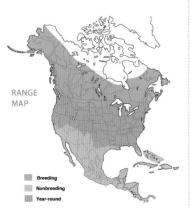

RANGE MAP

- Breeding
- Nonbreeding
- Year-round

KEYS TO IDENTIFICATION

FEMALE

MEASUREMENTS (Both sexes)

Length	Wingspan	Weight
11–13.8 in	18.9–22.8 in	4.9–6 oz
28–35 cm	48–58 cm	140–170 g

SIZE & SHAPE. Belted Kingfishers are stocky, large-headed birds with a shaggy crest on the top and back of the head and a straight, thick, pointed bill. Their legs and feet are surprisingly small, and their tails are medium length and square tipped.

COLOR PATTERN. Belted Kingfishers are steel blue above with fine white spotting on the wings and tail. The underparts are white with a broad blue breast band. Females also have a broad rusty band on their belly and sides. Juveniles show irregular rusty spotting in the breast band.

BEHAVIOR. Belted Kingfishers spend much of their time perched alone along the edges of streams, lakes, and estuaries, searching for small fish. They also fly quickly up and down rivers and shorelines giving loud rattling calls. They hunt either by plunging directly from a perch, or by hovering over the water, bill downward, before diving after a fish they've spotted.

Cool Facts

The Belted Kingfisher is one of comparatively few bird species in which the female is more brightly colored than the male.

Backyard Tips

Listen for this bird's loud rattle, given on the wing. Look up and you may see this stocky bird flashing white in its wings as it flies along a stream.

Reminiscent of a troupe of wide-eyed clowns, Acorn Woodpeckers live in large groups in western oak woodlands. They store thousands of acorns each year by jamming them into specially made holes in trees. A group member is always on alert to guard the hoard from thieves, while others race through the trees giving parrotlike *waka-waka* calls. Breeding involves multiple males and females that combine efforts to raise young in a single nest.

AT A GLANCE

Food Acorn Woodpeckers eat acorns, nuts, and insects. They harvest acorns directly from oak trees and store them and a variety of nuts in individually drilled holes in storage trees called "granaries." They grab insects on the wing by flying out from high perches.

Nesting Acorn Woodpeckers excavate cavities for nesting and nocturnal roosting, and reuse nest holes for many years. They don't build a nest, but as they dig, wood chips accumulate on the bottom. Throughout nesting, they add more by pecking at the cavity walls.

Habitat These woodpeckers live in oak and mixed oak-conifer forests on slopes and mountains. They do well around humans, sometimes choosing telephone poles or wood siding for their granaries.

RANGE MAP

Year-round

KEYS TO IDENTIFICATION

MALE

MEASUREMENTS (Both sexes)

Length	Wingspan	Weight
7.5–9.1 in	13.8–16.9 in	2.3–3.2 oz
19–23 cm	35–43 cm	65–90 g

SIZE & SHAPE. Acorn Woodpeckers are medium-sized woodpeckers with straight, chisel-like bills and stiff, wedge-shaped tails used for support as the birds cling to tree trunks.

COLOR PATTERN. These striking birds are mostly black above with a red cap, creamy white face, and black patch around the bill. In flight they show three patches of white: one in each wing and one on the rump. Females have less red on the crown than males.

BEHAVIOR. Acorn Woodpeckers live in large groups and breed cooperatively. They gather acorns by the hundreds and wedge them into holes they've made in a tree trunk or telephone pole. They also catch insects on the wing. They give raucous, scratchy *waka-waka* calls frequently.

Cool Facts

Acorn Woodpeckers store up to 50,000 acorns in a granary. Each acorn is jammed into a tight hole to foil squirrels. As the nuts begin to dry and shrink, the birds move them to new, better-fitting holes.

Backyard Tips

Acorn Woodpeckers visit seed and suet feeders near oak woodlands. Keep your eyes out for granaries—trees and telephone poles pock marked with acorn holes the whole way up—to know when they're near.

The Red-naped Sapsucker is a sharply marked, small woodpecker of lower elevations in the Rockies. Look for its bright-red crown and throat set off by neat black-and-white stripes. This and the closely related Yellow-bellied, Red-breasted, and Williamson's sapsuckers are unusual woodpeckers. They drill into trees not to extract insects but to make shallow holes in the bark. They then lap up the sap that flows out, along with any trapped insects.

AT A GLANCE

Food
The Red-naped Sapsucker drills rows of small holes in tree bark and returns to these "sap wells" to feed. It uses its brushy-tipped tongue to lap up sap and eat any insects trapped in the sticky fluid. It also feeds on many fruits, insects, and other arthropods.

Nesting
The male does most of the work excavating the nest cavity, usually in a tree infected with heart rot near feeding trees. No nest material is added to the cavity, but fresh wood chips from the excavation process line the bottom.

Habitat
Red-naped Sapsuckers breed in mountain forests, using willow, aspen, and conifers for sap wells. In winter they use woodlands along streams, oak or pine-oak woodlands, and orchards.

RANGE MAP

- Breeding
- Migration
- Winter
- Year-round

KEYS TO IDENTIFICATION

MALE

MEASUREMENTS (Both sexes)

Length	Wingspan	Weight
7.5–8.3 in	16-17 in	1.1–2.3 oz
19–21 cm	41-43 cm	32–66 g

SIZE & SHAPE. This fairly small woodpecker has a stout, straight bill, a smallish head, and a long, stiff tail. The wings are long. It may hold its crown feathers up to form a peak at the back of the head.

COLOR PATTERN. These are black-and-white birds with rich red on the crown and throat. The male's throat is entirely red; the female has a white patch on the chin. As in other sapsuckers, they have a bold white wing stripe and messy black-and-white barring on the back and flanks.

BEHAVIOR. Sapsuckers often sit still for extended periods as they tend sap wells, clinging to a tree trunk and leaning against their tails. They drum on trees with a stuttering rhythm.

Cool Facts
It's a lot of work to make sap wells, and the sticky-sweet flow attracts many other animals looking for a free meal. Red-naped Sapsuckers defend their sap wells by chasing away uninvited guests.

Backyard Tips
Sapsuckers seldom visit feeders, but often come to backyard trees to drill for sap. Trees usually survive sapsucker holes, but to protect a prized ornamental tree, wrap sections of trunk or limbs in burlap.

A small, mostly black-and-white woodpecker that lives in oak woodlands and suburbs, Nuttall's Woodpecker is nearly restricted to California. These active birds circle around trunks and limbs probing for insects, often clambering around horizontally in addition to hitching up a trunk the way other woodpeckers do. It looks very similar to the Ladder-backed Woodpecker, but there's almost no overlap in range.

AT A GLANCE

Food

Nuttall's Woodpeckers eat mostly insects, with about 20% of the diet made up of berries and seeds. They forage in oaks, cottonwoods, and willows, and rarely on the ground or by capturing insects on the wing.

Nesting

The male excavates a nest cavity in a dead trunk, tree limb, or, rarely, a fence post. He gets little or no help from the female. He may sleep in it during the last nights before it's finished.

Habitat

Nuttall's Woodpecker lives mainly in California's oak woodlands, as well as in tree-lined suburbs and woods along streams. It is seldom found in stands of coniferous trees.

RANGE MAP

▨ Year-round

KEYS TO IDENTIFICATION

MALE

MEASUREMENTS (Both sexes)

Length	Wingspan	Weight
6.3–7.1 in	13–16 in	1.1–1.6 oz
16–18 cm	33–41 cm	30–45 g

SIZE & SHAPE. This is a small woodpecker with a short, straight bill. It's only slightly larger than a Downy Woodpecker.

COLOR PATTERN. Nuttall's Woodpeckers are black-and-white birds with horizontal stripes down the back. Males have a small red patch at the back of the crown. A broad dark patch on the upper back helps distinguish it from the Ladder-backed Woodpecker.

BEHAVIOR. This little woodpecker often hops into tangles of twigs and onto small limbs where it perches crosswise—losing the classic woodpecker posture of leaning against its tail.

Cool Facts

Even though Nuttall's Woodpeckers are closely tied to California's oak woodlands, they do not eat acorns.

Backyard Tips

Nuttall's Woodpeckers visit backyards that have nearby oaks or cottonwoods. They visit suet feeders and sometimes sip sugar water at hummingbird feeders.

DOWNY WOODPECKER (Picoides pubescens)

The active little Downy Woodpecker is a familiar sight at backyard feeders and in parks and woodlots, where it joins flocks of chickadees and nuthatches. An often acrobatic forager, this woodpecker is at home on tiny branches or balancing on slender plant galls and suet feeders. The Downy and its larger lookalike, the Hairy Woodpecker, offer one of the first identification challenges that beginning bird watchers must master.

AT A GLANCE

Food Downy Woodpeckers eat insects such as ants, caterpillars, and beetle larvae living within wood and bark. About a quarter of their diet consists of plant material, especially berries, acorns, and grains. They are common at feeders, taking suet, sunflower seeds, and sometimes sugar water.

Nesting Downy Woodpeckers excavate cavities in dead trees or in dead parts of live trees. Entrance holes are round and 1–1.5 inches across. Cavities are 6–12 inches deep and widen toward the bottom. The cavity is lined only with wood chips.

Habitat You'll find Downy Woodpeckers in open woodlands, particularly among deciduous trees, and brushy or weedy edges. They're also at home in orchards, city parks, backyards and vacant lots.

RANGE MAP

Year-round

KEYS TO IDENTIFICATION

MALE

MEASUREMENTS (Both sexes)

Length	Wingspan	Weight
5.5–6.7 in	9.8–11.8 in	0.7–1 oz
14–17 cm	25–30 cm	21–28 g

SIZE & SHAPE. The Downy Woodpecker is a miniaturized version of the classic woodpecker body plan. It has a straight, chisel-like bill, blocky head, wide shoulders, and straight-backed posture as it leans away from tree limbs braced by its tail feathers. The bill seems short for a woodpecker.

COLOR PATTERN. The head is boldly striped black and white, and the gleaming white back stands out between folded black-and-white checkered wings. Males have a small red patch on the back of the head; male fledgings have a reddish crown. The outer tail feathers are white with a few black spots.

BEHAVIOR. Downy Woodpeckers hitch around tree limbs and trunks or drop into tall weeds to feed on galls, moving more acrobatically than larger woodpeckers. In spring and summer, Downy Woodpeckers are noisy, making shrill whinnying calls and drumming on trees.

Cool Facts

Downy Woodpeckers often feed on weed stalks, extracting insects larger woodpeckers can't get. They sometimes follow Pileated Woodpeckers to reach into their deep feeding holes.

Backyard Tips

Downy Woodpeckers are among the most frequent woodpeckers at bird feeders. They eat suet, black oil sunflower seeds, millet, and peanuts. They sometimes drink at hummingbird feeders.

The larger of two lookalikes, the Hairy Woodpecker is small but powerful, using its long, strong bill to forage along trunks and main branches of large trees. Hairy Woodpeckers have a somewhat soldierly bearing due to their erect, straight-backed posture on tree trunks and their neatly striped heads. Look for them at backyard suet or sunflower feeders, and listen for them calling in woodlots, parks, and forests.

AT A GLANCE

Food More than 75% of the Hairy Woodpecker's diet is insects, particularly beetle larvae, ants, and moth pupae. They also eat bees, wasps, caterpillars, spiders, and millipedes. Hairy Woodpeckers are common visitors at feeders, taking suet and sunflower seeds.

Nesting Hairy Woodpeckers typically excavate their nests in a dead stub of a living tree. The cavity is often in a branch or stub that isn't perfectly vertical, with the entrance hole on the underside. The entrance to the nest is about 1.5 inches wide, leading to a cavity 8–12 inches deep.

Habitat Hairy Woodpeckers are birds of mature forests across the continent. They're also found in woodlots, suburbs, parks, and cemeteries, as well as forest edges, open woodlands of oak and pine, recently burned forests, and stands infested by bark beetles.

RANGE MAP

Year-round

KEYS TO IDENTIFICATION

MALE

MEASUREMENTS (Both sexes)

Length	Wingspan	Weight
7.1–10.2 in	13–16.1 in	1.4–3.4 oz
18–26 cm	33–41 cm	40–95 g

SIZE & SHAPE. The Hairy Woodpecker is a medium-sized woodpecker with a fairly square head, a long, straight, chisel-like bill, and stiff, long tail feathers it braces against tree trunks. The bill is nearly the same length as the head.

COLOR PATTERN. Hairy Woodpeckers are contrasting bold black and bright white. The black wings are checkered with white; the head has two white stripes and, in males, a bright-red spot above the nape. The back is gleaming white between folded black-and-white wings.

BEHAVIOR. Hairy Woodpeckers hitch up tree trunks and along main branches. They sometimes feed at the bases of trees, along fallen logs, and, rarely, on the ground. They have the slowly undulating flight pattern of most woodpeckers.

Cool Facts

Hairy Woodpeckers sometimes drink sap leaking from wells made by sapsuckers. They've also been seen pecking into sugar cane to drink the sugary juice.

Backyard Tips

To attract Hairy Woodpeckers, offer suet, peanuts, and black oil sunflower seeds from hanging feeders, especially in winter when natural food is scarce.

Northern Flickers are large, brown woodpeckers with a gentle expression and handsome black-scalloped plumage. On walks, don't be surprised if you scare one up from the ground. Flickers eat a great many ants and beetles, digging into the ground with their strong, slightly curved bills. When they fly they show a flash of color in the underwings and undertail—yellow in the East, red in the West—and a bright white rump.

AT A GLANCE

Food Northern Flickers eat mainly insects, especially ants and beetles that they take on the ground. They often hammer at the soil much as other woodpeckers drill into wood, to dig out ant larvae from underground. They also eat fruits and seeds, especially in winter.

Nesting Northern Flickers usually excavate nest holes in dead or diseased tree trunks or large branches. Nests are generally placed 6–15 feet off the ground, but on rare occasions can be over 100 feet high. The entrance hole is about 3 inches in diameter, and the cavity is 13–16 inches deep.

Habitat Look for Northern Flickers in woodlands, forest edges, and open fields with scattered trees, as well as city parks and suburbs. You can also find them in wet areas such as streamside woods, flooded swamps, and marsh edges.

RANGE MAP

Breeding
Nonbreeding
Year-round

KEYS TO IDENTIFICATION

MALE
(RED-SHAFTED
FORM)

MEASUREMENTS (Both sexes)

Length	Wingspan	Weight
11–12.2 in	16.5–20.1 in	3.9–5.6 oz
28–31 cm	42–51 cm	110–160 g

SIZE & SHAPE. Flickers are fairly large woodpeckers with a slim, rounded head, long, slightly curved bill, and long, flared tail that tapers to a point.

COLOR PATTERN. Flickers appear brownish overall with a white rump patch that's conspicuous in flight and often visible when perched. The undersides of the wing and tail feathers are bright yellow in eastern birds, or red in western birds. With a closer look you'll see the brown plumage is richly patterned with black spots, bars, and crescents.

BEHAVIOR. Unlike most woodpeckers, Northern Flickers spend lots of time on the ground. When in trees they're often perched upright on horizontal branches instead of leaning against their tails on a trunk. They fly in an up-and-down path using heavy flaps interspersed with glides, like many woodpeckers.

Cool Facts

Woodpeckers drum on trees to seek mates, not to find food. They're interested in making the loudest possible noise, which is why you may see flickers drumming on metal objects such as lampposts.

Backyard Tips

Northern Flickers don't habitually visit bird feeders, but you can find them in your yard if you have a mixture of trees and open ground, especially if there is an anthill or two.

The American Kestrel, North America's smallest falcon, packs a predator's fierce intensity into its tiny body. It's one of the most colorful of all raptors, too: the male has slate-blue wings and a reddish back; the female is warm reddish-brown. Hunting for insects and other small prey in open territory, kestrels perch on wires or poles, or hover facing into the wind, flapping and adjusting their long tails to stay in place.

AT A GLANCE

Food American Kestrels eat mostly insects and other invertebrates, as well as small rodents and birds. Common foods include grasshoppers, dragonflies, spiders, butterflies, mice, bats, and small songbirds. They also sometimes eat small snakes, lizards, and frogs.

Nesting American Kestrels nest in cavities. They cannot excavate their own, so they use old woodpecker holes, natural tree hollows, rock crevices, and nooks in buildings and other structures. Once they've found a suitable hole, American Kestrels do not add any additional nesting materials.

Habitat American Kestrels occupy open habitats ranging from deserts and grasslands to alpine meadows and agricultural fields. They're most often seen perching on telephone wires along roadsides, in open country with short vegetation and few trees.

RANGE MAP

Breeding
Nonbreeding
Year-round

KEYS TO IDENTIFICATION

MALE

MEASUREMENTS (Both sexes)

Length	Wingspan	Weight
8.7–12.2 in	20.1–24 in	2.8–5.8 oz
22–31 cm	51–61 cm	80–165 g

SIZE & SHAPE. The slender American Kestrel is roughly the size and shape of a Mourning Dove, although it has a larger head; longer, narrower wings; and a long, square-tipped tail. In flight, the wings are often bent, the wingtips swept back.

COLOR PATTERN. American Kestrels are pale when seen from below and warm, rusty brown spotted with black above. Males have slate-blue wings; females' wings are reddish brown. Both sexes have two black vertical marks on each side of their pale face, the front one nicknamed a "mustache," the rear one a "sideburn." The tail has a black band near the tip.

BEHAVIOR. American Kestrels usually snatch their prey from the ground, though some catch quarry on the wing. They are gracefully buoyant in flight, and are small enough to get tossed around in the wind. When perched, kestrels often pump their tails as if they are trying to balance.

Cool Facts

Birds can see ultraviolet light. This ability enables kestrels to track their vole prey by following the trails of urine that the mammals leave as they run along the ground.

Backyard Tips

American Kestrels are declining in many parts of their range. One problem is availability of nest sites. You can help by putting up a nest box—find plans and instructions at *nestwatch.org/birdhouses*.

WESTERN WOOD-PEWEE *(Contopus sordidulus)*

A medium-sized, drab flycatcher, the Western Wood-Pewee is a common breeder in open forests and riparian zones across the West. It's very difficult to tell this and the Eastern Wood-Pewee apart visually, though their voices are very different. Their breeding ranges overlap in a very narrow zone in the Great Plains. Despite their similarity, no evidence has ever been found that the two species interbreed.

AT A GLANCE

Food
This sit-and-wait predator sallies from open perches in pursuit of flying insects, especially flies, ants, bees, wasps, and beetles. It usually returns over and over to the same or nearby perches.

Nesting
The nest is a shallow cup of woven grass placed in a horizontal fork. It's bound together with spiderwebs, covered with moss, bud scales, or insect cocoons, and lined with hair or fine grass.

Habitat
Western Wood-Pewees breed in open forests up to about 10,000 feet. Look for them in cottonwoods and sycamores along rivers, or in stands of pinyon pine, juniper, oak, ponderosa pine, spruce, or aspen. They spend winters in mature tropical forests of South America.

RANGE MAP

Breeding
Migration

KEYS TO IDENTIFICATION

MEASUREMENTS (Both sexes)

Length	Wingspan	Weight
5.5–6.3 in	10.2 in	0.4–0.5 oz
14–16 cm	26 cm	11–14 g

SIZE & SHAPE. This medium-sized flycatcher has a long tail and wings, short legs, an upright posture, and a peaked crown that tends to give the head a triangular shape. The long wings help separate it from many other flycatchers.

COLOR PATTERN. This pewee, almost identical to the Eastern Wood-Pewee, is olive-gray with dark wings, little to no yellow on the underparts, and no eyering. The dark sides of the breast, with an off-white throat and belly, give it a vested appearance. Adults have thin, white wingbars; those of juveniles are buffy.

BEHAVIOR. Pewees sit on exposed perches and sally out to grab flying insects. The call, a harsh, burry *pee-eer*, is quite unlike that of Eastern Wood-Pewee and the best way to tell the two apart.

Cool Facts

The Western Wood-Pewee makes a clapping noise with its bill while chasing and attacking intruders in nest defense.

Find This Bird

"Look" for Western Wood-Pewees with your ears— their bury, descending calls let you know they're around. When you hear one, look up—they'll be fairly high up on an exposed branch.

The Black Phoebe is a dapper flycatcher of the western U.S. with a sooty black body and clean white belly. It sits in the open on low perches to scan for insects, often keeping up a running series of shrill chirps. Black Phoebes use mud to build cup-shaped nests against walls, overhangs, culverts, and bridges. Look for them near any water source, including small streams, suburban gardens, and the salt-sprayed cliffs of the Pacific Ocean.

AT A GLANCE

Food
Black Phoebes eat insects and other arthropods including bees, wasps, flies, beetles, bugs, grasshoppers, damselflies, dragonflies, termites, and spiders. They also seize small minnows from just below the water's surface. On rare occasions they eat small berries.

Nesting
Black Phoebes nest on rock faces, streamside boulders, tree hollows, and structures such as eaves, irrigation culverts, and abandoned wells. The nest is a mud shell lined with plant fibers, plastered to a vertical wall an inch or two below a protective ceiling.

Habitat
These flycatchers virtually always live near water, including streams, rivers, lakes, cattle tanks, and seacoasts. They may show up anywhere they can find water and some kind of ledge or overhang on which to anchor a mud nest.

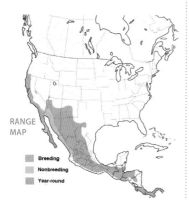

RANGE MAP

- Breeding
- Nonbreeding
- Year-round

KEYS TO IDENTIFICATION

MEASUREMENTS (Both sexes)

Length	Wingspan	Weight
6.3 in	11 in	0.5–0.8 oz
16 cm	28 cm	15–22 g

SIZE & SHAPE. Black Phoebes are small, plump songbirds with large heads and medium-long, squared tails. They often show a slight peak at the rear of the crown. The bill is straight and thin.

COLOR PATTERN. Black Phoebes are mostly sooty gray on the upperparts and chest, with a slightly darker black head. The belly is clean white, and the wing feathers are edged with pale gray.

BEHAVIOR. Black Phoebes sit upright on low perches near water and make short flights to catch insects. They pump their tails up and down incessantly when perched. They often keep up a string of sharp chip notes.

Cool Facts

The male Black Phoebe gives the female a tour of potential nest sites. He hovers in front of each likely spot for 5 to 10 seconds as she decides.

Backyard Tips

Black Phoebes don't come to feeders, but they may use your backyard as a place to catch insects, or even build nests under eaves of a building, especially if there is water or mud nearby.

SAY'S PHOEBE *(Sayornis saya)*

Like other phoebes, Say's Phoebe is seemingly undaunted by people and often nests on buildings. These open-country birds have cinnamon-washed underparts and a rather gentle expression. They breed farther north than any other flycatcher and are seemingly limited only by the lack of nest sites. The soft call has been described as "despondent"; others find it lends a soothing sound to dry open areas of the West.

AT A GLANCE

Food
This phoebe eats almost entirely insects such as beetles, grasshoppers, flies, and bees. It picks them off the ground or snatches them in midair.

Nesting
Female Say's Phoebes build cup nests on protected ledges such as caves, cliff faces, dirt banks, and buildings or other structures. They use stems, grasses, rocks, spiderwebs, and other items to form a cup, and then line it with hair, paper, fibers, and feathers.

Habitat
Say's Phoebes live in open country, sagebrush, badlands, dry foothills, canyons, desert borders, and ranches. They often gravitate to buildings. They avoid heavy forests and aren't closely tied to watercourses (unlike other phoebes).

RANGE MAP

- Breeding
- Migration
- Nonbreeding
- Year-round

KEYS TO IDENTIFICATION

MEASUREMENTS (Both sexes)

Length	Wingspan	Weight
6.7 in	13 in	0.7–0.8 oz
17 cm	33 cm	21–22 g

SIZE & SHAPE. This slender flycatcher appears large-headed for a bird of its size. The head often appears flat on top, but phoebes sometimes raise the head feathers into a small peak. The bill is straight and fairly flat; the tail is long.

COLOR PATTERN. Say's Phoebes are pale brownish gray above with a cinnamon belly, a darker tail, and a gray breast. The immature is similar to the adult, but is browner and may show a buffy wingbar.

BEHAVIOR. Say's Phoebes persistently wag their tails when perched. When foraging, they perch on exposed twigs, fly out to snatch an insect, and often return to the same perch.

Cool Facts

Say's Phoebes breed north beyond the treeline. They may be using the Alaska pipeline to extend their range, even nesting on the pipeline itself.

Backyard Tips

Say's Phoebes do well around humans. They don't come to feeders, but they may use your backyard as a place to catch insects, or even build nests under eaves of a building.

A common flycatcher of the dry, open West, Ash-throated Flycatchers are exceptionally tolerant of high temperatures and can survive without drinking water. These brownish-gray flycatchers have pale yellow bellies and cinnamon highlights in the wings and tail. They sit on low perches and carefully tip their head from side to side as they watch for unwary insects. They nest in cavities or holes including in dead trees, fence posts, pipes, and mailboxes.

AT A GLANCE

Food

Ash-throated Flycatchers eat mostly insects, larvae, and spiders. They eat some fruit in winter, and they occasionally catch small reptiles.

Nesting

These flycatchers build a nest in a rotted tree cavity, woodpecker hole, or nest box. The nest is made of dry grass, weed stems, manure, and dry leaves, lined with hair, feathers, soft plant fibers, and sometimes snakeskin.

Habitat

Look for these flycatchers in scrubby, dry habitats, open woodland, and woodlands along streams.

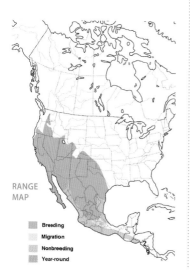

RANGE MAP

- Breeding
- Migration
- Nonbreeding
- Year-round

KEYS TO IDENTIFICATION

MEASUREMENTS (Both sexes)

Length	Wingspan	Weight
7.5–8.3 in	11.8–12.6 in	0.7–1.3 oz
19–21 cm	30–32 cm	21–38 g

SIZE & SHAPE. This is s a medium-large flycatcher with a big, slightly peaked head and a straight, thick bill.

COLOR PATTERN. The Ash-throated Flycatcher has a brownish gray back and head, a pale gray chest, and a pale yellow belly. The wings and tail have cinnamon patches that become especially apparent in flight. They have two white wingbars on each wing.

BEHAVIOR. These flycatchers often move from perch to perch through the understory, cocking their heads inquisitively as they look for prey to take from the vegetation or from the ground.

Cool Facts

Ash-throated Flycatchers are exceptionally tolerant of heat and can survive without drinking water. Instead they derive water from the food they eat.

Backyard Tips

Although Ash-throated Flycatchers do not visit feeders, you can put up a nest box to attract a breeding pair. Find plans and instructions to make your own at nestwatch.org/birdhouses.

An eye-catching bird with ashy gray and lemon-yellow plumage, the Western Kingbird is a familiar summertime sight in open habitats across western North America. This large flycatcher sallies out to capture flying insects from conspicuous perches on trees or utility lines, flashing a black tail with white edges. It's aggressive and will scold and chase intruders away, including Red-tailed Hawks and American Kestrels.

Food Like most flycatchers, Western Kingbirds are mainly insectivores. They hunt by sight during the day, using acrobatic maneuvers to catch flying insects out of the air. They also take some fruits of elderberry, hawthorn, Texas mulberry, woodbine, and other shrubs.

Nesting Western Kingbirds build nests in crotches of trees and shrubs, and on human-made structures such as utility poles, fence posts, and metal girders. The female weaves a bulky, open cup of plant fibers and lines it with a softer material such as wool, hair, feathers, or string.

Habitat Western Kingbirds live in open valleys and lowlands up to about 7,000 feet elevation. They perch on utility lines, fences, and trees in grasslands, deserts, sagebrush, agricultural fields, and open woodlands.

RANGE MAP

- Breeding
- Migration
- Nonbreeding

MEASUREMENTS (Both sexes)

Length	Wingspan	Weight
7.9–9.4 in	15–16 in	1.3–1.6 oz
20–24 cm	38–41 cm	37–46 g

SIZE & SHAPE. Western Kingbirds are fairly large flycatchers with large heads and broad shoulders. They have heavy, straight bills, long wings, and medium-length, square-tipped tails.

COLOR PATTERN. Western Kingbirds are gray-headed birds with a yellow belly and a whitish chest and throat. The tail is black with white outer tail feathers that are especially conspicuous in flight.

BEHAVIOR. Easily found perched upright on fences and utility lines, Western Kingbirds hawk insects from the air or fly out to pick prey from the ground. They ferociously defend their territories. Vocalizations include long series of squeaky, bubbling calls as well as single, accented *kip* notes.

Cool Facts

This flycatcher's breeding range has been spreading for the last century. Shade trees and utility poles have helped with this by providing hunting perches and nest sites. Cleared forests provide open habitats.

Find This Bird

A great way to find Western Kingbirds is to take a drive through open country in summer and scan the fences and utility lines, which are favorite hunting perches for these flycatchers.

The deceptively cute Gray Jay is one of the most intrepid birds in North America, living in northern forests year-round and rearing chicks in the dark and cold of winter. Highly curious and always on the lookout for food, Gray Jays eat just about anything, from berries to small animals. In some areas they visit campsites or even alight on hikers' hands to grab a raisin or peanut—giving rise to colorful nicknames such as "whiskey Jack" and "camp robber."

AT A GLANCE

Food

Gray Jays are smart and opportunistic foragers. They eat insects, berries, and fungi, raid birds' nests for eggs and young, and pick at carrion or roadkill. In areas where they frequently encounter people, they also look for handouts, investigate trash, and sometimes grab unattended items.

Nesting

Gray Jays often nest close to the south-facing edge of a forest patch for the extra warmth from sunlight. The pair builds the nest togther, with the male building a loose ball of twigs held together with cocoon silk. Then the jays build a nest cup of twigs over the ball, lined with feathers or fur.

Habitat

Gray Jays live in evergreen (especially spruce) and mixed evergreen-deciduous woods across the boreal forest of the northern United States and Canada, as well as in high mountain ranges of the West.

RANGE
MAP

☐ Year-round

KEYS TO IDENTIFICATION

MEASUREMENTS (Both sexes)

Length	Wingspan	Weight
10–11.5 in	18 in	2–3 oz
25–29 cm	46 cm	58–84 g

SIZE & SHAPE. Gray Jays are stocky, fairly large songbirds with short, stout bills. They have round heads and long tails, with broad, rounded wings.

COLOR PATTERN. Gray Jays are dark gray above and light gray below, with black on the back of the head forming a partial hood. Juveniles are grayish black overall, and usually show pale edges to the base of the bill.

BEHAVIOR. Gray Jays often travel in small groups. They swoop in silently, generally holding their wings below the horizontal. This is one bird species that will often come looking for you instead of the other way around. They are less noisy overall than other jays.

Cool Facts

Gray Jays store food year-round by molding the food into a sticky blob with their saliva and gluing it behind flakes of bark and other hiding places. They have a great memory for where they've stored food.

Backyard Tips

Gray Jays visit feeders within their northern range, eating almost any kind of food offered at tube, platform, or ground feeders. They especially go for peanut butter and suet.

A large, dark, crested jay of evergreen forests in the mountainous West, Steller's Jays are fixtures of campgrounds, parklands, and backyards, where they visit bird feeders and unattended picnic tables. When patrolling the woods they stick to the high canopy, their harsh, scolding calls revealing their presence. Graceful and almost lazy in flight, they make long swoops on broad, rounded wings.

AT A GLANCE

Food Steller's Jays eat seeds, berries, nuts, eggs, and small animals such as insects, lizards, mice, and nestlings. They can carry several acorns or pinyon pine seeds at once, to bury for later eating. They readily steal food from other animals and people.

Nesting The nest is a bulky cup of stems, leaves, moss, and sticks held together with mud and lined with pine needles, soft rootlets, or animal hair. Look for nests on horizontal branches close to the trunk and often near the tops of trees. Nests are 10–17 inches across, the inner cup 2.5–3.5 inches deep.

Habitat Look for Steller's Jays in evergreen forests of western North America, at elevations of 3,000–10,000 feet (lower along the Pacific Coast). They're most easily seen at campgrounds, picnic areas, parks, and backyards.

RANGE MAP

■ Year-round

KEYS TO IDENTIFICATION

MEASUREMENTS (Both sexes)

Length	Wingspan	Weight
11.8–13.4 in	17.3 in	3.5–4.9 oz
30–34 cm	44 cm	100–140 g

SIZE & SHAPE. Steller's Jays are large songbirds with large heads, chunky bodies, rounded wings, and a long, full tail. The straight, powerful bill has a slight hook. The prominent triangular crest often stands nearly straight up from the head.

COLOR PATTERN. At a distance, Steller's Jays are very dark, lacking any white underparts. The head is charcoal black and the body all blue, lightest on the wings.

BEHAVIOR. Steller's Jays are bold and inquisitive. They spend much of their time in the forest canopy, coming to the forest floor to investigate visitors and look for food, moving with decisive hops of their long legs.

Cool Facts

Steller's Jay, Steller's sea lion, and Steller's Sea-Eagle were all named for Georg Steller. He was a naturalist who collected specimens while on a Russian ship that visited Alaskan islands in 1741.

Backyard Tips

Steller's Jays visit feeders for peanuts, other large seeds and nuts, and suet. They often carry large amounts away to store in a cache to help them get through the winter.

This is the "blue jay" of dry lowlands from Nevada south to Mexico, It's dusty blue, gray-brown, and white, and looks very similar to the California Scrub-Jay (they were considered the same species, called Western Scrub-Jay, until 2016). The bird's rounded, crestless head sets it apart from Blue Jays and Steller's Jays. This species is a fixture of dry shrublands and woodlands of pinyon pine and juniper.

Food Woodhouse's Scrub-Jays eat insects, fruit, nuts, seeds, and small animals such as lizards and nestling birds. They can't break into unopened pine cones, but their relatively thin, straight, pointed bill helps them reach in and extract the rich pine nuts as soon as a gap opens.

Nesting Woodhouse's Scrub-Jays build their nests fairly low in small trees; they fashion a basket of twigs lined with rootlets, fine strands of plant fibers, and livestock hair. The nest is about 6 inches across when finished. It's usually well hidden amid foliage and vines.

Habitat Look for Woodhouse's Scrub-Jays in open habitats and pinyon-juniper woodlands of the intermountain West, and in backyards and pastures. They're usually, though not always, in lower and drier habitats than Steller's Jay.

RANGE MAP

▪ Year-round
▪ Year-round (scarce)

KEYS TO IDENTIFICATION

MEASUREMENTS (Both sexes)

Length	Wingspan	Weight
11–11.8 in	15.4 in	2.5–3.5 oz
28–30 cm	39 cm	70–100 g

SIZE & SHAPE. Woodhouse's Scrub-Jay is a fairly large, lanky songbird with a long, floppy tail and a hunched-over posture. The bill is fairly long and straight, with a pointed tip.

COLOR PATTERN. Light blue and gray above, with a whitish throat and grayish belly separated by an indistinct, partial breast band of blue. In birds, the color blue depends on lighting, so Woodhouse's Scrub-Jays can look simply dark.

BEHAVIOR. Like many jays, Woodhouse's Scrub-Jay is assertive, vocal, and inquisitive. Often one perches high on a tree, wire, or post, acting as a lookout for the rest of the flock. Its flight seems underpowered and slow, with bouts of fluttering alternating with glides.

Cool Facts

Along the West Coast, keep an eye out for a scrub-jay with deeper blue plumage and a more distinct blue necklace across the chest. That's the very similar, closely related California Scrub-Jay.

Backyard Tips

Woodhouse's Scrub-Jays sometimes come to feeders for sunflower seeds and peanuts. If you have dense shrubs or small trees, a pair might build a nest.

Black-billed Magpies are familiar and entertaining birds of western North America often seen sitting on fence posts and road signs. In flight, the wings flash large white patches and the very long tail trails behind. This flashy relative of jays and crows is a social creature, gathering in numbers to feed at carrion. They're also vocal birds and keep up a regular stream of raucous or querulous calls.

AT A GLANCE

Food

Black-billed Magpies eat fruit, seeds, insects, small mammals, bird eggs, and nestlings. Carrion is also a main food source, as are the fly maggots found within. Magpies also land on large animals, such as cows or moose, and pick ticks off them.

Nesting

Black-billed Magpie pairs share the work of building domed nests, which are typically about 30 inches high and 20 inches wide. The male gathers sticks for the exterior. The female builds the interior, forming a mud cup and lining it with grass. They build domed nests in trees, shrubs, on utility poles, and in deserted buildings.

Habitat

Black-billed Magpies occur in meadows, grasslands, and sagebrush plains. They prefer open areas and are not found in dense woods. Magpies also spend time near human developments such as barnyards, livestock areas, and grain elevators where they have ready access to food.

RANGE MAP

- Nonbreeding (scarce)
- Year-round

KEYS TO IDENTIFICATION

MEASUREMENTS (Both sexes)

Length	Wingspan	Weight
17.7–23.6 in	22–24 in	5.1–7.4 oz
45–60 cm	56–61 cm	145–210 g

SIZE & SHAPE. Black-billed Magpies are large, bulky birds. They are larger than jays with much longer, diamond-shaped tails and heavier bills.

COLOR PATTERN. These birds are black and white overall with blue-green iridescent flashes in the wing and tail. The upperparts are mostly black with a white patch in the outer wing and two white stripes on the back.

BEHAVIOR. Black-billed Magpies are social, inquisitive birds that give a variety of trilling, cackling, and whistling calls. They make sweeping flights with their long tails trailing behind. They flap steadily in flight, alternating deep and shallow wingbeats, and use their long tails to negotiate abrupt turns.

Cool Facts

Historical accounts tell of magpies following parties of Plains Indians to eat leftovers from bison kills. Lewis and Clark reported that magpies used to sneak into their tents to steal food.

Find This Bird

Black-billed Magpies are noisy and often sit conspicuously at the tops of trees or fence posts. In flight their trailing tail feathers and flashy white wing patches make them easy to spot.

American Crows, familiar over much of the continent, are large, intelligent, all-black birds with hoarse, cawing voices. Common in habitats ranging from open woods and empty beaches to town centers, they usually feed on the ground and eat a huge variety of foods, especially earthworms, insects, small animals, eggs and chicks taken from other birds' nests, seeds, and fruit. They scavenge on garbage and carrion.

Food American Crows are omnivores, taking a vast array of plant and animal foods, including crop pests and aquatic animals such as fish, crayfish, and clams. A frequent nest predator on eggs and nestlings of many species, it also eats carrion and garbage.

Nesting Both members of a breeding pair help build the nest. Young birds from the previous year sometimes help as well. The nest is made largely of medium-sized twigs with an inner cup lined with pine needles, weeds, soft bark, or animal hair. Nest size is quite variable, typically 6–19 inches across, with an inner cup about 6–14 inches across and 4–15 inches deep.

Habitat Highly adaptable, crows live in open areas, from big cities to wilderness. They're common on farms, pastures, landfills, feedlots, and towns. They avoid deserts and unbroken forest, but show up on campgrounds and venture into forests along roads and rivers.

RANGE MAP

■ Breeding
■ Nonbreeding
■ Year-round

MEASUREMENTS (Both sexes)

Length	Wingspan	Weight
15.7–20.9 in	33.5–39.4 in	11.1–21.9 oz
40–53 cm	85–100 cm	316–620 g

SIZE & SHAPE. The American Crow is a long-legged, thick-necked, oversized songbird with a heavy, straight bill. In flight, the wings are fairly broad and rounded with the wingtip feathers spread like fingers. The short tail is rounded or squared off at the end.

COLOR PATTERN. American Crows are all black, including the legs and bill. As crows molt, the old feathers can appear brownish or scaly compared to the glossy new ones.

BEHAVIOR. American Crows are very social, usually seen hanging out with family members or large flocks. Inquisitive and sometimes mischievous, they often raid garbage cans and pick over discarded food containers. They often chase away larger birds including hawks, eagles, owls, and herons.

Cool Facts

American Crows don't breed until they are 2 years old and most wait until they are 4 or more. The offspring often help their parents raise young for a few years before setting out on their own.

Backyard Tips

Crows don't regularly visit feeders, but they may steal garbage or pet food if it's not well contained. Peanuts left in an open place are a good attractant if you want crows in your yard.

The Common Raven has accompanied people around the Northern Hemisphere for centuries, following their wagons, sleighs, and hunting parties in hopes of a quick meal. Ravens are among the smartest of all birds, solving complicated problems invented by scientists. These big, sooty birds thrive among humans, stretching across the sky on easy, flowing wingbeats and filling empty spaces with their resounding croaks.

AT A GLANCE

Food Common Ravens are omnivores. They prey on animals ranging from mice and baby tortoises up to pigeons and nestling herons. They also eat eggs, insects, fish, dung, carrion, and garbage.

Nesting The female builds the 5-foot-wide nest platform from large sticks she and her mate take from live trees and old nests. She weaves more sticks, bones, wire, etc. into a basket. The inner cup, 9–12 inches across and 5–6 inches deep, is lined with softer materials.

Habitat Common Ravens occur over most of the Northern Hemisphere, in nearly every wild habitat except the open Great Plains. Once driven from eastern forests, they've been reappearing in recent years. They gravitate to landfills and have adapted to city life in some places.

RANGE MAP

▨ Year-round

KEYS TO IDENTIFICATION

MEASUREMENTS (Both sexes)

Length	Wingspan	Weight
22–27.2 in	45.7–46.5 in	24.3–57.3 oz
56–69 cm	116–118 cm	689–1625 g

SIZE & SHAPE. Significantly more massive than a crow, the Common Raven has a thick neck, shaggy throat feathers, and a Bowie knife of a beak. In flight, it has a long, wedge-shaped tail. Its wings are longer and more slender than a crow's, with longer, thinner "fingers" at the wingtips.

COLOR PATTERN. Common Ravens are entirely black, including the legs, eyes, and beak. Adult plumage can be beautifully glossy, especially in good light.

BEHAVIOR. Common Ravens are less sociable than crows, spending most days alone or in pairs except at food sources such as landfills. On the ground, they strut or occasionally bound forward with light, two-footed hops. In flight they are buoyant and graceful, interspersing soaring, gliding, and slow flaps.

Cool Facts

Common Ravens can mimic the calls of other bird species. When raised in captivity, they can even imitate human words; one Common Raven raised from birth was taught to say the word "nevermore."

Backyard Tips

Ravens can cause problems in yards where garbage or pet food is left out. Keeping these attractants under wraps is typically a good idea.

Look through any bare, brown field, especially in winter, and you may notice little brownish birds milling about. These Horned Larks are widespread songbirds of fields, deserts, and tundra, where they forage for seeds and insects, often in mixed flocks with pipits, longspurs, and Snow Buntings. They sing a high, tinkling song on the ground, from a perch, or in flight. Though still common, they have undergone a sharp decline in the last half-century.

AT A GLANCE

Food Adult Horned Larks eat seeds taken from the ground or pulled from seedheads. They also eat sprouted seedlings and insects such as grasshoppers, beetles, and caterpillars. They feed their young mostly insects and such invertebrates as sowbugs and earthworms.

Nesting The Horned Lark's nest, set in a 3–4-inch-wide depression on bare ground, is a basket woven of fine grasses, shredded corn stalks, and other plant material, lined with down, fur, fine rootlets, and other fine fibers. The inner cup is about 2.5 inches wide and 1.5 inches deep.

Habitat Horned Larks favor deserts, tundra, beaches, dunes, heavily grazed pastures, plowed fields, mowed expanses around airstrips, roadsides, and feedlots. They are drawn to fields spread with waste grain and manure. In winter, they mostly feed in areas free of snow.

RANGE MAP

- Breeding
- Migration
- Nonbreeding
- Nonbreeding (scarce)
- Year-round

KEYS TO IDENTIFICATION

MEASUREMENTS (Both sexes)

Length	Wingspan	Weight
6.3–7.9 in	11.8–13.4 in	1.0–1.7 oz
16–20 cm	30–34 cm	28–48 g

SIZE & SHAPE. Horned Larks are small, long-bodied songbirds that usually adopt a horizontal posture. They have short, thin bills, short necks, and rounded heads, the shape sometimes broken by two small "horns" of feathers sticking up toward the back of the head.

COLOR PATTERN. Male Horned Larks are brown above and white beneath, with a black chest band, curving black mask, and head stripes that extend to the back of the head. These are sometimes raised into tiny "horns." The face and throat are yellow or white. Females have similar, less crisply defined markings.

BEHAVIOR. Horned Larks are social birds, usually found in flocks except during the breeding season. They creep along bare ground searching for small seeds and insects. They often join in winter flocks with other open-country species.

Cool Facts

Horned Larks inhabit an extensive elevation range, from sea level to altitudes of 13,000 feet. Linnaeus named this bird *Alauda alpestris*: "lark of the mountains."

Find This Bird

To find them, look for the barest ground around and scan carefully, watching for movement or for the birds to turn their black-and-yellow faces toward you.

Tree Swallows are a familiar sight in summer fields and wetlands across northern North America. They chase after flying insects with acrobatic twists and turns, their steely blue-green feathers flashing in the sunlight. Tree Swallows nest in tree cavities and also in nest boxes, which has allowed scientists to study their breeding biology in detail. Their beauty and insect-eating habits make them a great addition to backyards and everywhere else.

AT A GLANCE

Food
Tree Swallows eat all kinds of flying insects, and, rarely, other small animals; They can eat plant foods when prey is scarce. They usually forage no more than 40 feet above the ground. They sometimes converge in large numbers where insects swarm.

Nesting
The female collects grasses to construct the cup nest, about 2–3 inches across and 1–2 inches deep, inside a natural cavity, woodpecker hole, or bird box. She lines the nest with feathers of other bird species; the male gathers at least half of the feathers.

Habitat
Tree Swallows breed in fields, marshes, and swamps, and around shorelines and beaver ponds, preferring bodies of water that produce multitudes of flying insects for food. Dead and old trees with cavities are used for nesting and sometimes roosting.

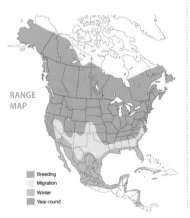

RANGE MAP

- Breeding
- Migration
- Winter
- Year-round

KEYS TO IDENTIFICATION

MALE

MEASUREMENTS (Both sexes)

Length	Wingspan	Weight
4.7–5.9 in	11.8–13.8 in	0.6–0.9 oz
12–15 cm	30–35 cm	16–25 g

SIZE & SHAPE. Tree Swallows are streamlined small songbirds with long, pointed wings and a short, squared or slightly notched tail. Their bills are very short and flat. They tend to perch with a vertical posture.

COLOR PATTERN. Adult males are blue-green above and white below with blackish flight feathers and a thin black eye mask. Females have more brown in their upperparts, and juveniles are completely brown above. Juveniles and some females can show a weak, blurry gray-brown breast band.

BEHAVIOR. Tree Swallows feed on small, aerial insects that they catch in their mouths during acrobatic flight. After breeding, they gather in large flocks to molt and migrate. In the nonbreeding season, they form huge communal roosts.

Cool Facts

The Tree Swallow—which is most often seen in open, treeless areas—gets its name from its habit of nesting in tree cavities. They also take readily to nest boxes.

Backyard Tips

Tree Swallows may supplement their insect diet with berries, such as bayberry and wax myrtle fruits. They often nest in birdhouses—find plans for making your own at nestwatch.org/birdhouses.

These aerial insectivores swoop over lakes and streams performing acrobatic stunts high in the sky in search of flying insects. As Violet-green Swallows dip and dive, their true colors come to life when sunlight illuminates their metallic green backs and iridescent purple rumps. Violet-green Swallows constantly chitter and chatter to each other each other as they gracefully fly through the sky.

AT A GLANCE

Food Violet-green Swallows feed on flying insects such as flies, leafhoppers, beetles, and winged ants, which they eat in midair.

Nesting Violet-green Swallows nest in nest boxes, natural cavities inside trees, or natural holes along cliffs. Inside these cavities they build a shallow cup nest made of grasses, small twigs, and straw. Nests are lined with feathers and measure about 3 inches across.

Habitat Violet-green Swallows breed in a variety of open woodlands including deciduous, coniferous, and mixed woodlands as well as areas near human habitation. These swallows also frequent open water, where they forage for flying insects.

RANGE MAP

- Breeding
- Nonbreeding
- Year-round

KEYS TO IDENTIFICATION

MALE

MEASUREMENTS (Both sexes)

Length	Wingspan	Weight
4.7 in	10.6 in	0.5 oz
12 cm	27 cm	14 g

SIZE & SHAPE. Violet-green Swallows are small, sleek songbirds with long, pointed wings and a short, slightly forked tail. Swallows have short necks and streamlined bodies for acrobatic flight.

COLOR PATTERN. Violet-green Swallows appear dark above and crisp white below, but in good light the greenish-bronze back and iridescent violet rump come to life. They have white bellies that wrap around to the upper side of the rump. Adult males have white cheek patches while females and juveniles have dusky cheeks. Juveniles have grayish-brown backs and crowns.

BEHAVIOR. Violet-green Swallows are graceful aerial acrobats that fly at various heights in search of flying insects. When not foraging Violet-green Swallows perch on wires or exposed tree branches. They are social songbirds and often occur in groups with other swallows and swifts.

Cool Facts

Violet-green Swallows have been recorded flying at 28 miles per hour.

Backyard Tips

Violet-green Swallows might nest in your backyard if you put up a nest box. To find out how to build your own nest box, visit nestwatch.org/birdhouses.

These common swallows are nearly always found in large groups, whether chasing insects in the sky, perching on wires, or dipping into a river for a bath. Cliff Swallows often swarm around bridges in summer, offering passers-by a chance to admire avian architecture. Their mud nests cling to vertical walls, and the birds' pale foreheads can sometimes be seen glowing from the dim entrance.

AT A GLANCE

Food
Cliff Swallows eat flying insects all year, foraging during the day in groups of 2 to more than 1,000. They feed on the wing, often taking advantage of thermal air currents that bring together swarms of insects.

Nesting
Both sexes build nests on cliffsides, caves, building eaves, or bridges. They gather mud in their bills from stream banks or lakesides and mold them into place. They line the nest with dried grass and continue to patch it up with mud throughout the breeding season. The nest is gourd shaped, about 8 inches deep, 6 inches wide, and 4.5 inches high.

Habitat
Cliff Swallows occur in grasslands, towns, open forest, and river edges, but avoid heavy forest and deserts. Most colony sites are close to a water source, open fields or pastures for foraging, and a source of mud for nest building.

RANGE MAP

■ Breeding
■ Migration

KEYS TO IDENTIFICATION

MEASUREMENTS (Both sexes)

Length	Wingspan	Weight
5.1 in	11–11.8 in	0.7–1.2 oz
13 cm	28–30 cm	19–34 g

SIZE & SHAPE. These compact swallows have rounded, broad wings, a small, square head, and a medium-length, squared tail.

COLOR PATTERN. In poor light, Cliff Swallows look brownish with dark throats and white underparts. In good light, their metallic, dark-blue backs and pale, pumpkin-colored rumps shine. They have brick-red faces and a buff-white forehead patch. Some juveniles show whitish throats in summer and fall.

BEHAVIOR. Cliff Swallows zoom around in intricate aerial patterns to catch insects on the wing. When feeding in flocks with other species of swallows, they often stay higher in the air.

Cool Facts
When young Cliff Swallows leave the nest they congregate in large groups called creches. A pair of swallows can find its own young in the creche primarily by recognizing the youngster's voice.

Find This Bird
One easy way to find Cliff Swallows is to look for their gourd-shaped mud nests clustered under a highway overpass or a river bridge. Also look for them foraging in flocks at lakes, rivers, or wetlands.

Barn Swallows dart gracefully over fields, barnyards, and open water in search of flying insect prey. Look for the long, deeply forked tail that streams out behind this agile flyer and sets it apart from all other North American swallows. Barn Swallows often cruise low, flying just a few inches above the ground or water. True to their name, they build their cup-shaped mud nests almost exclusively on human-made structures.

AT A GLANCE

Food
Barn Swallows mostly eat flies, along with beetles, bees, wasps, ants, butterflies, moths, and other flying insects. They usually take single insects rather than feeding on swarms of small ones. They eat grit and pebbles to help digest insects and get calcium.

Nesting
Barn Swallows plaster their heavy mud nests on eaves and rafters of buildings and beneath bridges, culverts, etc. They form mud and grasses into mouth-sized pellets to build the cup, and line it with grass and feathers. The inner cup is 3 inches wide and 2 inches deep.

Habitat
Barn Swallows forage in open areas throughout most of the continent, especially over fields or near water. Breeding habitat must include open areas for foraging, structures to build nests on, and a source of mud for building their nests.

RANGE MAP

- ▨ Breeding
- ▨ Migration
- ▨ Nonbreeding
- ▨ Year-round

KEYS TO IDENTIFICATION

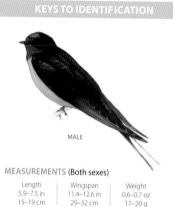

MALE

MEASUREMENTS (Both sexes)

Length	Wingspan	Weight
5.9–7.5 in	11.4–12.6 in	0.6–0.7 oz
15–19 cm	29–32 cm	17–20 g

SIZE & SHAPE. When perched, this sparrow-sized swallow appears cone shaped, with flattened head, no visible neck, and broad shoulders that taper to long, pointed wings. The tail extends well beyond the wingtips and the long outer feathers give the tail a deep fork. In flight, the "swallow tail" is distinctive.

COLOR PATTERN. Barn Swallows have a steely blue back, wings, and tail with rufous to tawny underparts. The blue crown and face contrast with the cinnamon-colored forehead and throat. White spots under the tail can be difficult to see except in flight. Males are more boldly colored than females.

BEHAVIOR. Barn Swallows fly with fluid wingbeats in bursts of straight flight, and execute quick, tight turns and dives to feed on the wing. They catch insects from just above the ground or water to heights of 100 feet or more. They often join other swallows in mixed foraging flocks.

Cool Facts

Barn Swallow parents sometimes get help from other birds to feed their young. These "helpers at the nest" are usually older siblings from previous clutches, but unrelated juveniles may help as well.

Backyard Tips

Putting up a nest box may attract a breeding pair. Find plans for a Barn Swallow–specific nest box you can make yourself at nestwatch.org/birdhouses.

The Black-capped Chickadee is a bird almost universally considered "cute" thanks to its oversized round head, tiny body, and unbounded curiosity. The chickadee's black cap and bib; white cheeks; gray back, wings, and tail; and whitish underside with buffy sides are distinctive. Its habit of investigating its home territory and its quickness to discover bird feeders make it one of the first birds most people learn.

AT A GLANCE

Food In winter Black-capped Chickadees eat about half plant matter (seeds, berries, etc.) and half animal matter (insects, spiders, suet, etc.). The rest of the year, animal matter makes up 80%-90% of the diet. At feeders they take sunflower seeds, peanuts, suet, peanut butter, and mealworms.

Nesting Chickadees nest in nest boxes, natural cavities, abandoned woodpecker cavities, or holes they excavate themselves, usually between 4 and 25 feet high. The female builds the cup-shaped nest of moss and other coarse material, lined with soft items such as rabbit fur.

Habitat Chickadees are found in deciduous and mixed forests, open woods, parks, willow thickets, cottonwood groves, disturbed areas, and big cities as long as there are some trees and shrubs.

RANGE MAP

Year-round

KEYS TO IDENTIFICATION

MEASUREMENTS (Both sexes)

Length	Wingspan	Weight
4.7–5.9 in	6.3–8.3 in	0.3–0.5 oz
12–15 cm	16–21 cm	9–14 g

SIZE & SHAPE. This tiny songbird has a short neck and large head, giving it a distinctive, rather spherical body shape. It also has a long, narrow tail and a short bill a bit thicker than a warbler's but thinner than a finch's.

COLOR PATTERN. Black-capped Chickadees have black-and-white heads, soft gray backs, and buffy to white underparts. The wing feathers are strongly edged with white. The black cap extends down just beyond the black eyes, making the small eyes tricky to see.

BEHAVIOR. Black-capped Chickadees often visit feeders but seldom remain for long. They are acrobatic and associate in flocks—the sudden activity when a flock arrives is distinctive. They often fly across roads and open areas one at a time with a bouncy flight.

Cool Facts

Every autumn Black-capped Chickadees replace old brain neurons with new ones, allowing them to discard old information and adjust to new developments in their flocks and the environment.

Backyard Tips

Chickadees eat suet, sunflower seeds, and peanuts. They use hanging feeders and window feeders. They also use nest boxes—find plans for building a chickadee-sized box at *nestwatch.org/birdhouses*.

The tiny Mountain Chickadee is a busy presence overhead in the dry evergreen forests of the mountainous West. Often the nucleus in mixed flocks of small birds, Mountain Chickadees flit through high branches, hang upside down to pluck insects or seeds from cones, and give their scolding *chick-a-dee* call seemingly to anyone who will listen.

AT A GLANCE

Food Mountain Chickadees eat many kinds of insects including beetles, caterpillars, wasp larvae, aphids, and leafhoppers. They also eat spiders, seeds, and nuts. They come to bird feeders all year round.

Nesting Mountain Chickadees nest in cavities but they don't excavate them unless the wood is very soft. Instead, they rely on holes made by other birds such as small woodpeckers and nuthatches. Inside the cavity the female makes a neat cup from fur. Mountain Chickadees also nest in natural crevices and nest boxes.

Habitat They are common across most evergreen forests of the Western mountains, particularly pine, mixed conifer, spruce-fir, and pinyon-juniper forests. Mountain Chickadees tend to use coniferous trees, typically leaving deciduous stands to the Black-capped Chickadee.

RANGE MAP

■ Year-round

KEYS TO IDENTIFICATION

MEASUREMENTS (Both sexes)

Length	Wingspan	Weight
4.3–5.5 in	8.5 in	0.4 oz
11–14 cm	22 cm	11 g

SIZE & SHAPE. Mountain Chickadees are tiny, large-headed but small-bodied songbirds, with a long, narrow tail, small bill, and full, rounded wings.

COLOR PATTERN. Like most chickadees, this species is strikingly black and white on the head, gray elsewhere. The white stripe over the eye distinguishes Mountain Chickadees from all other chickadees.

BEHAVIOR. Mountain Chickadees are quick, agile, and curious birds that hop and flit through the outer twigs, often hanging upside down as they look for insects and seeds. In winter, Mountain Chickadees flock with kinglets and nuthatches, following each other one by one from tree to tree. At feeders, chickadees have a distinct pecking order, with males typically forcing females aside except early in the breeding season.

Cool Facts

Chickadees store food when they find a ready supply. They often shell sunflower seeds by holding one between their feet and hammering it apart with their beak. Then they fly off to stash it.

Backyard Tips

Mountain Chickadees come to black oil sunflower seed feeders. As spring approaches, consider putting up a nest box—find plans and tips at *nestwatch.org/birdhouses*.

CHESTNUT-BACKED CHICKADEE (*Poecile rufescens*)

A handsome chickadee that matches the rich brown bark of the coastal trees it lives among, the Chestnut-backed Chickadee is the species to look for up and down the West Coast. Active, sociable, and noisy as any chickadee, you'll find these birds at the heart of foraging flocks moving through tall conifers with titmice, nuthatches, and sometimes other chickadee species.

AT A GLANCE

Food Most of the Chestnut-backed Chickadee's diet is made up of spiders and insects including caterpillars, leafhoppers, scale insects, wasps, and aphids. They also eat seeds and berries.

Nesting Female chickadees build a nest of moss and strips of bark that is lined with fur, grass, and feathers, placed inside a cavity, nest box, or natural crevice. Chickadees can excavate cavities if the wood is soft enough; otherwise they use old woodpecker or nuthatch holes.

Habitat Chestnut-backed Chickadees live mainly in dense, wet evergreen forests along the Pacific Coast. They also occur in willow and alder stands along streams, eucalyptus groves, and sometimes along the edges of oak woodlands. They're also commonly seen at backyard feeders in urban, suburban, and rural areas where extensive trees and shrubs are present.

RANGE MAP

Year-round

KEYS TO IDENTIFICATION

MEASUREMENTS (Both sexes)

Length	Wingspan	Weight
3.9–4.7 in	7.5 in	0.2–0.4 oz
10–12 cm	19 cm	7–12 g

SIZE & SHAPE. This is a tiny, large-headed but small-bodied songbird with a rather long, narrow tail, small bill, and short, rounded wings.

COLOR PATTERN. The Chestnut-backed Chickadee is boldly black and white on the head like other chickadees, but the back is a rich chestnut. The flanks can be either rich brown (north of San Francisco) or dull gray (central and southern California).

BEHAVIOR. Chestnut-backed Chickadees are active and acrobatic, clinging to small limbs and twigs or hanging upside down from cones. In winter, they flock with kinglets and nuthatches. Flight is short and undulating, with flock members crossing openings one at a time.

Cool Facts

The Chestnut-backed Chickadee uses fur from rabbits, coyotes, and deer in its nest. The adults use a layer of fur about a half-inch thick to cover the eggs when they leave the nest.

Backyard Tips

This species often comes to bird feeders that offer black oil sunflower seed or suet. Try setting up a nest box before spring to entice them to nest—find plans and tips at *nestwatch.org/birdhouses*.

Nondescript save for its crest, the Oak Titmouse might not wow many bird watchers at first sight. But these vocal, active birds characterize the warm, dry oak woods from southern Oregon to Baja California—they're "the voice and soul of the oaks," according to one early naturalist. Birds pair for life and both partners noisily defend their territory year-round. This and the Juniper Titmouse of the Great Basin were once considered a single species.

AT A GLANCE

Food The Oak Titmouse eats a variety of seeds, insects, spiders, and plant materials, such as willow catkins and leaf buds. Oak Titmice glean their prey from bark and foliage, usually less than 30 feet off the ground. They use their stout bills to peck and probe crevices, chip away bark, and pull apart leaf galls, flowers, acorns, curled dead leaves, and lichens in search of prey.

Nesting Female Oak Titmice build nests in naturally occurring cavities, old woodpecker holes, and nest boxes. Sometimes females partially excavate a nest hole if the wood is soft. Nests are made of grass, moss, hair, and feathers.

Habitat Oak Titmice live in open, dry oak or oak-pine woodlands. In a few areas within their range, they use habitats without oaks, including open pine forests and pinyon-juniper woodlands.

RANGE
MAP

▨ Year-round

KEYS TO IDENTIFICATION

MEASUREMENTS (Both sexes)

Length	Wingspan	Weight
5.75 in	9 in	0.4–0.7 oz
14.5 cm	23 cm	10–21 g

SIZE & SHAPE. Oak Titmice are small songbirds with short, stubby bills, a short crest on the head, and a medium-long tail.

COLOR PATTERN. Oak Titmice are plain gray-brown birds. They are slightly darker above than below and may show a slight buffy wash on the flanks.

BEHAVIOR. Oak Titmice flit between branches and trees, flying with a shallow undulating motion. They form pair bonds in their first year and mate for life. Both sexes defend territories year-round, meaning they don't flock in the winter the way many other titmice and relatives do. When defending against an intruding member of its species, the Oak Titmouse raises its crest, quivers its wings, and scolds.

Cool Facts

In pursuit of insects and plant material, the Oak Titmouse forages at a rate of about 40 food-catching attempts every 15 minutes.

Backyard Tips

Oak Titmice visit feeders with sunflower seeds and other birdseed, particularly when tree cover is nearby. They prefer seeds on raised trays or tubes rather than ground feeders.

BUSHTIT (Psaltriparus minimus)

Bushtits are sprightly, social songbirds that twitter as they fly between shrubs and thickets. Almost always found in lively flocks, they move constantly, often hanging upside down to pick at insects or spiders on the undersides of leaves. They often mix with warblers, chickadees, and kinglets while foraging. Bushtits weave a very unusual hanging nest, shaped like a soft pouch or sock, from moss, spiderwebs, and grasses.

AT A GLANCE

Food Bushtits eat mostly small insects and spiders, including very tiny scale insects that adhere to leaves and twigs. They less frequently eat plant material, but have been seen eating olives and willow seeds.

Nesting Bushtits suspend their oversized, sac-like nests on a branch at any height from about 3 to 100 feet. The nest droops a foot or so below its anchor point and has a hole in the side near the top leading into the nest bowl. The stretchy sac is made of spiderwebs and plant material. The nest may be reused for a second brood.

Habitat Bushtits live in oak forest, evergreen woodlands, dry scrublands, streamsides, and suburbs. You can find them at elevations from sea level to over 10,000 feet.

RANGE MAP

▪ **Year-round**

KEYS TO IDENTIFICATION

MALE

MEASUREMENTS (Both sexes)

Length	Wingspan	Weight
2.8–3.1 in 7–8 cm	6 in 15 cm	0.1–0.2 oz 4–6 g

SIZE & SHAPE. Bushtits are tiny, kinglet-sized birds, plump and large headed, with long tails and short, stubby bills.

COLOR PATTERN. Bushtits are fairly plain brown and gray. Slightly darker above than below, they have brown-gray heads, gray wings, and tan-gray underparts. Males in parts of the range have a blackish face mask.

BEHAVIOR. Bushtits move quickly through vegetation, almost always in flocks, continuously making soft chips and twitters. They forage much as chickadees do, frequently hanging upside down to grab small insects and spiders from leaves. Their active little flocks seem to materialze out of nowhere and disappear just as suddenly.

Cool Facts

A breeding Bushtit pair often has helpers at the nest, usually adult males, that help them raise the nestlings. The whole family shares the nest until the young fledge.

Backyard Tips

Bushtits eat mostly small insects, so they don't visit feeders much but they often come to backyards—especially if the yard features dense shrubs and tangles.

An intense bundle of energy at your feeder, the Red-breasted Nuthatch is a tiny, active songbird of northern woods and western mountains. Long-billed and short-tailed, it travels through tree canopies with chickadees, kinglets, and woodpeckers but mostly sticks to tree trunks and branches, where it searches bark furrows and cones for hidden food items. Its excitable _yank-yank_ call sounds like a tiny tin horn being honked in the treetops.

AT A GLANCE

Food

In summer, Red-breasted Nuthatches eat mainly insects and spiders. In fall and winter they switch to conifer seeds. During outbreaks of spruce budworm, they feast on the pests. They select the heaviest food item available, sometimes jamming it into bark to hammer it open.

Nesting

The female excavates a cavity with her mate in the soft wood of a dead tree, or finds an existing cavity. She builds a bed of grass, bark strips, and pine needles, then lines it with fur, feathers, fine grasses, or shredded bark. The pair applies sticky conifer resin to the entrance.

Habitat

Red-breasted Nuthatches live mainly in coniferous forests of spruce, fir, pine, hemlock, larch, and western red cedar. Eastern populations use some deciduous woods. During some winters they may "irrupt" or move far south of their normal range.

RANGE MAP

Nonbreeding
Year-round

KEYS TO IDENTIFICATION

MALE

MEASUREMENTS (Both sexes)

Length	Wingspan	Weight
4.3 in	7.1–7.9 in	0.3–0.5 oz
11 cm	18–20 cm	8–13 g

SIZE & SHAPE. Red-breasted Nuthatches are small, compact songbirds with slightly upturned, pointed bills; extremely short tails; and almost no neck. The body is plump or barrel chested, and the short wings are very broad.

COLOR PATTERN. The Red-breasted Nuthatch is blue-gray above. The male's underparts are rich rusty-cinnamon, the female's a softer peachy color. The male's head is strongly patterned with a black cap, white stripe above the eye, and black stripe through the eye. The female's head markings are softer gray.

BEHAVIOR. Red-breasted Nuthatches creep up, down, and sideways over trunks and branches, probing for food in crevices and under flakes of bark. They don't lean against their tail as woodpeckers do. Flight is short and bouncy.

Cool Facts

Red-breasted Nuthatches sometimes steal nest-lining material from the nests of other birds, including Pygmy Nuthatches and Mountain Chickadees.

Backyard Tips

Red-breasted Nuthatches visit feeders for sunflower seeds, suet, and peanuts. Make sure peanuts don't get wet or they'll mold. In their breeding range, Red-breasted Nuthatches sometimes use nest boxes.

A common feeder bird with clean black, gray, and white markings, the White-breasted Nuthatch is an active, agile little bird with an appetite for insects and large, meaty seeds. It gets its common name from its habit of jamming large nuts and acorns into tree bark, then whacking them with its sharp bill to "hatch" out the seed from the inside. It may be small, but its voice is loud and carries well. The insistent nasal yammering can lead you right to one.

AT A GLANCE

Food

White-breasted Nuthatches eat a wide variety of insects and spiders; also seeds and nuts including acorns, hawthorn fruits, sunflower seeds, and sometimes crops such as corn. At bird feeders they eat sunflower seeds, peanuts, suet, and peanut butter.

Nesting

White-breasted Nuthatches nest in natural cavities or old woodpecker holes, but rarely excavate their own. They don't seem bothered by nest holes considerably larger than they are. They sometimes use nest boxes.

Habitat

White-breasted Nuthatches are birds of mature deciduous woods. They're found more rarely in coniferous woods, where Red-breasted Nuthatches are more likely. They also occur in woodland edges and areas such as parks, wooded suburbs, and backyards.

RANGE MAP

▇ Nonbreeding
▇ Year-round

KEYS TO IDENTIFICATION

MALE

MEASUREMENTS (Both sexes)

Length	Wingspan	Weight
5.1–5.5 in	7.9–10.6 in	0.6–1.1 oz
13–14 cm	20–27 cm	18–30 g

SIZE & SHAPE. North America's largest nuthatch, the White-breasted Nuthatch is still fairly small, with a large head and almost no apparent neck. The tail is very short, and the long, narrow, sharp bill is straight or slightly upturned.

COLOR PATTERN. White-breasted Nuthatches are gray-blue on the back, with a frosty white face and underparts. The lower belly and under the tail are often chestnut. The black or gray cap and neck frame the face and make it look like this bird is wearing a hood.

BEHAVIOR. Like other nuthatches, white-breasteds creep along trunks and large branches, probing into bark furrows with their straight, pointed bills. They often turn sideways and upside down on vertical surfaces as they forage. They don't use their tails to brace against a vertical trunk as woodpeckers do.

Cool Facts

In winter, White-breasted Nuthatches join foraging flocks led by chickadees or titmice, perhaps partly because it makes food easier to find and partly because more birds can keep an eye out for predators.

Backyard Tips

White-breasted Nuthatches take suet, sunflower, and peanuts at feeders. Make sure the peanuts are fresh and dry to protect the birds from mold. Nuthatches sometimes nest in nest boxes.

Small even by nuthatch standards, Pygmy Nuthatches are tiny bundles of hyperactive energy that climb up and down ponderosa pines giving rubber-ducky calls to their flockmates. Their buffy-white underparts set off a crisp brown head, slate-gray back, and sharp, straight bill. Pygmy Nuthatches breed in large extended-family groups, which is one reason why you'll often see a half-dozen at a time.

AT A GLANCE

Food Pygmy Nuthatches forage up and down tree trunks and out to the outermost tips of the branches in search of insects and seeds. Pygmy Nuthatches cache seeds year-round by hammering them into crevices or under flakes of bark on the tree.

Nesting Pygmy Nuthatches nest in cavities in live or dead trees, and in nest boxes. Both the male and the female, and sometimes their offspring from a previous year, help dig out the nest cavity. In the bottom of the hole they build a nest cup of bark shreds, fine moss, grass, plant down, fur, wool, snakeskin, cocoons, and feathers.

Habitat Pygmy Nuthatches live almost exclusively in forests of long-needled pine species, particularly ponderosa pine. They occur in open, parklike stands of older, large trees as well as forests with a mix of oak, quaking aspen, maple, Douglas-fir, and white fir.

RANGE MAP

▩ Year-round

KEYS TO IDENTIFICATION

MEASUREMENTS (Both sexes)

Length	Wingspan	Weight
3.5–4.3 in	8 in	0.3–0.4 oz
9–11 cm	20 cm	9–11 g

SIZE & SHAPE. Pygmy Nuthatches are tiny songbirds with short, square tails, large, rounded heads, and straight, sharp bills. The legs are short and the wings are short and broad.

COLOR PATTERN. Pygmy Nuthatches have a slate-gray back and wings, with a rich brown cap that ends in a sharp line through the eye. The underparts are whitish to pale buff.

BEHAVIOR. Pygmy Nuthatches move constantly and give short, squeaky calls, often mixing with chickadees, kinglets, and other songbirds. They are highly social: they breed cooperatively and also pile in to cavities in groups to roost communally on cold winter nights.

Cool Facts

They survive cold nights by sheltering in tree cavities, huddling with other Pygmy Nuthatches, and letting their body temperature drop into hypothermic states.

Backyard Tips

Pygmy Nuthatches may come to backyard feeders for suet, and to sunflower feeders. They may use dead trees or trees with dead limbs as nest sites.

BROWN CREEPER (Certhia americana)

Brown Creepers are tiny woodland birds with an affinity for the biggest trees they can find. Look for these long-tailed scraps of brown and white spiraling up stout trunks and main branches, sometimes passing downward-facing nuthatches along the way. They probe into crevices and pick at loose bark with their slender, curved bills. Listening for their thin but piercing calls can make it easier to find this well-camouflaged species.

AT A GLANCE

Food Brown Creepers forage for insects and larvae in the furrowed bark of large, live trees. In winter they supplement this diet with small amounts of seeds. They occasionally visit suet feeders.

Nesting The female builds the hammock-shaped nest behind peeling flakes of bark using twigs, strips of bark, bits of leaves, and lichens, using cocoons and spider egg cases as adhesives. The nest cup is about 2.5 inches deep and 6 inches across.

Habitat Look for Brown Creepers in deciduous or coniferous forests with large, live trees. In summer they are often among evergreens such as hemlock, pine, fir, redwood, and cypress. In winter they use a wider variety of wooded habitats, parks, and yards.

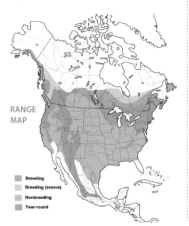

RANGE MAP

- Breeding
- Breeding (scarce)
- Nonbreeding
- Year-round

KEYS TO IDENTIFICATION

MEASUREMENTS (Both sexes)

Length	Wingspan	Weight
4.7–5.5 in	6.7–7.9 in	0.2–0.4 oz
12–14 cm	17–20 cm	5–10 g

SIZE & SHAPE. Brown Creepers are tiny, slender songbirds. They have a long, spine-tipped tail that curves slightly downward, a slim body, and a thin, curved bill.

COLOR PATTERN. Streaked brown and buff above, with the white underparts usually in shadow and hidden against a tree trunk, Brown Creepers blend easily into bark. Their brownish heads show a broad, buffy stripe over the eye.

BEHAVIOR. Brown Creepers hunt for insects by hitching upward in a spiral around tree trunks and limbs, using their stiff tails for support. Then they fly weakly to the base of another tree and resume climbing up. They sing a high, warbling song and give a high, wavering call note.

Cool Facts

Tiny Brown Creepers burn only an estimated 4 to 10 calories per day.

Backyard Tips

Though they eat mostly insects, in winter Brown Creepers will visit backyard feeders, especially to eat suet and peanut butter.

A plain brown bird with an exuberant voice, the House Wren is a common backyard bird over nearly the entire Western Hemisphere. Listen for its rush-and-jumble song in summer and you'll find this species zipping through shrubs and low tree branches, snatching at insects. House Wrens readily use nest boxes, and you may find their twig-filled nests in old cans, boots, or boxes lying around in your garage.

AT A GLANCE

Food House Wrens eat a wide variety of insects and spiders, including both sluggish and quick species. They also eat snail shells, probably for the calcium they contain and to provide grit for digestion.

Nesting House Wrens nest in all kinds of cavities and crevices within 100 feet of woody vegetation. The male piles twigs into several cavities. When he attracts a female, she chooses one, and builds a nest cup into a depression in the twigs, lined with softer materials.

Habitat House Wrens have a huge geographic range and live in many habitats featuring trees, shrubs, and tangles interspersed with clearings. They thrive around human habitations, often exploring the nooks and crannies in houses, garages, and play spaces.

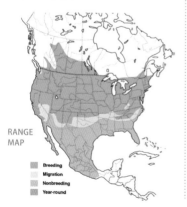

RANGE
MAP

- Breeding
- Migration
- Nonbreeding
- Year-round

KEYS TO IDENTIFICATION

MEASUREMENTS (Both sexes)

Length 4.3–5.1 in 11–13 cm	Wingspan 5.9 in 15 cm	Weight 0.4 oz 10–12 g

SIZE & SHAPE. The House Wren is small and compact, with a flat head and fairly long, thin, curved bill. It has short wings and a longish tail that it keeps either cocked above the line of the body or slightly drooped.

COLOR PATTERN. The House Wren is subdued brown overall with darker barring on the wings and tail. The pale eyebrow that is characteristic of so many wren species is much fainter in House Wrens.

BEHAVIOR. Bubbly and energetic, just like their songs, House Wrens hop or flit quickly through tangles and low branches. They call attention to themselves year-round with harsh scolding chatter and, in spring and summer, frequent singing.

Cool Facts

The House Wren has an enormous range—from Canada to the tip of South America. The map above shows only the range of the North American subspecies.

Backyard Tips

Wrens use brush piles for cover, protection, and a source of insects. If you prune trees or cut brush in your yard, consider heaping the cuttings into a pile for them.

Pacific Wrens are tiny brown wrens with a vocal repertoire much larger than themselves. One researcher deemed them a "pinnacle of song complexity." This tinkling, bubbly songster hides in the dark understory of old-growth evergreen forests or darts between patches of cover, looking almost mouselike. When they sing they hold their tail upright and their entire body shakes with sound.

AT A GLANCE

Food Pacific Wrens eat spiders and insects such as beetles, caterpillars, and flies. They hop slowly on the ground or just above the ground inspecting crevices, decaying wood, upturned roots, and vegetation for food.

Nesting Pacific Wrens nest in natural cavities and also build domed, globular nests. Males build nests in roots of upturned trees, under creek banks, in decaying logs, in hanging moss, or in dead trees. Males use moss, bark, rootlets, and other plant material to build nests. Females only help line the interior of the nest.

Habitat Pacific Wrens live in old-growth evergreen forests in the West, but they can also occur in hardwood forests. They favor areas with fallen logs, upturned tree roots, and a thick understory of mosses and ferns, often near water.

RANGE MAP

■ Breeding
■ Nonbreeding
■ Year-round

KEYS TO IDENTIFICATION

MEASUREMENTS (Both sexes)

Length	Wingspan	Weight
3.1–4.7 in	4.7–6.3 in	0.3–0.4 oz
8–12 cm	12–16 cm	8–12 g

SIZE & SHAPE. This very small wren has a short, stubby tail which it usually holds upright. Their small size and short tail give them a rather round appearance. They have short, rounded wings and a thin bill.

COLOR PATTERN. This wren is brown overall with darker brownish-black barring on the wings, tail, and belly. The chest is brown and unmarked. The face is also brown with a slight pale mark over the eyebrow.

BEHAVIOR. Pacific Wrens quickly hop through the understory, moving more like a mouse than a bird as they forage. Pacific Wrens also often bob their heads or entire bodies. In flight they rapidly beat their tiny wings to move short distances between cover. During the breeding season males sing vigorously from prominent perches in the understory.

Cool Facts

Male Pacific Wrens build multiple nests within their territory. During courtship, the male leads the female around to each nest and the female chooses which nest to use.

Find This Bird

Pacific Wrens are very vocal, so listen for their rapid, trilling songs in old-growth forests. When you hear one, patiently look for a mouselike flurry of motion along fallen logs or in upturned roots.

If you come across a noisy, hyperactive little bird with bold white eyebrows, flicking its long tail as it hops from branch to branch, you may have spotted a Bewick's Wren. These master vocalists belt out a string of short whistles, warbles, burrs, and trills to attract mates and defend their territory; you may also hear them scolding visitors with raspy calls.

AT A GLANCE

Food

Bewick's Wrens eat caterpillars, spiders, flies, grasshoppers, and other insects, including eggs, larvae, and pupae. Bewick's Wrens also occasionally eat seeds, fruit, and other plant matter, especially in winter. Bewick's Wrens pick insects from trees and leaves, quickly shake or bash them into submission, and eat them whole.

Nesting

Males and females build nests inside cavities, rock crevices, ledges, or deep within thick brush piles. Nests are made of sticks, grasses, rootlets, leaves, moss, or other plant material. The birds line the open cup with feathers, wool, hair, or plant down, and may add a final inner lining of snakeskin.

Habitat

Bewick's Wrens favor brushy areas, chaparral, scrub, thickets in open country, and open woodlands near rivers and streams. They also use gardens, residential areas, and scrubby areas in city or suburban parks.

RANGE MAP

- Breeding
- Nonbreeding
- Year-round

KEYS TO IDENTIFICATION

MEASUREMENTS (Both sexes)

Length	Wingspan	Weight
5.1 in	7.5 in	0.3–0.4 oz
13 cm	18 cm	8–12 g

SIZE & SHAPE. Bewick's Wrens are medium-sized wrens with a slender body and a long tail often held upright. They have slender, long bills that are slightly curved.

COLOR PATTERN. Bewick's Wrens are subdued brown and gray with a long white stripe over the eye. The back and wings are plain brown; underparts gray-white; and the tail is barred with black and tipped with white spots.

BEHAVIOR. Bewick's Wrens cock their tails up over their backs, often flicking them from side to side or fanning them. During breeding season, males sing vigorously from prominent perches. Bewick's Wrens make quick, direct, and level flights when moving from shrub to shrub.

Cool Facts

A young male Bewick's Wren learns his song from neighboring adult males. The melodious signature he acquires between the ages of about 30 and 60 days will be his for life.

Backyard Tips

You might attract Bewick's Wrens by adding thick shrubs to your yard—try planting native shrubs such as willow, mesquite, elderberry, and chaparral plants, or by keeping a brush pile in your yard.

No bird exemplifies Southwestern deserts better than the noisy Cactus Wren. At all hours of the day they give a raw scratchy noise that sounds like they are trying to start a car. Cactus Wrens are always up to something, whether hopping on the ground, fanning their tails, scolding their neighbors, or singing from the tops of cacti. Cactus Wrens are true desert dwellers; they can survive without needing to drink freestanding water.

AT A GLANCE

Food Cactus Wrens eat mostly spiders and insects such as beetles, ants, wasps, grasshoppers, and butterflies, which they find while hopping on the ground. Cactus Wrens occasionally eat fruit, particularly cactus fruits.

Nesting Male and female Cactus Wrens build large football-shaped nests with a tunnel-shaped entrance in cacti or other thorny shrubs. Nests are made out of coarse grass or plant fibers and lined with feathers.

Habitat Cactus Wrens live in deserts, arid foothills, coastal sage scrub, and urban areas throughout the Southwestern deserts, especially among thorny shrubs, cholla, and prickly pear cacti.

RANGE MAP

■ Year-round

KEYS TO IDENTIFICATION

MEASUREMENTS (Both sexes)

Length	Wingspan	Weight
7.1–8.7 in 18–22 cm	11 in 28 cm	1.1–1.7 oz 32–47 g

SIZE & SHAPE. The Cactus Wren is a large chunky wren with a long heavy bill and a long rounded tail. The Cactus Wren is the largest wren in the United States and is similar in size to a Spotted Towhee.

COLOR PATTERN. The Cactus Wren is a speckled brown bird with a bright-white eyebrow stripe that extends from the red eye to the side of the neck. They have pale cinnamon sides and a white chest with dark speckles on the breast. The back is brown with white streaks, and the tail is barred white and black—especially noticeable from below.

BEHAVIOR. Cactus Wrens perch atop tall shrubs to announce their presence and defend their territory. When another bird intrudes, Cactus Wrens spread their tails, fluff up their feathers, scold, and even give chase. In flight Cactus Wrens make short and direct flights alternating between rapid wingbeats and a glide.

Cool Facts

Male and female Cactus Wrens build multiple nests and use them as roosting sites even during the nonbreeding season.

Find This Bird

Cactus Wrens are conspicuous; listen for the rusty old car that just won't start and look for them on the tops of cholla cactus, prickly pear cactus, yuccas, and mesquite shrubs.

A tiny songbird overflowing with energy, the Ruby-crowned Kinglet forages almost frantically through lower branches of shrubs and trees, often at or below eye level. Its restless habit of constantly flicking its wings is a key identification clue. The male's brilliant ruby crown patch stays hidden unless he's agitated. Your best chance of seeing the crown is to track down a singing male.

AT A GLANCE

Food

Ruby-crowned Kinglets prey on spiders, insects, and other tiny invertebrates, taken at any height in trees and shrubs. They hover and peck to glean this prey from leaves and branches. They also eat some seeds and fruit, including poison-oak berries and dogwood berries.

Nesting

Ruby-crowned Kinglets nest high in trees. The female builds the compact structure using grasses, feathers, mosses, spiderwebs, and cocoon silk for the outer structure, and fine plant material and fur for the inner lining. The nest is elastic, stretching as the brood grows.

Habitat

Ruby-crowned Kinglets breed in spruce-fir forests, mixed woodlands, and shrubby meadows in northern North America. During migration and winter they occur in woods and thickets.

RANGE MAP

▦ Breeding
▦ Migration
▢ Nonbreeding
▦ Year-round

KEYS TO IDENTIFICATION

MALE

MEASUREMENTS (Both sexes)

Length	Wingspan	Weight
3.5–4.3 in	6.3–7.1 in	0.2–0.4 oz
9–11 cm	16–18 cm	5–10 g

SIZE & SHAPE. Kinglets are tiny songbirds with relatively large heads, almost no apparent neck, and thin tails. They have a very small, thin, straight bill.

COLOR PATTERN. Ruby-crowned Kinglets are olive-green songbirds with a prominent white eyering and white wingbar. This wingbar contrasts with an adjacent blackish bar on the wing. The "ruby crown" of the male is only occasionally visible.

BEHAVIOR. Ruby-crowned Kinglets are restless, acrobatic birds that move quickly through foliage, typically at lower and middle levels. They flick their wings almost constantly as they go.

Cool Facts

Metabolic studies on Ruby-crowned Kinglets suggest that these tiny birds use only about 10 calories per day.

Backyard Tips

These are fast-moving but quiet little birds, best seen in winter in much of the U.S. Watch for their near-constant activity and habit of flicking their wings.

The Wrentit's characteristic bouncing-ball song is a classic sound of coastal scrub and chaparral areas along the West Coast. Seeing a Wrentit is a challenge as they skulk among the shrubs, rarely making an appearance. With patience, a brownish-gray bird with a piercing white eye might pop out of the shrubs and cock its long tail off to the side. Wrentits rarely travel far from their territories, which they defend year-round.

AT A GLANCE

Food
Wrentits pick beetles, caterpillars, ants, and spiders from twigs and bark. They also stretch their necks to reach fruits and seeds from the tips of branches. Poison oak seeds are an important food source during the winter.

Nesting
Males and females build tidy cup nests made of bark strips held together with cobwebs and lined with soap plant or grass. Wrentits build nests about 2.5 feet off the ground in shrubs, ferns, or other dense vegetation.

Habitat
The Wrentit occurs in coastal scrub and chaparral along the West Coast, including suburban yards and parks with shrubs. Away from the coast the Wrentit occurs in thickets along creeks, oak woodlands, and mixed-species evergreen forests.

RANGE MAP

■ Year-round

KEYS TO IDENTIFICATION

MEASUREMENTS (Both sexes)

Length	Wingspan	Weight
5.5–5.9 in	7 in	0.5–0.6 oz
14–15 cm	17.5 cm	13–16 g

SIZE & SHAPE. Wrentits are chickadeelike birds with rather large, round heads and short rounded wings giving them an overall plump appearance. The legs are long. They often hold their long tails up and away from the body at different angles.

COLOR PATTERN. Wrentits are plain brownish-gray with paler, slightly streaked, pinkish bellies. They have a distinctive pale eye.

BEHAVIOR. Males and females sing from deep inside shrubs, making them difficult to find. Wrentits move slowly, often pausing to look around before hopping to the next spot. When they fly between shrubs they fly slowly and pump their tails slightly to maintain elevation. Males and females defend territories year-round and tend to stay in the same vicinity throughout their lives.

Cool Facts

Both males and females incubate eggs. Females incubate at night; males incubate early in the morning and again just before dark.

Find This Bird

Next time you go to the Pacific Ocean, linger a while in the dense coastal scrub. Listen for this bird's long, bouncing-ball trill, and look for it low in the shrubs.

In open parklands of the American West, brilliant Western Bluebirds sit on low perches and swoop lightly to the ground to catch insects. The deep blue, rusty, and white males are considerably brighter than the gray-brown, blue-tinged females. These small thrushes nest in holes in trees or nest boxes. They often gather in small flocks to feed on insects or berries, giving their quiet, chortling calls.

AT A GLANCE

Food
Western Bluebirds eat insects in summer, switching to mostly fruits and seeds in winter. They catch insects such as grasshoppers, caterpillars, beetles, and ants on the ground, and catch small marine invertebrates on beaches.

Nesting
Each pair selects a cavity or nest box. The female builds the nest with grasses, straw, pine needles, and other fibers. She lines the nest cup with grasses, rootlets, feathers, horsehair, and sometimes bits of plastic.

Habitat
Look for Western Bluebirds in open woodland, both coniferous and deciduous. They also live in backyards, burned areas, and farmland, from sea level far up into the mountains.

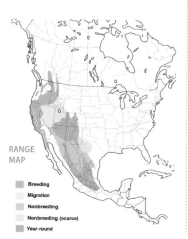

RANGE MAP

- Breeding
- Migration
- Nonbreeding
- Nonbreeding (scarce)
- Year-round

KEYS TO IDENTIFICATION

MALE

MEASUREMENTS (Both sexes)

Length	Wingspan	Weight
6.3–7.5 in	11.5–13.5 in	0.8–1.1 oz
16–19 cm	29–34 cm	24–31 g

SIZE & SHAPE. Western Bluebirds are small thrushes that usually perch upright. They are stocky with thin, straight bills and fairly short tails.

COLOR PATTERN. Male Western Bluebirds are shiny blue above with rust-orange extending from a vest on the breast onto the upper back. Females are gray-buff with a pale orange wash on the breast and blue tints to the wings and tail. The throat is blue in males and gray-buff in females; the lower belly is whitish.

BEHAVIOR. Western Bluebirds are highly social, feeding in flocks during the nonbreeding season. They hunt for insects by dropping to the ground from a low perch. They also eat berries in trees. They depend on trees for nesting cavities and hunting perches, and also perch on fences and utility lines.

Cool Facts

Western Bluebirds nest in holes in trees—but lacking strong bills they rely on woodpeckers to make holes for them. This is one reason why dead trees are a valuable resource in many habitats.

Backyard Tips

Western Bluebirds take readily to nest boxes. Their numbers have improved as people have set up dozens of boxes on so-called "bluebird trails."

MOUNTAIN BLUEBIRD (Sialia currucoides)

Male Mountain Bluebirds lend a bit of cerulean sparkle to open habitats across much of western North America. These cavity nesters flit between perches in mountain meadows, in burned or cut-over areas, or where prairie meets forest—especially in places where people have provided nest boxes. Unlike many thrushes, Mountain Bluebirds hunt insects from perches or while on the wing with hovering flights or quick dives.

AT A GLANCE

Food

Mountain Bluebirds eat insects including beetles, grasshoppers, and caterpillars. In winter they eat insects, seeds, and small fruits such as elderberries, sumac, and mistletoe.

Nesting

Mountain Bluebirds nest in tree cavities and nest boxes. The female entirely fills the cavity floor with coarse, dry grass stems and other vegetation, hollowing out a cup just large enough to allow her to cover her eggs snugly, with an interior diameter of about 2 inches.

Habitat

Mountain Bluebirds occur in open areas with a mix of short grasses, shrubs, and trees, at elevations of up to 12,500 feet. Habitats include prairie and tundra edges, meadows, sagebrush flats, alpine hillsides, pastures, and recently burned or clearcut areas.

RANGE MAP

- Breeding
- Nonbreeding
- Year-round

KEYS TO IDENTIFICATION

MALE

MEASUREMENTS (Both sexes)

Length	Wingspan	Weight
6.3–7.9 in	11–14 in	1.1 oz
16–20 cm	28–36 cm	30 g

SIZE & SHAPE. Mountain Bluebirds are fairly small thrushes with round heads and straight, thin bills. Compared with other bluebirds they are lanky and long winged, with a long tail.

COLOR PATTERN. Male Mountain Bluebirds are sky-blue, a bit darker on the wings and tail and a bit paler below, with white under the tail. Females are mostly gray-brown with tinges of pale blue in the wings and tail. They occasionally show a hint of orange-brown on the chest. Juveniles have an unspotted gray back, blue tail, and gray chest with diffuse spotting.

BEHAVIOR. Unlike other bluebirds, Mountain Bluebirds often hover while foraging; they also pounce on their insect prey from elevated perches. In winter, the species often occurs in large flocks wandering the landscape and feasting on berries, particularly those of junipers.

Cool Facts

A male Mountain Bluebird frequently feeds his mate while she is on the nest. As the male approaches with food, the female may beg like a fledgling, with open beak and quivering wings.

Backyard Tips

Mountain Bluebirds take readily to nest boxes. If you live in suitably open habitat within their range, consider putting one up—find instructions and tips at *nestwatch.org/birdhouses.*

The Townsend's Solitaire is an elegant wide-eyed bird, but its overall gray plumage can make it easy to overlook. In mountain evergreen forests, its sweet jumbling song is a common sound. They frequently perch atop trees and shrubs to advertise their territories all year long. In winter they switch from eating primarily insects to eating fruit, particularly juniper berries.

AT A GLANCE

Food
The Townsend's Solitaire eats insects, butterflies, moths, and spiders during the breeding season but switches to eating fruit, especially juniper berries, during the nonbreeding season. They capture insects by flying out from perches and snapping them up in midair. They also take berries from the ground or pick them from trees.

Nesting
Female Townsend's Solitaires build cup nests using pine needles, lined with grasses or strips of bark. They build nests on the ground or along banks or small cliffs where small pockets or overhanging objects provide protection.

Habitat
Townsend's Solitaires prefer open pine, fir, and spruce forests in mountainous regions from about 1,100–11,500 feet. During the nonbreeding season some Townsend's Solitaires migrate short distances to lower elevations, especially where juniper berries are abundant.

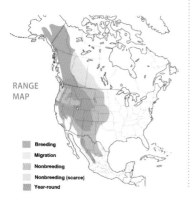

RANGE MAP

- ■ Breeding
- ■ Migration
- ■ Nonbreeding
- ■ Nonbreeding (scarce)
- ■ Year-round

KEYS TO IDENTIFICATION

MEASUREMENTS (Both sexes)

Length	Wingspan	Weight
7.9–8.7 in	13–14.5 in	1.1–1.2 oz
20–22 cm	33–37 cm	30–35 g

SIZE & SHAPE. This medium-sized songbird has a long tail, a short bill, and a small round head. Its upright posture and long tail give it a long and slender appearance.

COLOR PATTERN. Townsend's Solitaires are gray birds with a prominent white eyering and a buffy wing patch that is often easier to see in flight. In flight they also flash white outer tail feathers. Juveniles are dark gray overall and are heavily spotted with buff and white.

BEHAVIOR. The Townsend's Solitaire perches upright and sings from tall perches all year. When they leave their perch they fly with leisurely wingbeats. In the nonbreeding season, adults vigorously defend juniper patches.

Cool Facts

The Townsend's Solitaire is in the thrush family. Unlike most thrushes, they sit upright and fly out and back from a perch to capture food, similar to how many flycatchers behave.

Find This Bird

Townsend's Solitaires are often heard before they are seen. To find a Townsend's Solitaire during the breeding season listen for its sweet jumbling song and scan the tops of trees and shrubs.

HERMIT THRUSH *(Catharus guttatus)*

An unassuming bird with a lovely, melancholy song, the Hermit Thrush spends summer lurking in the understories of forests in the mountains and far north. They winter in the southern states and along the Pacific Coast. The first brown thrush to return to northern forests in spring, it's the last to leave in fall. It forages for insects on the forest floor. To identify this small thrush, look for its distinctive rusty tail.

AT A GLANCE

Food In spring, the Hermit Thrush eats mainly insects such as beetles, caterpillars, bees, ants, wasps, and flies. It also occasionally eats small amphibians and reptiles. In winter, it eats far more fruit, including wild berries.

Nesting In the East, most Hermit Thrushes nest on the ground; in the West they build fairly low in shrubs or trees. Made of grass, leaves, pine needles, and bits of wood, the nest is lined with finer fibers inside and mud and lichen around the outside. The nest measures 4–6 inches across.

Habitat Hermit Thrushes breed in open areas inside boreal forests, deciduous woods, and mountain forests. In winter, they often occupy lower-elevation forests with dense understory and berry bushes, including pine, evergreen, and deciduous woods.

RANGE MAP

- Breeding
- Migration
- Nonbreeding
- Year-round

KEYS TO IDENTIFICATION

MEASUREMENTS (Both sexes)

Length	Wingspan	Weight
5.5–7.1 in	9.8–11.4 in	0.8–1.3 oz
14–18 cm	25–29 cm	23–37 g

SIZE & SHAPE. Hermit Thrushes have a chunky shape similar to an American Robin, but smaller. They stand upright, often with the slender, straight bill slightly raised. Like other thrushes, the head is round and the tail fairly long.

COLOR PATTERN. The Hermit Thrush is soft brown on the head and back, with a distinctly warm, reddish tail. The underparts are pale with distinct spots on the throat and smudged spots on the breast. With a close look you may see a thin pale eyering (not a bold one).

BEHAVIOR. Hermit Thrushes hop and scrape in leaf litter while foraging. They perch low to the ground on fallen logs and shrubs, often wandering into open areas such as forest clearings or trails. Hermit Thrushes have a distinctive habit of raising the tail and then lowering it slowly.

Cool Facts

Hermit Thrushes usually make their nests in and around trees and shrubs, but they can also get more creative. Nests have been found on a cemetery grave, on a golf course, and in a mine shaft.

Backyard Tips

Look for Hermit Thrushes in forest openings or along trails, and check the range map to know whether to search during summer or winter. In winter, look for them around shrubs and vines with berries.

The quintessential early bird, American Robins are common sights on lawns across North America, where you often see them tugging earthworms out of the ground. Robins are popular birds for their warm orange breast, cheery song, and early appearance at the end of winter. Though they're familiar town and city birds, American Robins are at home in wilder areas, too, including mountain forests and Alaskan wilderness.

AT A GLANCE

Food American Robins eat worms, snails, and other invertebrates, as well as fruit and berries. One study suggested that robins may try to round out their diet by selectively eating fruits that have bugs in them.

Nesting Robins build their sturdy grass-and-mud nests on thick branches, horizontal structures on buildings, or the ground. The finished nest is 6–8 inches across and 3–6 inches high. They usually choose an evergreen rather than a deciduous tree for the first nest of spring.

Habitat American Robins are common across the continent in gardens, parks, yards, golf courses, fields, pastures, and tundra, as well as deciduous woodlands, pine forests, shrublands, and forests regenerating after fires or logging.

RANGE MAP

■ Breeding
■ Year-round
■ Winter

KEYS TO IDENTIFICATION

MALE

MEASUREMENTS (Both sexes)

Length	Wingspan	Weight
7.9–11 in	12.2–15.7 in	2.7–3 oz
20–28 cm	31–40 cm	77–85 g

SIZE & SHAPE. American Robins are the largest North American thrush, with a large, plump body, long legs, and fairly long tail. Their profile offers a good chance to learn the basic shape of most thrushes, and they make a good reference point for comparing the size and shape of other birds, too.

COLOR PATTERN. American Robins are gray-brown birds with warm-orange underparts and dark heads. In flight, a white patch on the lower belly and under the tail can be conspicuous. Compared with males, females have paler heads that contrast less with the gray back.

BEHAVIOR. American Robins are industrious birds that run or hop across lawns or stand erect, beak tilted upward, to survey their environs. When alighting they habitually flick their tails downward several times. In fall and winter they form large flocks and gather in trees to roost or eat berries.

Cool Facts

Winter robin roosts can sometimes number a quarter-million birds. In summer, adult females sleep at or near the nest; adult males and fledged young gather at roosts to sleep.

Backyard Tips

Robins visit fruit trees and lawns much more than feeders. Pesticides kill the invertebrates they eat and can be toxic to the birds. Robins often use nest platforms on houses and often visit birdbaths.

The Varied Thrush's simple, ringing song gives a voice to the quiet forests of the Pacific Northwest. Catch a glimpse of this shy bird and you'll see a handsome thrush with a slaty gray back and breast band set against a burnt-orange breast and belly. Common in the Cascades, Northern Rockies, and along the Pacific Coast, Varied Thrushes forage for insects in summer and switch to berries and seeds in winter.

Food Varied Thrushes eat insects found in leaf litter. They pick up dead leaves in their bill and hop backward to clear a spot on the ground before examining the space for insects. In winter they eat mostly berries and nuts.

Nesting Females build open-cup nests about 10 feet above the ground in evergreen trees. The outer layer of the nest is made of fir, hemlock, or alder twigs and the middle layer is made of moss or mud that forms a hard layer. The female then lines the cup with leaves or moss.

Habitat The Varied Thrush breeds in dark, wet, mature forests in the Pacific Northwest. In nonbreeding season it may be found in a broader range of habitats, including parks, gardens, lakeshores, and along streams where fruit and berries are abundant.

RANGE MAP

- ■ Breeding
- ■ Nonbreeding
- ■ Nonbreeding (scarce)
- ■ Year-round

MALE

MEASUREMENTS (Both sexes)

Length	Wingspan	Weight
7.5–10.2 in	13.4–15 in	2.3–3.5 oz
19–26 cm	34–38 cm	65–100 g

SIZE & SHAPE. Varied Thrushes are stocky songbirds with large, rounded heads, straight bills, and long legs. Usually seen standing horizontally on the ground or in a tree, they often look plump-bellied with a relatively short tail.

COLOR PATTERN. Male Varied Thrushes are dark blue-gray on the back and rich burnt-orange below with a sooty breastband and orange line over the eye. The wings are blackish with two orange bars and orange edging to the flight feathers. Females have the same patterns, but are paler gray-brown.

BEHAVIOR. Varied Thrushes forage on the ground, periodically moving to higher perches in the understory to sing. Males arrive on the breeding grounds before females and start singing to establish territories.

Cool Facts

Long-term data collected by participants of Project FeederWatch have shown that Varied Thrush populations go up and down on a 2-year cycle.

Backyard Tips

In the winter Varied Thrushes often eat seed from ground feeders. Planting native fruiting shrubs such as snowberry, toyon, or dogwood is also a good way to attract them to your yard.

If you've been hearing an endless string of 10 or 15 different birds singing in your yard, it might have been just one Northern Mockingbird. This gray bird apparently pours all its color into its songs, sometimes singing all night long. By day it harasses birds, cats, and other intruders in its territory, flying slowly around them or prancing toward them, legs extended, flaunting the white patches in its wings.

AT A GLANCE

Food

Northern Mockingbirds eat mainly small animal prey such as beetles, earthworms, moths, and grasshoppers in summer. They switch to mostly fruit and berries in fall and winter.

Nesting

Northern Mockingbirds nest in shrubs and trees, usually 3–10 feet up but sometimes as high as 60 feet. The nest is made of dead twigs shaped into an open cup, lined with grasses, rootlets, leaves, and sometimes shreds of trash.

Habitat

Year-round the Northern Mockingbird is found in parkland, cultivated land, suburban areas, and regenerating habitat at low elevations. It prefers grassy areas rather than bare spots for foraging.

RANGE MAP

■ Breeding
■ Nonbreeding (scarce)
■ Year-round

KEYS TO IDENTIFICATION

MEASUREMENTS (Both sexes)

Length	Wingspan	Weight
8.3–10.2 in	12.2–13.8 in	1.6–2 oz
21–26 cm	31–35 cm	45–58 g

SIZE & SHAPE. The Northern Mockingbird is a medium-sized songbird, a bit more slender than a thrush and with a longer tail. It has a small head, long, thin bill with a hint of a downward curve, and long legs. The wings are short, rounded, and broad, making the tail seem particularly long in flight.

COLOR PATTERN. The Northern Mockingbird is overall gray-brown, paler on the breast and belly, with two white wingbars on each wing. A white patch in each wing is often visible when the bird is perched, and in flight these become large white flashes. The white outer tail feathers are also flashy in flight.

BEHAVIOR. The Northern Mockingbird usually sits conspicuously on high vegetation, fences, eaves, or telephone wires, or runs and hops along the ground. Found alone or in pairs throughout the year, it aggressively chases off intruders on its territory.

Cool Facts

People once kept mockingbirds as pets, endangering some populations. In New York in 1828, good singers could cost $50. President Jefferson had a pet mocker in the White House.

Backyard Tips

Northern Mockingbirds are common in backyards, but don't often visit feeders. They're attracted to open lawns with fruiting trees and brambles.

First brought to North America by Shakespeare enthusiasts in the nineteenth century, European Starlings are now among the continent's most numerous songbirds. These stocky brown birds with triangular wings are sometimes disliked for their abundance and aggressiveness. For much of the year, they wheel through the sky and mob lawns in big, noisy flocks. They're excellent mimics and are related to mynas.

AT A GLANCE

Food

Starlings are omnivores but focus on small invertebrates such as grasshoppers, beetles, caterpillars, snails, earthworms, millipedes, and spiders. They also eat fruits and berries, seeds, nectar, livestock feed, and garbage.

Nesting

Starlings nest in cavities, nest boxes, and nooks and crannies of human-made structures including streetlights and traffic-signal supports. The male fills the cavity with grass, pine needles, feathers, trash, cloth, and string. The nest cup is lined with soft material.

Habitat

Starlings are common in towns, suburbs, farms, and countryside near human settlements. They feed on the ground on lawns, fields, sidewalks, and parking lots. They perch and roost high on wires, trees, and buildings.

RANGE MAP

■ Nonbreeding
■ Year-round

KEYS TO IDENTIFICATION

MEASUREMENTS (Both sexes)

Length	Wingspan	Weight
7.9–9.1 in	12.2–15.7 in	2.1–3.4 oz
20–23 cm	31–40 cm	60–96 g

SIZE & SHAPE. Starlings are chunky and blackbird-sized, but with short tails and long, slender bills. In flight their wings are short and pointed, creating the starlike silhouette that gives them their name.

COLOR PATTERN. At a distance, starlings look black. In summer they are an iridescent purplish-green with a yellow beak; in fresh winter plumage they are brown, covered in bright white spots.

BEHAVIOR. Starlings are boisterous and loud, and they travel in large groups, sometimes with blackbirds. They shuffle across fields with beak down, probing the grass for food; or they sit high on wires or trees making a constant stream of rattles, whirs, and whistles.

Cool Facts

Every European Starling in North America is descended from 100 birds released in New York in the early 1890s. Genetically, those in Virginia are almost identical to those in California.

Backyard Tips

Starlings often come to bird feeders and nest in nest boxes—often driving away native species in the process. See *nestwatch.org/birdhouses* for ways to help with this problem.

Cedar Waxwings have plumage so silky it hardly looks real. Sociable year-round, waxwings are rarely seen alone. In spring and summer, flocks are small, but several pairs may nest in a small stand of trees, seldom squabbling except when one steals another's nesting materials. In fall, they gather by the hundreds to eat berries or perch in dead trees, sallying out to capture flying insects. WInter flocks are mainly found in fruit trees.

AT A GLANCE

Food Cedar Waxwings feed on insects, many caught on the wing, but also eat fruit year-round, even feeding their nestlings more fruit than insects, unlike most songbirds. Cowbirds seldom survive in a waxwing nest because of the relatively low-protein diet.

Nesting Cedar Waxwings nest in the fork of a tree, anywhere from 3 to 50 feet up. The female weaves twigs, grasses, cattail down, etc., into a bulky cup about 5 inches across and 3 inches high, lined with fine fibers. She often takes these materials from other birds' nests.

Habitat Cedar Waxwings live in deciduous or coniferous woodlands, old fields, and sagebrush, especially near water. They're increasingly common in towns and suburbs, where ornamental fruit trees flourish.

RANGE MAP

Breeding
Nonbreeding
Year-round

KEYS TO IDENTIFICATION

MEASUREMENTS (Both sexes)

Length	Wingspan	Weight
5.5–6.7 in	8.7–11.8 in	1.1 oz
14–17 cm	22–30 cm	32 g

SIZE & SHAPE. The Cedar Waxwing is a medium-sized, sleek bird with a large head, short neck, and short, wide bill. Waxwings have a crest that often lies flat and droops over the back of the head. The wings are broad and pointed, like a starling's. The tail is fairly short and square-tipped.

COLOR PATTERN. Cedar Waxwings are pale brown on the head and chest fading to soft gray on the wings. The belly is pale yellow, and the tail is gray with a bright-yellow tip. The face has a narrow black mask neatly outlined in white. The red waxy tips to the wing feathers are not always easy to see.

BEHAVIOR. Cedar Waxwings are social birds that associate in flocks year-round. They sit in fruiting trees swallowing berries whole, or pluck them from outer twigs with a brief fluttering hover. They also course over water for insects, flying like tubby, slightly clumsy swallows.

Cool Facts

The name "waxwing" comes from waxy red secretions found on the tips of the secondary feathers in the wings.

Backyard Tips

Cedar Waxwings feed primarily on fruit. To attract them to your yard, plant native trees and shrubs that bear small fruits, such as dogwood, serviceberry, cedar, juniper, and others.

Orange-crowned Warblers aren't the most dazzling birds in their family, but they're a helpful one to learn. These grayish to olive-green birds vary in color geographically, have few markings, and rarely show any sign of an orange crown. They are most recognizable by their slim shape, sharply pointed bill, and yellow under the tail. These busy birds forage low in shrubs, and are one of the few warblers that's more common in the West than the East.

AT A GLANCE

Food Orange-crowned Warblers eat mainly spiders and insects including ants, beetles, flies, and caterpillars. They supplement their diet with berries, seeds, and plant galls. These warblers also pierce the bases of flowers to obtain nectar, and visit sapwells drilled by sapsuckers.

Nesting Females build nests on the ground on shady hillsides, road cuts, the bases of snowmelt drainages, and gullies or canyons, often sheltered by vegetation. Females use leaves, grasses, twigs, bark, and moss to construct the nest.

Habitat Orange-crowned Warblers breed in dense shrubby areas, usually within or adjacent to forest. They occur from low-elevation oak scrub to stunted forest near timberline. During migration they occur in many areas, but still prefer dense vegetation.

RANGE MAP

- Breeding
- Migration
- Nonbreeding
- Year-round

KEYS TO IDENTIFICATION

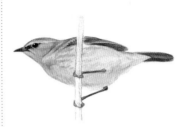

MEASUREMENTS (Both sexes)

Length	Wingspan	Weight
4.3–5.5 in	7.5 in	0.2–0.4 oz
11–14 cm	19 cm	7–11 g

SIZE & SHAPE. Orange-crowned Warblers are small songbirds. Compared with other warblers, they have noticeably thin, sharply pointed bills. They have short wings and short, square tails.

COLOR PATTERN. Orange-crowned Warblers are plain yellowish or olive birds. They have a thin white or yellowish stripe over the eye, a faint blackish line through the eye, and a pale partial eyering. The brightest yellow part of the bird is usually the area under the tail. Birds of the West Coast are brighter yellow; in the interior West the head is usually gray.

BEHAVIOR. Orange-crowned Warblers tend to be unobtrusive as they forage low in shrubs and tangles. They feed among branches and twigs, but sometimes sally like a flycatcher to snag a flying insect or hover to reach the undersides of leaves. They often give a high, faint contact call while foraging.

Cool Facts

The male Orange-crowned Warbler's song is far more variable than that of other wood warblers—so much so that the males can be told apart by their distinctive song patterns.

Find This Bird

In the West this species is widespread during summer and migration. On the breeding grounds listen for the rapidly trilled song—similar to a Chipping Sparrow, but dropping in pitch at the end.

A broad black mask lends a touch of highwayman's mystique to the male Common Yellowthroat. The female lacks the mask and is much browner, though it usually shows a hint of warm yellow at the throat. One of our most numerous warblers, the yellowthroat skulks through tangled vegetation, often at the edges of marshes and wetlands. Both the *witchety-witchety-witchety* songs and distinctive call notes help reveal its presence.

AT A GLANCE

Food Common Yellowthroats forage on or near the ground, eating insects and spiders in low vegetation, sometimes sallying out from a perch to catch prey. They also eat grit, which helps them digest food and may also add minerals to their diet.

Nesting The well-concealed, bulky nest is usually set on or near the ground and supported by sedges, cattails, or other low plants. Nests in marshes are usually higher off the ground, to be safer from flooding. Some nests are roofed, like the nest of an Ovenbird.

Habitat Yellowthroats live in open areas with thick, low vegetation, ranging from marsh to grassland to open pine forest. During migration, they use an even broader suite of habitats including backyards and forests.

RANGE MAP

- Breeding
- Breeding (scarce)
- Migration
- Nonbreeding
- Year-round

KEYS TO IDENTIFICATION

MALE

MEASUREMENTS (Both sexes)

Length	Wingspan	Weight
4.3–5.1 in	5.9–7.5 in	0.3–0.4 oz
11–13 cm	15–19 cm	9–10 g

SIZE & SHAPE. Common Yellowthroats are small songbirds with chunky, rounded heads and medium-length, slightly rounded tails.

COLOR PATTERN. Adult males are bright yellow below, with a sharp black mask and olive upperparts. Immature males show traces of the mask. Females are olive-brown, usually with yellow brightening the throat and under the tail. They lack the black mask.

BEHAVIOR. Common Yellowthroats skulk low to the ground in dense thickets and fields, searching for small insects and spiders. Males sing a rolling *wichety-wichety-wichety* song, and both sexes give a full-sounding *chuck* note. During migration, this is often the most common warbler found in fields and edges.

Cool Facts

The Common Yellowthroat was one of the first bird species to be catalogued from the New World, when a specimen from Maryland was described by Linnaeus in 1766.

Backyard Tips

Look for yellowthroats in reeds, rushes, brambles, and shrubs around wet areas. Though they live deep in tangles, they are inquisitive and often pop up to take a look if you pish or squeak at them.

North America has more than 50 species of warblers, but few combine brilliant color and easy viewing quite like the Yellow Warbler. In summer, males sing their sweet whistled song from willows, wet thickets, and roadsides across almost all of North America. The females and immatures aren't as bright, and lack the male's rich chestnut streaking, but their overall warm yellow tones, unmarked faces, and prominent black eyes help distinguish them.

AT A GLANCE

Food
Yellow Warblers eat mostly insects that they pick from foliage or capture on short flights. Typical prey include midges, caterpillars, beetles, leafhoppers and other bugs, and wasps.

Nesting
Yellow Warblers nest in the vertical fork of a bush or small tree, often within about 10 feet of the ground. The female builds a cup of grasses, bark strips, etc. She places plant fibers, spiderwebs, and plant down around the outside, and lines the inner cup with fine soft fibers.

Habitat
Yellow Warblers breed in shrubby thickets and woods, especially near water. Favorite trees include willows, alders, and cottonwoods. In winter they mainly occur in mangrove forests of Central and South America.

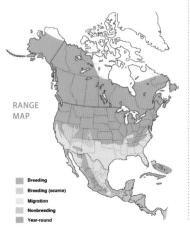

RANGE MAP

- Breeding
- Breeding (scarce)
- Migration
- Nonbreeding
- Year-round

KEYS TO IDENTIFICATION

BREEDING MALE

MEASUREMENTS (Both sexes)

Length	Wingspan	Weight
4.7–5.1 in	6.3–7.9 in	0.3–0.4 oz
12–13 cm	16–20 cm	9–11 g

SIZE & SHAPE. Yellow Warblers are small, evenly proportioned songbirds with medium-length tails and rounded heads. For a warbler, the straight, thin bill is relatively large.

COLOR PATTERN. Yellow Warblers are yellow from head to tail. Males are a bright, egg-yolk yellow with reddish streaks on the underparts. Both sexes flash yellow patches in the tail. The face is unmarked, accentuating the large black eye.

BEHAVIOR. Look for Yellow Warblers near the tops of tall shrubs and small trees. They forage restlessly, with quick hops along small branches and twigs to glean caterpillars and other insects. Males sing their sweet, whistled songs from high perches.

Cool Facts

Yellow Warblers have to watch out for strange eggs that appear in their nests, laid by Brown-headed Cowbirds. The warbler responds by building a new nest directly on top of the previous one.

Find This Bird

Yellow Warblers don't visit feeders. Keep an eye out for them in shrubs and trees along streams, where the males often sing a sweet, whistled song from outer branches.

Scads of these abundant warblers flood the continent each fall. Shrubs and trees fill with the streaky birds giving their distinctive, sharp chips. Their colors are subdued all winter, but spring molt brings a transformation, leaving them a dazzling mix of bright yellow, charcoal gray and black, and bold white. The "Audubon's" form of this species is common in the West and has a yellow throat. In the East look for the white throat of the "myrtle" form.

AT A GLANCE

Food
In summer, Yellow-rumped Warblers eat mainly insects, including spruce budworm. On migration and in winter they eat secretions from scale insects, fruits such as bayberry, wax myrtle, juniper berries, and poison ivy, and some wild seeds. They sometimes visit feeders.

Nesting
Yellow-rumped Warblers nest on horizontal branches of conifers. The nest is a cup of twigs, pine needles, etc., sometimes with moose, horse, or deer hair, moss, and lichens, lined with feathers that may curl up and over the eggs.

Habitat
In summer, Yellow-rumped Warblers live in open coniferous forests and edges, and to a lesser extent in deciduous forests. In fall and winter they move to open woods and shrubby habitats, including coastal vegetation, parks, and residential areas.

RANGE MAP

- ■ Breeding
- ■ Migration
- ■ Winter
- ■ Winter (scarce)
- ■ Year-round

KEYS TO IDENTIFICATION

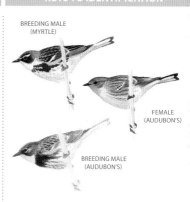

BREEDING MALE (MYRTLE)

FEMALE (AUDUBON'S)

BREEDING MALE (AUDUBON'S)

MEASUREMENTS (Both sexes)

Length	Wingspan	Weight
4.7–5.5 in	7.5–9.1 in	0.4–0.5 oz
12–14 cm	19–23 cm	12–13 g

SIZE & SHAPE. The Yellow-rumped Warbler is a small songbird, fairly large and full bodied for a warbler, with a large head, sturdy but slender bill, and fairly long, narrow tail.

COLOR PATTERN. In summer, both sexes are a smart gray or black with yellow on the crown, sides, and rump. Males are bright; females are duller and may show some brown. Winter birds are paler brown and streaky, with bright yellow rumps and usually some yellow on the sides.

BEHAVIOR. Yellow-rumped Warblers forage in the outer tree branches at middle heights. They're active, often sallying out to catch insects in midair, sometimes on long flights. In winter they spend lots of time eating berries from shrubs, and they often travel in large flocks.

Cool Facts

Yellow-rumped Warblers can digest the waxes found in bayberries and wax myrtles, so they can winter farther north than other warblers. They're also the most versatile at catching insects.

Backyard Tips

During migration and winter, Yellow-rumped Warblers sometimes come to bird feeders for suet and peanut butter. They and other warblers are very vulnerable to window collisions.

A bird of the Pacific Northwest, the beautiful Townsend's Warbler nests in coniferous forests from Alaska to Oregon. It winters in two distinct areas: a narrow strip along the Pacific Coast, and Mexico and Central America. Although thought of as a treetop bird, some individuals spend a lot of time in flowering and fruiting trees during winter, making them fairly easy to see and even photograph.

AT A GLANCE

Food

Townsend's Warblers feed on insects, and also the "honeydew" or plant sap excreted by scale insects. They typically forage in treetops, where they can be hard to spot, but they may feed at lower heights in winter.

Nesting

The nest is a bulky open cup of bark, pine needles, small twigs, dried grass, lichens, and spiderweb or insect silk, lined with fine grasses, moss, or hair. The nest is built on a main limb of a coniferous tree, well concealed by foliage.

Habitat

Townsend's Warblers breed in tall coniferous and mixed forests. They winter in a variety of habitats, including chaparral, mature forest, suburban yards, and parks.

RANGE MAP

- Breeding
- Migration
- Nonbreeding
- Year-round

KEYS TO IDENTIFICATION

MALE

MEASUREMENTS (Both sexes)

Length	Wingspan	Weight
4.7 in	7.9 in	0.2–0.4 oz
12 cm	20 cm	7–11 g

SIZE & SHAPE. Townsend's Warblers are small songbirds with a standard warbler shape including a medium-length tail and a thin, fairly straight bill.

COLOR PATTERN. The adult male's crown, throat, and cheek patches are black. The rest of the face and breast are bright yellow, the breast and sides streaked with black. The lower belly, undertail, and wingbars are white. The back is olive-green with black streaks or spots. Females and young are duller.

BEHAVIOR. Townsend's Warblers pick insects from leaf surfaces and needles, usually in the upper third of a tree's canopy. In fall and winter they may leave the conifers and spend time in ornamental trees and shrubs. They also catch flying insects and hover to take insects from the outermost leaves.

Cool Facts

In winter, Townsend's Warblers feed heavily on the sugary excretions of scale insects. It's such a good resource that one individual will defend a good spot against other birds looking for a meal.

Find This Bird

To find them in summer you'll want to visit evergreen forests and listen for their buzzy songs, then look for them high in the canopy. In winter, try flowering shrubs in yards along the West Coast.

Small even by warbler standards, the energetic Wilson's Warbler dances through wet thickets to the rapid beat of its chattering song. These bright-yellow, black-capped birds breed in the north and in Western mountains, but are widespread on migration. They rarely slow down as they dash between shrubs, grabbing insects from leaves or popping up onto low perches.

AT A GLANCE

Food

Wilson's Warblers pick insect larvae, spiders, beetles, and caterpillars from leaves and twigs. They also hover to grab flies, bees, and mayflies from leaves. They sometimes eat berries.

Nesting

Wilson's Warblers nest on the ground in small depressions at the bases of small trees and shrubs or under bunches of grass or flowering plants. Females use large leaves or sedges to form the base of the nest; then they add moss, strips of bark, fine plant material, and grass.

Habitat

Wilson's Warblers breed in mountain meadows and thickets near streams, especially those with willows and alders. They also breed along the edges of lakes, bogs, and aspen stands. Pacific Coast populations breed in shrubby habitat or young stands of conifers, alders, or maples. During migration Wilson's Warblers use woodlands, suburban areas, desert scrub, and shrubby areas near streams.

RANGE MAP

- Breeding
- Migration
- Nonbreeding

KEYS TO IDENTIFICATION

MALE

MEASUREMENTS (Both sexes)

Length	Wingspan	Weight
3.9–4.7 in	5.5–6.7 in	0.2–0.4 oz
10–12 cm	14–17 cm	5–10 g

SIZE & SHAPE. Wilson's Warblers are one of the smallest warblers. They have long, thin tails and small thin bills.

COLOR PATTERN. Wilson's Warblers are bright yellow below and yellowish-olive above. Their black eyes stand out on their yellow cheeks. Adult males have a distinctive black cap. Females are similar in color but show variations in the amount of black on the top of the head.

BEHAVIOR. Wilson's Warblers flit restlessly between perches and make direct flights with rapid wingbeats through the understory. Unlike many warblers, they spend much of their time in the understory.

Cool Facts

Wilson's Warblers are small even by warbler standards—a detail reflected in the "pusilla" part of the scientific name. It's Latin for "very small."

Find This Bird

During spring migration Wilson's Warblers are quite vocal; listen for their chattering song and look for a little bright-yellow bird at eye level in shrubby vegetation.

Spotted Towhees are large, striking sparrows of sun-baked thickets of the West. They are gleaming black above (females are grayish), spotted and striped with brilliant white. Their warm rufous flanks match the dry leaves they hop around in. The birds can be hard to see in the leaf litter, so your best chance for an unobstructed look at this handsome bird may be in the spring, when males climb into the shrub tops to sing their buzzy songs.

AT A GLANCE

Food
In the breeding season, Spotted Towhees eat mainly insects including beetles, weevils, ladybugs, crickets, grasshoppers, caterpillars, moths, bees, and wasps. In fall and winter they also eat acorns, berries, and seeds.

Nesting
Female Spotted Towhees build nests on the ground, often in small depressions at the base of a shrub, log, or clump of grass. Nests are made of dry leaves, stems, and bark strips and lined with grass, pine needles, and hair.

Habitat
Spotted Towhees are birds of dry thickets, brushy tangles, forest edges, old fields, shrubby backyards, chaparral, and canyon bottoms—places with dense shrub cover and plenty of leaf litter for the towhees to scratch around in.

RANGE MAP

- Breeding
- Nonbreeding
- Nonbreeding (scarce)
- Year-round

KEYS TO IDENTIFICATION

MALE

MEASUREMENTS (Both sexes)

Length	Wingspan	Weight
6.7–8.3 in	11 in	1.2–1.7 oz
17–21 cm	28 cm	33–49 g

SIZE & SHAPE. The Spotted Towhee is a large sparrow with a thick, pointed bill, short neck, chunky body, and long, rounded tail.

COLOR PATTERN. Male Spotted Towhees have jet-black upperparts and throat; the wings and back are spotted bright white. The flanks are warm rufous and the belly is white. Females have the same pattern but are warm brown where males are black. In flight, look for white corners to the black tail.

BEHAVIOR. Spotted Towhees rummage in the leaf litter or creep through thick shrubs. Towhees tend to hop wherever they go, moving deliberately and giving themselves plenty of time to spot food items. They scratch at leaves with a characteristic two-footed backward hop, then pounce on anything they've uncovered. Towhees can fly long distances, but more often make short, slow flights between patches of cover.

Cool Facts

Male towhees have been recorded spending up to 90% of their mornings singing. Almost as soon as they attract a mate, their attention shifts and they sing only about 5% of the time.

Backyard Tips

Spotted Towhees may come to backyard feeders near the ground. Dense, low shrubs and brushy borders in your yard may encourage them to visit or nest.

This big, warm-brown sparrow of the Desert Southwest is common on the ground and beneath shrubs in scrubby habitats, but blends into the background. It's a fairly long-legged, long-tailed sparrow the same color as dirt, with rusty brown under the tail. It looks very similar to the widespread California Towhee (the two were once considered the same species), but the ranges don't overlap.

Food
Canyon Towhees eat mostly small seeds of grasses and weeds, as well as berries such as elderberry and poison oak. They eat small invertebrates, too. At feeders they take milo (sorghum), millet, sunflower seeds, and rolled oats.

Nesting
Canyon Towhees hide their bulky nests in trees, shrubs, or vines, against the main trunk and supported by strong branches. They often incorporate flowers, including mustards and daisies, into the nest, which is about 4 inches across. The inner cup is 2.5 inches across and 3 inches deep.

Habitat
Canyon Towhees are found in desert grasslands with scattered dense shrubs, rocky terrain, dry watercourses with mesquite, and other dry, scrubby areas. Unlike California Towhees, they shy away from suburban neighborhoods, favoring sparsely settled and remote areas.

RANGE MAP

■ Year-round

KEYS TO IDENTIFICATION

MEASUREMENTS (Both sexes)

Length	Wingspan	Weight
8.3–9.8 in	11.5 in	1.3–1.9 oz
21–25 cm	29.2 cm	37–53 g

SIZE & SHAPE. The Canyon Towhee is a large sparrow with a fairly long tail, chunky body, and short rounded wings. The bill is short and thick at the base, and the legs are long.

COLOR PATTERN. Overall, the Canyon Towhee is about as plain brown as a bird gets—although it does have rusty undertail coverts, a buffy throat, and a hint of a reddish crown.

BEHAVIOR. Canyon Towhees scurry along the ground from one bush to another, scratching and pecking for seeds and insects on the ground. Sometimes they linger in the open for a bit. The male perches atop short shrubs and cacti to sing in the breeding season.

Cool Facts

As desert creatures, Canyon Towhees pay close attention to water supplies. They nest twice a year, timed with winter and summer rains, when the most seeds and insects are available.

Backyard Tips

Canyon Towhees feed on spilled seed on the ground or at platform feeders. They are among the few birds that readily take milo (sorghum); they also eat millet and black oil sunflower seeds.

Your first encounter with a California Towhee may be prompted by a tireless knocking at your window or car mirror: these common backyard birds habitually challenge their reflections. But California Towhees are, at heart, birds of the tangled chaparral and other scrublands of California and Oregon. You're as likely to hear their bright chip notes along a secluded trail as outside your front door. If you live in the Southwest, look for this bird's twin, the Canyon Towhee.

AT A GLANCE

Food California Towhees eat mostly seeds from grasses and herbs, supplemented with insects (mostly beetles and grasshoppers) during the breeding season. They also eat acorns and berries such as elderberry, coffeeberry, and poison oak.

Nesting Female California Towhees weave nests of twigs, grasses, and dried flowers. They line the nest with hair and downy seeds. Females build their nests in a low fork (3–12 feet high) in a shrub or small tree.

Habitat California Towhees are birds of chaparral scrub. They also occur in suburban yards and along streams and canyon bottoms, where they live amid manzanita, buckthorn, madrone, foothill pines, and oaks.

RANGE MAP

■ Year-round

KEYS TO IDENTIFICATION

MEASUREMENTS (Both sexes)

Length	Wingspan	Weight
8.3–9.8 in	11.4 in	1.3–2.4 oz
21–25 cm	29 cm	37–67 g

SIZE & SHAPE. California Towhees are large sparrows with short, rounded wings, long tails, and a thick, seed-cracking beak. The long tail and short wings can give this bird an ungainly look in flight.

COLOR PATTERN. Few birds are as uniformly matte brown as a California Towhee. A patch under the tail (called the crissum, giving the bird its scientific name) is a noticeably warmer ruddy brown. Males look the same as females.

BEHAVIOR. California Towhees hop or run on the ground but tend to stay close to the protection of low shrubs and trees. When not foraging they may perch on shrubs, rooftops, and backyard fences, to sit and chip for long periods. In flight they look out of practice, using lots of wing power to travel short distances. Look for California Towhees doing the classic towhee foraging maneuver, the double-scratch—a quick backwards hop while scratching the ground.

Cool Facts

Poison oak might be hazardous to you, but California Towhees build their nests in the oily bushes and feast on the plant's copious crops of pale white berries.

Backyard Tips

In much of California, there's a good chance you have California Towhees in your neighborhood. Offer sunflower, cracked corn, milet, milo, or peanuts from feeders at or near ground level.

This is a crisp, pretty sparrow whose bright reddish cap and black eyeline provide a splash of color and make adults fairly easy to identify. Chipping Sparrows are common across North America wherever trees are interspersed with grassy openings. Their loud, trilling songs are one of the most common sounds of spring woodlands and suburbs.

AT A GLANCE

Food Chipping Sparrows eat seeds of a great variety of grasses and herbs. During the breeding season they also hunt for protein-rich insects, and these form a large part of their summer diet. Sometimes they eat small fruits such as cherries.

Nesting Females typically build their nests between 3 and 10 feet off the ground, hidden in foliage at the tip of a branch. They gravitate toward evergreen trees, but also nest in crabapples, honeysuckle tangles, ornamental shrubs, and other deciduous species. Females can be finicky about placement, often beginning to build a nest, then leaving to begin in another spot.

Habitat Look for Chipping Sparrows in open woodlands and forests with grassy clearings across North America, all the way up to the highest elevations. You'll also see them in parks, along roadsides, and in your backyard, particularly if you have feeders and trees.

RANGE MAP

- Breeding
- Migration
- Nonbreeding
- Year-round

KEYS TO IDENTIFICATION

BREEDING

NONBREEDING

MEASUREMENTS (Both sexes)

Length	Wingspan	Weight
4.7–5.9 in	8.3 in	0.4–0.6 oz
12–15 cm	21 cm	11–16 g

SIZE & SHAPE. The Chipping Sparrow is a slender, fairly long-tailed sparrow with a medium-sized bill that is a bit small compared to those of other sparrows.

COLOR PATTERN. Summer Chipping Sparrows look clean and crisp, with frosty underparts, pale face, and black line through the eye, topped off with a bright rusty crown. In winter, Chipping Sparrows are subdued, buff brown, with darkly streaked upperparts. The black line through the eye is still visible, and the cap is a warm but more subdued reddish brown.

BEHAVIOR. Chipping Sparrows feed on the ground, take cover in shrubs, and sing from the tops of small trees (often evergreens). You'll often see loose groups of them flitting up from open ground. When singing, they cling to high outer limbs.

Cool Facts

A naturalist in 1929 memorably described the Chipping Sparrow as "the little brown-capped pensioner of the dooryard and lawn."

Backyard Tips

Chipping Sparrows will eat many kinds of birdseed, particularly black oil sunflower seeds from feeders, but also seed mixes scattered on the ground.

Some streaky brown birds are easier to identify than others. Savannah Sparrows are understated but distinctive, with a short tail, small head, and telltale yellow spot before the eye. They're one of the most abundant songbirds in North American grasslands and fields, despite sometimes being overlooked. In summer, their soft but distinctive insectlike song drifts lazily over farm fields and grasslands.

AT A GLANCE

Food During the breeding season, these sparrows eat mostly insects and spiders, foraging on the ground and hopping onto weeds to devour foods such as spittlebug nymphs. In winter they eat seeds. In coastal areas, they take tiny crustaceans.

Nesting Savannah Sparrows hide their nests in a thatch of dead grasses on or near the ground. The nest exterior is about 3 inches across and made of coarse grasses. Inside is a finely woven, tiny cup of thin grass about 2 inches across and 1 inch deep.

Habitat Savannah Sparrows breed on tundra, grasslands, marshes, and farmland. On their winter range, they stick to the ground or in low vegetation in open areas; look for them along the edges of roads adjacent to farms.

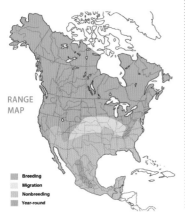

RANGE MAP

- ■ Breeding
- ■ Migration
- ■ Nonbreeding
- ■ Year-round

KEYS TO IDENTIFICATION

MEASUREMENTS (Both sexes)

Length	Wingspan	Weight
4.3–5.9 in	7.9–8.7 in	0.5–1 oz
11–15 cm	20–22 cm	15–28 g

SIZE & SHAPE. Savannah Sparrows are medium-sized sparrows with short, notched tails. The head appears small for the plump body, and the crown feathers often flare up to give the bird's head a small peak. The thick-based, seed-eating bill is small for a sparrow.

COLOR PATTERN. Savannah Sparrows are brown above with dark streaks. They are white below with thin brown or black streaks on the breast and flanks. They usually show a small yellow mark above and in front of the eye.

BEHAVIOR. Savannah Sparrows forage on or near the ground. When flushed, they usually fly up, flare their short tails, and circle before landing a few yards away. Males sing from exposed, low perches such as fence posts.

Cool Facts

Savannah Sparrows have a strong tendency to return each year to the area where they hatched. This is called "natal philopatry" and has led to several distinct Savannah Sparrow subspecies.

Backyard Tips

Savannah Sparrows are not feeder birds, though they may visit backyards adjoining fields. A brush pile may lure them to swoop in and take cover during migration or over the winter.

Typically seen sending up a spray of leaf litter as they kick around in search of food, Fox Sparrows are dark, splotchy birds of dense thickets. Named for their rich red hues, this species is one of our most variable birds, with four main forms that can range from foxy red to gray to dark brown. Most breed in remote areas, so many people see them only during migration and in winter, when the birds move into backyard thickets or visit feeders.

AT A GLANCE

Food

Fox Sparrows forage for insects and seeds in leaf litter and bare ground, often under dense cover. They find their prey with a characteristic "double-scratch" involving a hop forward and an immediate hop back, during which they simultaneously scratch both feet backwards through the leaf litter.

Nesting

Fox Sparrows nest on or near the ground. Nests vary a lot in size. The outer wall is made of twigs, strips of bark, shredded or rotting wood, moss, coarse dry grass, and lichens. The inner cup is often lined with fine grass, rootlets, mammal hair, or feathers.

Habitat

Fox Sparrows breed in coniferous forest and dense mountain scrub. They spend winters in scrubby habitat and forest, when they are most likely to be seen kicking around under backyard bird feeders.

RANGE MAP

- Breeding
- Migration
- Nonbreeding
- Nonbreeding (scarce)
- Year-round

KEYS TO IDENTIFICATION

ADULT
(SLATE-COLORED FORM)

ADULT
(SOOTY FORM)

MEASUREMENTS (Both sexes)

Length	Wingspan	Weight
6–7.5 in 15–19 cm	10.5–11.5 in 26.7–29 cm	0.9–1.5 oz 26–44 g

SIZE & SHAPE. Fox Sparrows are large, round-bodied sparrows with stout bills and medium-length tails.

COLOR PATTERN. Fox Sparrows are generally rust-brown above with a mix of rust and gray on the head and heavy brownish splotches on the flanks and the center of the chest. Those of interior mountains are dull gray above with brownish splotches below, and those along the Pacific Coast are very dark brown above. The bill can range from yellowish to dark gray.

BEHAVIOR. Fox Sparrows spend a lot of time on the ground, using their sturdy legs to kick away leaf litter in search of insects and seeds. They rarely venture far from cover and frequently associate with other sparrows. In spring and summer, listen for Fox Sparrows' sweet, whistled song from scrub or forest, and also for a sharp *smack* call.

Cool Facts

People have spotted Fox Sparrows in Greenland, Iceland, Ireland, Germany, and Italy. Some of these vagrant birds probably went part of the way on a ship after landing on one to rest.

Backyard Tips

Fox Sparrows feed on the ground close to dense vegetation. To attract them, scatter millet and sunflower seeds close to a brush pile, and plant native berry bushes.

SONG SPARROW (Melospiza melodia)

A rich, russet-and-gray bird with bold streaks down its white chest, the Song Sparrow is one of the most familiar North American sparrows. Don't let its bewildering variety of regional plumage differences deter you: this is one of the first species you should suspect if you see a streaky sparrow in an open, shrubby, or wet area. If it perches on a low shrub, leans back, and sings a stuttering, clattering song, so much the better.

AT A GLANCE

Food Song Sparrows eat mainly seeds and fruits, adding invertebrates in summer. Food types vary greatly depending on what's most available. In British Columbia, Song Sparrows have even been observed picking at the droppings of Glaucous-winged Gulls.

Nesting Song Sparrows nest in grasses or weeds, often near water, from ground level up to 15 feet. The female builds a simple, sturdy cup of grasses, weeds, and bark lined with finer material. The finished nest is 4–8 inches across and 2.5–4 inches deep.

Habitat Look for Song Sparrows in nearly any open habitat, including marsh edges, overgrown fields, backyards, desert washes, and forest edges. Song Sparrows commonly visit bird feeders and build nests in residential areas.

RANGE MAP

Breeding
Nonbreeding
Year-round

KEYS TO IDENTIFICATION

MEASUREMENTS (Both sexes)

Length	Wingspan	Weight
4.7–6.7 in	7.1–9.4 in	0.4–1.9 oz
12–17 cm	18–24 cm	12–53 g

SIZE & SHAPE. Song Sparrows are medium-sized and fairly bulky sparrows. For a sparrow, the bill is stout and the head fairly rounded. The tail is long and rounded and the wings are broad.

COLOR PATTERN. Song Sparrows are streaky and brown with thick streaks on a white chest and flanks. The breast streaks usually coalesce in a dark central spot. The head is strongly striped with russet on gray, with conspicuous dark, triangular "malar" stripes bordering the throat.

BEHAVIOR. Song Sparrows flit through dense, low vegetation or low branches, occasionally moving onto open ground to feed. Flights are short and fluttering, with a characteristic downward pumping of the tail. Male Song Sparrows sing from exposed perches such as small trees.

Cool Facts

Song Sparrows of coastal areas have more dark pigment (melanin) in their feathers. The melanin toughens the feathers, reducing damage caused by mites that flourish in humid climates.

Backyard Tips

Song Sparrows visit feeding stations, or more often the ground beneath feeders, for many seeds, especially sunflower and white millet. They often nest in shrubs, flower beds, and woodpiles.

The handsome Lincoln's Sparrow is understated yet elegant. It's a streaky bird with the color pattern of a Song Sparrow but with warmer colors and more delicate markings, as if painted by a finer-tipped brush. They're hardy birds that nest in bogs and meadows of the far north or in mountains just below treeline. Males sing rich, warbling songs that have been called "wrenlike" in complexity.

AT A GLANCE

Food Throughout the breeding season, Lincoln's Sparrows primarily eat insects, spiders, and other arthropods. In winter, their diet consists of small seeds and invertebrates. They occasionally visit feeding stations.

Nesting The female builds the nest, usually on slightly raised ground under cover of willow shrubs or mountain birches; it's less often built in elevated branches. The nest is a cup of woven, dried sedges and grasses lined with soft vegetation.

Habitat Lincoln's Sparrows breed in bogs, wet meadows, and riparian thickets, mostly in the far north or at high elevations. They winter in brushy areas, thickets, hedgerows, understory of open woodlands, forest edges, and sometimes backyards.

RANGE MAP

- Breeding
- Migration
- Nonbreeding
- Year-round

KEYS TO IDENTIFICATION

MEASUREMENTS (Both sexes)

Length	Wingspan	Weight
5.1–5.9 in	7.5–8.5 in	0.6–0.7 oz
13–15 cm	19–22 cm	17–19 g

SIZE & SHAPE. The Lincoln's Sparrow is a small songbird, a bit smaller than a Song Sparrow, and with a more delicate bill and shorter tail.

COLOR PATTERN. Lincoln's Sparrow is brown or grayish-brown overall, with delicate streaking and a creamy buff wash across the breast. The head shows warm brown stripes on a gray face, and a strong pale eyering.

BEHAVIOR. Lincoln's Sparrows walk and hop on the ground searching for food. They tend to forage alone or in very small numbers, but may join larger mixed flocks of sparrows at feeding stations.

Cool Facts

Each male Lincoln's Sparrow has from one to six song types in his repertoire, and no two males sing the same song type. They improvise to create their own rich, warbling, complex songs.

Backyard Tips

Lincoln's Sparrows visit feeding stations, especially during migration. They sometimes feed in elevated feeders, but usually take millet and sunflower scattered on the ground near cover.

The striking Harris's Sparrow is rarely found far east or west of the middle of North America. The only bird species that breeds in Canada and nowhere else in the world, it nests along the edge of boreal forest and tundra, and winters in the very center of the United States, where it's a beloved backyard visitor. Its remote breeding habitat and secretive nesting behavior made it one of the last songbirds in North America to have its nest and eggs described.

AT A GLANCE

Food

Harris's Sparrows eat a variety of seeds and some fruits, especially during migration and winter. They focus on insects and other arthropods mainly in the nesting season. They sometimes eat young conifer needles.

Nesting

Harris's Sparrows place their nest on the ground, sunken into moss and lichens. The open cup nest is constructed of mosses, small twigs, and lichens, lined with dried grass and often some caribou hair.

Habitat

Harris's Sparrows breed at the edge of boreal forest and tundra. They winter along hedgerows, shelterbelts, agricultural fields, weed patches, and pastures, often visiting feeders, especially near brush piles or other low hiding places.

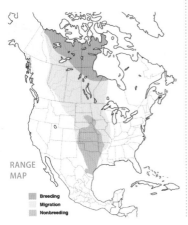

RANGE MAP

- ■ Breeding
- ■ Migration
- ■ Nonbreeding

KEYS TO IDENTIFICATION

MEASUREMENTS (Both sexes)

Length	Wingspan	Weight
6.7–7.9 in	10.6 in	0.9–1.7 oz
17–20 cm	27 cm	26–49 g

SIZE & SHAPE. This medium-sized songbird is fairly large for a sparrow. It has a rounded head and a moderately long tail.

COLOR PATTERN. Spring adults have a striking black hood covering the crown, nape, throat, and upper breast that contrasts with the gray face and white underparts. In fall and winter, brown obscures some of the black hood. Immatures have very little black on the face or crown.

BEHAVIOR. Harris's Sparrows feed on the ground, picking up seeds and occasionally insects. They often scratch in litter with both feet to reveal food. They also visit feeding stations, concentrating on the ground beneath feeders near cover.

Cool Facts

Winter flocks of Harris's Sparrows have a pecking order that's based on who's got the largest black bib marking. That usually means older birds, but younger birds with large bibs also rank highly.

Backyard Tips

Harris's Sparrows visit bird feeders or, more often, the ground beneath them. Scatter white millet and black oil sunflower seeds near shrubs or a brush pile to attract them.

White-crowned Sparrows appear in droves each winter over much of North America, gracing gardens and trails. The smart black-and-white head, pale beak, and crisp gray breast give them a dashing look and make identification fairly simple. Flocks scurry through brushy borders, overgrown fields, and backyards. As spring approaches, they start singing their thin, sweet whistle before and during migration.

AT A GLANCE

Food White-crowned Sparrows eat mainly seeds of weeds and grasses. In summer they also eat considerable numbers of caterpillars, wasps, beetles, and other insects. They also eat grains such as oats, wheat, barley, and corn, and fruit including elderberries and blackberries.

Nesting White-crowned Sparrows nest fairly low in shrubs or on the ground, hiding the cup nest among mats of mosses, lichens, and ground-hugging shrubs. The nest, about 5 inches across and 2 inches deep, is built from twigs, grasses, pine needles, moss, bark, and dead leaves, lined with grasses and hairs.

Habitat White-crowned Sparrows live where safe tangles of brush mix with open or grassy ground for foraging. In much of the United States, they're most common in winter; they're found year-round in parts of the West.

RANGE MAP

- Breeding
- Migration
- Nonbreeding
- Nonbreeding (scarce)
- Year-round

KEYS TO IDENTIFICATION

MEASUREMENTS (Both sexes)

Length	Wingspan	Weight
5.9–6.3 in	8.3–9.4 in	0.9–1 oz
15–16 cm	21–24 cm	25–28 g

SIZE & SHAPE. The White-crowned Sparrow is a large sparrow with a small bill and a long tail. The head can look either distinctly peaked or smooth and flat, depending on the bird's posture and activity.

COLOR PATTERN. White-crowned Sparrows are gray-and-brown birds with large, bold black-and-white stripes on the head. The bill can be pale pink or yellow. Young birds have brown, not black, markings on the head.

BEHAVIOR. White-crowned Sparrows usually stay low at the edges of brushy habitat, hopping on the ground or on branches, usually below waist height. They're also found on open ground, usually with shrubs or trees nearby for when they need to retreat quickly to a hiding place.

Cool Facts

A migrating White-crowned Sparrow was tracked flying 300 miles in a single night. In the lab they've been tracked running on a treadmill at about a third of a mile per hour without tiring.

Backyard Tips

White-crowned Sparrows visit feeders or the ground beneath for millet and sunflower and other seeds. A brush pile encourages them to spend more time in your yard.

GOLDEN-CROWNED SPARROW (*Zonotrichia atricapilla*)

The large, handsome Golden-crowned Sparrow is a common bird of weedy or shrubby lowlands and city edges in winter along the Pacific Coast. It seems to vanish for the summer into tundra and shrublands from British Columbia to Alaska, where little is known of its breeding habits. Gold-rush miners took cold comfort from this bird's melancholy-sounding song, which seems to reflect the bleak beauty of its surroundings.

AT A GLANCE

Food

In winter and migration, Golden-crowned Sparrows eat a wide variety of seeds. They also eat fruits, buds, flowers, sprouts, and some insects. Their diet in summer is not well known, but probably includes more insects and spiders.

Nesting

The well-insulated ground nest of twigs, dry bark flakes, and other plant fibers is lined with fine grasses, ptarmigan feathers, and hair from moose, deer, or caribou. It's hidden near ferns or other plants. When the ground is still snow covered, it may be built in a shrub or small tree.

Habitat

Golden-crowned Sparrows are most often seen in fall and winter, in forest edges, shrubs, chaparral, and backyards of the West Coast. They nest much farther north, in low, shrubby areas of tundra and at the edges of boreal forests.

RANGE MAP

- Breeding
- Migration
- Nonbreeding

KEYS TO IDENTIFICATION

IMMATURE

BREEDING ADULT

MEASUREMENTS (Both sexes)

Length	Wingspan	Weight
5.9–7.1 in	9–10 in	1.1–1.2 oz
15–18 cm	23–25 cm	30–33 g

SIZE & SHAPE. Golden-crowned Sparrows are large, plump, long-tailed sparrows with small heads, thick necks, and short but stout seed-eating bills.

COLOR PATTERN. In summer, adult Golden-crowned Sparrows are streaked brown above and smooth gray to brown below, with a black crown and bright-yellow forehead. Winter and immature Golden-crowned Sparrows are duller, with brown replacing black on the head and less obvious yellow on the crown.

BEHAVIOR. Golden-crowned Sparrows feed on seeds and insects on the ground and in low vegetation. They whistle their slow, mournful-sounding songs from high perches and nest in dense, low vegetation. In migration and winter, they gather in loose flocks and mix with other sparrows, especially White-crowned Sparrows.

Cool Facts

Miners during the Alaska Gold Rush interpreted the sad-sounding, three-noted Golden-crowned Sparrow song as "I'm so tired," nicknaming it "Weary Willie," and also the "no gold here" bird.

Backyard Tips

These big sparrows eat seeds in and below feeders and take fruits, buds, and flowers from garden plants. They also sometimes nibble on cabbages, beets, and peas.

Dark-eyed Juncos are neat, even flashy little sparrows that flit about forest floors of the western mountains and Canada, then flood the rest of North America for winter. They're easy to recognize by their simple (though extremely variable) markings and the bright white tail feathers they flash in flight. One of the most abundant forest birds of North America, you'll see juncos on woodland walks as well as in flocks at your feeders or on the ground beneath them.

AT A GLANCE

Food Seeds make up about 75% of the Dark-eyed Junco's year-round diet. At feeders it seems to prefer millet over sunflower seeds. During the breeding season, it also preys on insects including beetles, moths, butterflies, caterpillars, ants, wasps, and flies.

Nesting Juncos usually build nests on the ground, sheltered by tree roots, rocks, or sloping ground. Nests are made of grasses, pine needles, and other plant material. The nest is 3–5.5 inches across and up to 3 inches deep.

Habitat Dark-eyed Juncos breed in coniferous or mixed-coniferous forests across Canada, the western U.S., and the Appalachians. During winter you'll find them in open woodlands, fields, parks, roadsides, and backyards.

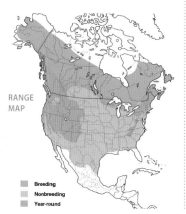

RANGE MAP

- ▩ Breeding
- ▩ Nonbreeding
- ▩ Year-round

KEYS TO IDENTIFICATION

MALE
(OREGON FORM)

MEASUREMENTS (Both sexes)

Length	Wingspan	Weight
5.5–6.3 in	7.1–9.8 in	0.6–1.1 oz
14–16 cm	18–25 cm	18–30 g

SIZE & SHAPE. The Dark-eyed Junco is a medium-sized sparrow with a rounded head, a short, stout bill, and a fairly long tail.

COLOR PATTERN. Juncos vary across the country but in general are dark gray or brown with a white belly, pink bill, and white outer tail feathers that flash when the bird spreads its tail, particularly in flight.

BEHAVIOR. Dark-eyed Juncos hop around the bases of trees and shrubs in forests or venture out onto lawns looking for fallen seeds. They give high chip notes almost absent-mindedly while foraging, or more insistently as they take short, low flights through cover.

Cool Facts

Some juncos live in the Appalachian mountains year-round. These residents have shorter wings than migrants that join them each winter. Longer wings are better suited to flying long distances.

Backyard Tips

Dark-eyed Juncos visit feeders, the ground beneath feeders, and wood or brush piles. They have a preference for white millet and sunflower seed. They also visit birdbaths.

The male Western Tanager looks like a flame with his orange-red head, yellow body, and coal-black wings, back, and tail. The females and immature are a duller yellow-green and blackish. These birds live in open woods all over the West, often staying hidden in the canopies of evergreens. Nevertheless, they're a quintessential woodland bird of summertime, filling the air with their short, burry song and low, chuckling call notes.

AT A GLANCE

Food In summer, Western Tanagers eat mostly insects. Before swallowing dragonflies, they clip off the wings. They also eat fruit, especially during fall and winter, when it may dominate the diet. Winter stragglers have also been seen eating seeds at feeders.

Nesting Western Tanagers usually nest in relatively open areas of the canopy. The female builds the nest of twigs, roots, and finer fibers. The final product has a hastily assembled look: a loosely woven, open, flat bowl with a relatively small cup for eggs.

Habitat Western Tanagers breed in coniferous forests, from juniper-pine mixtures at low elevations up to spruce-fir near treeline. During migration they appear in nearly any shrubby or wooded habitat, and even in fairly open country.

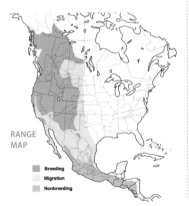

RANGE MAP

Breeding
Migration
Nonbreeding

KEYS TO IDENTIFICATION

FEMALE

MALE

MEASUREMENTS (Both sexes)

Length	Wingspan	Weight
6.3–7.5 in	11.5 in	0.8–1.3 oz
16–19 cm	29 cm	24–36 g

SIZE & SHAPE. Western Tanagers are stocky songbirds, fairly small yet noticeably larger and heavier bodied than warblers. They have short, thick-based bills and medium-length tails.

COLOR PATTERN. Adult males are yellow with a flaming orange-red head and black wings. The wings show a yellow shoulder patch and a white wingbar. The back and tail are black. Adult females have little to no red on the face and subdued yellow-green plumage. Immatures show less red on the head than adults.

BEHAVIOR. Western Tanagers forage slowly and methodically along branches and among leaves or needles for insects, supplemented with small fruits in fall and winter. They sometimes catch insects in the air. In spring and summer, males sing a hoarse, robinlike song frequently.

Cool Facts

Male Western Tanagers sometimes perform an antic, eye-catching display, apparently a courtship ritual, in which they tumble past a female, their showy plumage flashing yellow and black.

Backyard Tips

If you live in a wooded area within their range, providing moving water or a birdbath or pond may help attract them to your yard.

The male Northern Cardinal is perhaps responsible for getting more people to open up a field guide than any other bird. The male is a conspicuous red; the female is brown with a sharp crest and red accents. Cardinals don't migrate and the male doesn't molt into a dull plumage, so it's still breathtaking in winter's backyards. In summer, the sweet whistled song is one of the first sounds of morning.

AT A GLANCE

Food
Northern Cardinals eat mainly seeds and fruit, supplemented with insects. Cardinals eat many kinds of birdseed, particularly black oil sunflower seed and, in some areas, safflower. They feed their young almost entirely insects.

Nesting
Nests are usually wedged into a fork of small branches in dense vegetation, up to about 15 feet high. The female builds the cup, about 2–3 inches tall and 4 inches across, of coarse twigs covered in a leafy mat, lined with grapevine bark and finer fibers.

Habitat
Northern Cardinals live in open or fragmented habitat such as backyards, parks, woodlots, and shrubby forest edges, nesting in dense tangles of shrubs and vines. They're virtually never found in large forest interiors.

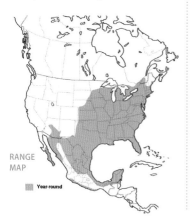

RANGE
MAP

■ Year-round

KEYS TO IDENTIFICATION

FEMALE

MALE

MEASUREMENTS (Both sexes)

Length	Wingspan	Weight
8.3–9.1 in	9.8–12.2 in	1.5–1.7 oz
21–23 cm	25–31 cm	42–48 g

SIZE & SHAPE. The Northern Cardinal is a fairly large, long-tailed songbird with a short, very thick bill and a prominent pointed crest. Cardinals often sit with a hunched-over posture and with the tail pointed straight down.

COLOR PATTERN. Male cardinals are brilliant red all over, with a reddish bill and a solid black area around the bill. Adult females are pale brown overall with warm reddish tinges in the wings, tail, and crest, with black around the red-orange bill. Fledglings lack the black face and red bill.

BEHAVIOR. Northern Cardinals tend to sit low in shrubs and trees and forage on or near the ground, often in pairs. They are common at bird feeders but may be inconspicuous away from them, at least until you learn their loud, metallic chip note.

Cool Facts

Unlike most songbirds, female Northern Cardinals sing, sometimes even from the nest. A pair shares song phrases, but the female's song may be longer and slightly more complex than the male's.

Backyard Tips

Cardinals come to feeders with sunflower or safflower seeds. In spring they sometimes fight their reflections in windows. If this happens, cover the window with paper on the outside for a few days.

BLACK-HEADED GROSBEAK *(Pheucticus melanocephalus)*

In western North America, the sweet song of the Black-headed Grosbeak caroling down from the treetops sounds like a tipsy robin welcoming spring. The flashy black, white, and cinnamon male and the less flamboyant female sing from perches in suburbs, desert thickets, and mountain forests. At feeders they effortlessly shuck sunflower seeds with their heavy bills. Both sexes incubate the eggs, feed the young, and feistily defend their nesting territory.

AT A GLANCE

Food Black-headed Grosbeaks use their massive bills to crack seeds and crush hard-bodied insects or snails. They also eat fruits and berries, and visit feeders. In winter they eat monarch butterflies; they are apparently immune to the toxins that keep monarchs safe from other predators.

Nesting The female builds the nest in the outer branches of a small tree or bush near a stream. The nest, 5–7 inches across and 2–4 inches deep, may be so loosely constructed that the eggs can be seen from beneath; this may provide ventilation to keep nest and eggs cool.

Habitat Look for Black-headed Grosbeaks in mixed woodlands and edges including mountain forests, thickets along desert streams, backyards, and gardens. Ideal habitat includes some large trees and a diverse understory.

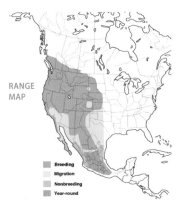

RANGE MAP

- Breeding
- Migration
- Nonbreeding
- Year-round

KEYS TO IDENTIFICATION

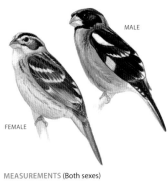

MALE

FEMALE

MEASUREMENTS (Both sexes)

Length 7.1–7.5 in 18–19 cm	Wingspan 12.6 in 32 cm	Weight 1.2–1.7 oz 35–49 g

SIZE & SHAPE. Black-headed Grosbeaks are hefty songbirds with a huge, conical bill that is very thick at the base. They have a large head and short, thick neck. A short tail imparts a compact, chunky look.

COLOR PATTERN. Breeding males are rich orange-cinnamon with a black head and black-and-white wings. Females and immature males are brown above with warm orange or buff on the breast; some have streaks on the sides. All have grayish bills. In flight, the bright yellow under the wings is conspicuous.

BEHAVIOR. Black-headed Grosbeaks are often hidden as they hop about in dense foliage gleaning insects and seeds, but are conspicuous at feeders. Males sing in a rich, whistled lilt from treetops in spring and summer. The short, squeaky chip note is distinctive and can be a good way to find them.

Cool Facts

The males sport showy feathers, but that doesn't mean they're only obsessed with courtship. They share parenting duties about equally with females.

Backyard Tips

Attract Black-headed Grosbeaks by setting out sunflower seed feeders. Grosbeaks may also visit nectar feeders set out for orioles.

A large, vibrantly blue bunting with an oversized silver bill and chestnut wingbars, the male Blue Grosbeak sings a rich, warbling song from trees and roadside wires. He and his cinnamon-colored mate often raise two broods in a single breeding season. These birds of shrubby habitats can be hard to spot unless you hear them singing or calling first. The species is widespread but not abundant across the southern U.S., and is expanding its range.

AT A GLANCE

Food

Blue Grosbeaks feed mostly on insects, especially grasshoppers and crickets, and also seeds of wild and cultivated grains. Before feeding an insect to their nestlings, they remove the head, wings, and most of the legs.

Nesting

Blue Grosbeaks build their nests low in small trees, shrubs, and tangles, often near open areas. The compact, cup-shaped nest is woven from twigs, bark strips, rootlets, snakeskin, and sometimes trash. It's lined with rootlets, hair, and fine grasses.

Habitat

Look for Blue Grosbeaks in old fields beginning to grow back into woodland. They breed in areas covered with grass, forbs, and shrubs, with a few taller trees. In dry areas, they often concentrate in the shrubby growth along watercourses.

RANGE MAP

■ Breeding
■ Nonbreeding
■ Year-round

KEYS TO IDENTIFICATION

MALE

FEMALE

MEASUREMENTS (Both sexes)

Length	Wingspan	Weight
5.9–6.3 in	11 in	0.9–1.1 oz
15–16 cm	28 cm	26–31 g

SIZE & SHAPE. The Blue Grosbeak is a stocky songbird with a very large, triangular bill that seems to cover the entire front of its face, from throat to forehead.

COLOR PATTERN. Adult males are deep, rich blue with a tiny black mask in front of the eyes, chestnut wingbars, and a black-and-silver beak. Females are rich cinnamon-brown, richer on the head and paler on the underparts; the tail is bluish. Both sexes have two wingbars, the upper chestnut and the lower grayish to buffy. Immature Blue Grosbeaks are a rich, dark chestnut brown, with chestnut wingbars.

BEHAVIOR. Blue Grosbeaks are unobtrusive despite their bright colors and frequent rich, warbling songs. They sing while perched on high points in shrubs and small trees of their open habitats. Listen for their loud, almost metallic *chink* call. Also watch for their odd habit of twitching the tail sideways.

Cool Facts

For such a widespread bird with a conspicuous song, very little field research has been done on the Blue Grosbeak. According to genetic evidence, its closest relative is the Lazuli Bunting.

Backyard Tips

Blue Grosbeaks are sometimes attracted to grains and seeds at feeders in shrubby backyards.

These brilliant blue-and-orange buntings bring a double splash of color to brushy hillsides, thickets, and gardens throughout the West. Stocky, finchlike Lazuli Buntings are fun to watch as they teeter on tiny stems to reach seeds and other fare. In the spring, males show off their vivid colors from exposed perches and sing a sweet warbling song.

Food Lazuli Buntings pick caterpillars, spiders, grasshoppers, and the like from understory leaves and grasses. They also eat berries and seeds such as serviceberry, chokecherry, wild oats, and chickweed, as well as millet from bird feeders.

Nesting Female Lazuli Buntings build cup nests about 3 feet off the ground in shrubs. Females collect grasses, strips of bark, and leaves, which they weave together with spiderweb or silk from tent caterpillars. Construction takes between 2 days and a week.

Habitat Lazuli Buntings live in brushy hillsides, streamside habitats, wooded valleys, sagebrush, chaparral, thickets, hedges along agricultural fields, recently burned areas, and residential gardens.

RANGE MAP

- Breeding
- Migration
- Winter

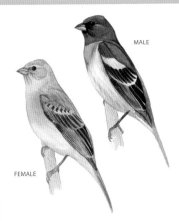

MALE

FEMALE

MEASUREMENTS (Both sexes)

Length	Wingspan	Weight
5.1–5.9 in	8.7 in	0.5–0.6 oz
13–15 cm	22 cm	13–18 g

SIZE & SHAPE. Lazuli Buntings are small, finchlike, stocky songbirds with stout, cone-shaped bills, and gently sloping foreheads. The tail is notched at the tip.

COLOR PATTERN. Adult males have a brilliant blue head, back, and tail offset by a pumpkin-colored breast and white belly. Males also have a white shoulder patch. Females are warm grayish-brown above, with a blue tinge to the wings and tail, two tan wingbars, and a tan breast.

BEHAVIOR. Lazuli Buntings do most of their foraging in the understory, hopping and reaching for insects or seeds. Males perch upright and sing from exposed perches in low trees and shrubs.

Cool Facts

After arriving on the breeding grounds, a yearling male forms his unique song by picking up sounds from nearby males. This creates a "song neighborhood" where all males sound fairly similar.

Backyard Tips

Lazuli Buntings often visit feeding stations, including hanging tube feeders and platform feeders. They mostly eat white millet, sunflower seeds, and nyjer (thistle) seeds.

One of the most abundant birds in North America, the Red-winged Blackbird is a familiar sight atop cattails, along roadsides, and on telephone wires. Glossy-black males have scarlet-and-yellowish shoulder patches they can puff up or hide almost completely. Females are a subdued, streaky brown, almost like a large, dark sparrow. In the North, their early arrival and tumbling song are happy indications of the return of spring.

AT A GLANCE

Food Red-winged Blackbirds eat mainly insects in the summer and a wide variety of seeds and grains in the winter. They probe the bases of aquatic plants with their slender bills, prying them open to get at insects hidden inside.

Nesting Red-winged Blackbirds build their nests low among shrubs, trees, and vertical shoots of marsh vegetation. The female winds stringy plant material around several upright stems, weaves a platform of coarse, wet vegetation, and plasters the inside with mud to form the cup.

Habitat Red-winged Blackbirds breed in wetlands, salt marshes, along streams, water hazards on golf courses, wet roadsides, and old fields. In winter, look for them in crop fields, feedlots, and pastures.

RANGE MAP

■ Breeding
■ Nonbreeding
■ Year-round

KEYS TO IDENTIFICATION

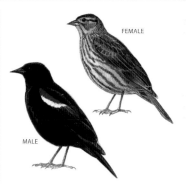

FEMALE

MALE

MEASUREMENTS (Both sexes)

Length	Wingspan	Weight
6.7–9.1 in	12.2–15.7 in	1.1–2.7 oz
17–23 cm	31–40 cm	32–77 g

SIZE & SHAPE. This stocky, broad-shouldered blackbird has a slender, conical bill and a medium-length tail. It often shows a humpbacked silhouette while perched; males often sit with tail slightly flared.

COLOR PATTERN. Male Red-winged Blackbirds are hard to mistake. They're glossy black with red-and-yellow shoulder badges. Females are streaked and dark brownish overall, paler on the breast, with a whitish or buffy eyebrow.

BEHAVIOR. In spring, male Red-winged Blackbirds sit conspicuously on high perches to belt out their *conk-la-ree* song. Females skulk through vegetation for food and quietly attend to nesting. In winter they all gather in huge flocks to eat grains with other blackbirds.

Cool Facts

Male Red-winged Blackbirds typically defend territories big enough for several females to nest in. The technical term for this system of one male mating with multiple females is "polygyny."

Backyard Tips

Red-winged Blackbirds may come to your yard for mixed grains and seeds, particularly during migration. Spread some grain or seed on the ground where they prefer to feed.

The buoyant, flutelike melody of the Western Meadowlark ringing out across a field can brighten anyone's day. Meadowlarks are often more easily heard than seen, unless you spot a male singing from a fence post. This colorful member of the blackbird family flashes a vibrant yellow breast crossed by a distinctive, black, V-shaped band. Look and listen for these stout ground feeders in grasslands.

AT A GLANCE

Food

Western Meadowlarks eat aseeds and insects. They forage for grain during winter and early spring, and for weed seeds in the fall. In late spring and summer they probe the soil or poke beneath dirt clods and manure piles seeking beetles, ants, grasshoppers, cutworms, crickets, and other insects.

Nesting

Female Western Meadowlarks make a small depression on the ground in which they build a nest of grasses and stems. They weave together the surrounding vegetation to create a roof or dome over the nest.

Habitat

Western Meadowlarks live in open grasslands, prairies, meadows, and agricultural fields ranging from sea level to 10,000 feet. They avoid wooded edges and areas with dense shrubs.

RANGE
MAP

- ■ Breeding
- ■ Nonbreeding
- ■ Year-round

KEYS TO IDENTIFICATION

MEASUREMENTS (Both sexes)

Length	Wingspan	Weight
6.3–10.2 in	16.1 in	3.1–4.1 oz
16–26 cm	41 cm	89–115 g

SIZE & SHAPE. The Western Meadowlark is the size of a robin but chunkier and shorter tailed, with a flat head, long, slender bill, and a round-shouldered posture that nearly conceals its neck.

COLOR PATTERN. Western Meadowlarks have yellow underparts with intricately patterned brown, black, and buff upperparts. A black V crosses the bright-yellow breast. The outer tail feathers flash white in flight.

BEHAVIOR. Western Meadowlarks fly in brief, quail-like bursts, alternating rapid, stiff wingbeats with short glides. In spring, males perform a "jump flight," springing straight up into the air and fluttering their wings over their back with their legs hanging limp below.

Cool Facts

A male Western Meadowlark usually has two mates at the same time. The females do all the incubating and brooding and most of the feeding of the young.

Find This Bird

In summer look for Western Meadowlarks perched on fence posts or foraging in open grasslands and meadows. In winter they often forage with blackbirds and starlings on almost-bare fields.

With a golden head, a white patch on black wings, and a call that sounds like a rusty farm gate opening, the Yellow-headed Blackbird demands attention. Find them in western and prairie wetlands, where they nest in reeds directly over the water. They're just as impressive in winter, when huge flocks seem to roll across farm fields. Each bird picks seeds from the ground, then leapfrogs over its flock mates to the front edge of the advancing troupe.

AT A GLANCE

Food Yellow-headed Blackbirds eat mostly insects in summer and seeds the rest of the year. They catch aquatic insects at the water's surface, including beetles, grasshoppers, dragonflies, caterpillars, and flies. Outside of the breeding season they forage in uplands, eating grains and seeds.

Nesting The female Yellow-headed Blackbird collects strands of wet vegetation from the surface of the water. She weaves them around stems of 4–5 cattails, bulrushes, or reeds in standing water to make the nest base. Nests are 5–6 inches across.

Habitat Yellow-headed Blackbirds breed in wetlands in prairies, mountain meadows, quaking aspen parklands, and shallow areas of marshes, ponds, and rivers. To forage, they may move to grasslands or croplands. In winter they use open agricultural areas.

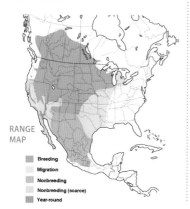

RANGE MAP

- ■ Breeding
- ■ Migration
- ■ Nonbreeding
- ■ Nonbreeding (scarce)
- ■ Year-round

KEYS TO IDENTIFICATION

MALE

MEASUREMENTS (Both sexes)

Length	Wingspan	Weight
8.3–10.2 in	16.5–17.3 in	1.6–3.5 oz
21–26 cm	42–44 cm	44–100 g

SIZE & SHAPE. Yellow-headed Blackbirds are fairly large blackbirds with stout bodies, large heads, and long, conical bills.

COLOR PATTERN. Males are striking black birds with a yellow head and chest. Their wings have prominent white patches at the bend, forming a white stripe at rest. Females and immatures are brown instead of black, with duller yellow heads. Immature males show some white at the bend of the wing, while females don't.

BEHAVIOR. Yellow-headed Blackbirds breed in loose colonies, and males mate with several females. Each male attracts up to 8 females that nest within his territory, which he defends from other males. They form huge flocks in winter, often mixing with other species of blackbirds, and feed on seeds and grains in cultivated fields.

Cool Facts

Yellow-headed Blackbirds seem to preferentially nest and forage near Forster's Terns when possible, cooperating with the terns to mob predators or give alarm calls.

Find This Bird

Look for these blackbirds in freshwater wetlands and farm fields. Scan marshes for yellow heads and white wing patches, and listen for their bizarre grinding, squeaky, and buzzing songs.

A bird to be seen in the full sun, the male Brewer's Blackbird is a glossy, almost liquid combination of black, midnight blue, and metallic green. Females are a staid brown, without the male's bright eye or the female Red-winged Blackbird's streaks. Common in towns and open habitats within their range, these long-legged birds forage on sidewalks and city parks, and gather in flocks atop shrubs, trees, and reeds.

Food Brewer's Blackbirds eat mostly seeds and grains, and also, when available, insects, small frogs, young voles, and some nestling birds. Around marshes, you may see them walk on lily pads to hunt aquatic insects.

Nesting Brewer's Blackbirds nest in colonies of a few to more than 100 pairs in shrubs, trees, reeds or cattails, on the ground, or sometimes even in tree cavities. The nest cup of plant stems and twigs is lined with fine dried grasses, sometimes cemented with mud or manure.

Habitat Look for Brewer's Blackbirds in open habitats such as coastal scrub, grasslands, riversides, meadows, and city parks and streets. Where they overlap with Common Grackles, Brewer's Blackbirds stick to fields and grasslands.

RANGE MAP

- ■ Breeding
- ■ Migration
- ■ Nonbreeding
- ■ Year-round

KEYS TO IDENTIFICATION

MALE

MEASUREMENTS (Both sexes)

Length	Wingspan	Weight
7.9–9.8 in	14.6 in	1.8–3 oz
20–25 cm	37 cm	50–86 g

SIZE & SHAPE. Brewer's Blackbirds are medium-sized, fairly long-legged songbirds. The fairly long tail is balanced by a full body, round head, and long, thick-based beak. The tail often appears widened and rounded toward the tip.

COLOR PATTERN. Males are glossy black with a blue sheen on the head and greenish sheen on the body; their eyes are yellow. Females are brown with darker wings and tail and a dark eye. Immatures look like pale females.

BEHAVIOR. Brewer's Blackbirds feed on open ground or underfoot in parks and busy streets. Their long legs give them a halting walk, head jerking with each step like a chicken's. Flying flocks seem to rise and fall; they often circle in slow fluttering flight before landing.

Cool Facts

Most birds fly south for the winter, but a small number of Brewer's Blackbirds fly west–leaving the frigid Canadian prairies for the milder coastal regions of British Columbia and Washington.

Backyard Tips

Brewer's Blackbirds visit feeders, though they're a bit clumsy when perching. Scattering seed on the ground or using an open platform feeder usually is most effective at attracting them.

Common Grackles are blackbirds that look like they've been stretched and shined. They strut on lawns and fields on their long legs or gather in noisy groups high in trees, especially evergreens. They eat many crops (notably corn) and nearly anything else as well, including garbage. Gardeners appreciate that they feed voraciously on slugs. In flight their long tails trail behind them, sometimes folded down the middle into a shallow V shape.

AT A GLANCE

Food Common Grackles eat mostly seeds, including agricultural grains such as corn and rice. They also take acorns, fruits, and garbage. In summer, one-quarter or more of their diet is animal, including insects, fish, salamanders, mice, and birds.

Nesting The nest is usually set high in a conifer but may be just off the ground. Sites can include cattails, nest boxes, woodpecker holes, crevices, or in an Osprey or Great Blue Heron nest. The bulky cup is made of twigs, leaves, and grasses along with bits of debris, reinforced with mud and lined with mammal hair.

Habitat Common Grackles thrive around agricultural fields, feedlots, city parks, and suburban lawns. They're also common in open habitats including woodland, forest edges, meadows, and marshes.

RANGE MAP

Breeding
Nonbreeding
Year-round

KEYS TO IDENTIFICATION

MEASUREMENTS (Both sexes)

Length	Wingspan	Weight
11–13.4 in	14.2–18.1 in	2.6–5 oz
28–34 cm	36–46 cm	74–142 g

SIZE & SHAPE. Common Grackles are large, lanky blackbirds with long legs and long tails. The head is flat and the bill is longer than in most blackbirds, with the hint of a downward curve. In flight, the wings appear short in comparison to the tail. Males are slightly larger than females.

COLOR PATTERN. Common Grackles appear black from a distance, but up close their glossy purple heads contrast with bronzy-iridescent bodies. A bright golden eye gives grackles an intent expression. Females are slightly less glossy than males. Young birds are dark brown with a dark eye.

BEHAVIOR. Common Grackles form large flocks, flying or foraging on lawns and in agricultural fields. They peck for food rather than scratching. At feeders they dominate smaller birds. When resting they sit atop trees or on telephone lines, keeping up a raucous chattering. Flight is direct, with stiff wingbeats.

Cool Facts

Common Grackles are versatile eaters: they follow plows to catch invertebrates and mice, wade into water to catch small fish, pick leeches off the legs of turtles, and steal worms from American Robins.

Backyard Tips

Where slugs are a problem, grackles are welcome visitors in backyards. They can be aggressive to other birds at feeders, but switching to feeders with small perches can keep these big birds at bay.

A big, brash blackbird, the male Great-tailed Grackle shimmers in iridescent black and purple, trailing a tail that will make you look twice. The rich brown female is about half the male's size. Flocks of these long-legged, social birds strut and hop on suburban lawns, golf courses, fields, and marshes. In the evening, raucous flocks pack neighborhood trees, filling the sky with their amazing and, some might say, ear-splitting voices.

AT A GLANCE

Food
Great-tailed Grackles eat grains, fruits, insects, spiders, slugs, amphibians, reptiles, fish, small mammals, bird eggs, and nestlings. In summer and early fall, about 80% of the female's diet and half of the male's is animal.

Nesting
The bulky nest is placed as high as possible in a tree or shrub, rushes or other marsh vegetation, or a structure such as a duck blind or telephone pole. Nest material can include plastic strips and bags, ribbons, feathers, and string. The nest is lined with mud or cow dung and fine grasses.

Habitat
Great-tailed Grackles forage in agricultural fields and feedlots, golf courses, cemeteries, parks, and neighborhood lawns. Large trees and vegetation edging marshes, lakes, and lagoons provide roosting and breeding sites.

RANGE MAP

■ Breeding
■ Year-round

KEYS TO IDENTIFICATION

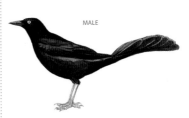

MALE

MEASUREMENTS (Both sexes)

Length	Wingspan	Weight
15–18.1 in	18.9–22.8 in	3.7–6.7 oz
38–46 cm	48–58 cm	105–190 g

SIZE & SHAPE. Males are big, long-legged, slender blackbirds with a flat-headed profile and stout, straight bill. The tapered tail, nearly as long as the body, folds into a distinctive V or keel shape. Females are half the size of males and have long, slender tails.

COLOR PATTERN. Adult males are iridescent black with yellow eyes and black bills and legs. Adult females are dark brown above, paler below. Juveniles have the female colors, but with streaked underparts and a dark eye.

BEHAVIOR. Great-tailed Grackles hang out in flocks, pecking for food on lawns, fields, and at marsh edges, vying for trash in urban settings, or crowding in trees and on telephone lines in noisy roosts.

Cool Facts

Boat-tailed Grackles are very similar, but their eyes are dark instead of yellow. They live almost exclusively in salt marshes along the East and Gulf coasts, while Great-tailed is more widespread.

Backyard Tips

Great-tailed Grackles take cracked corn, milo, and other seed from beneath feeders, often chasing off smaller birds. Using feeders with small perches can give the littler birds a chance.

The Brown-headed Cowbird is a stocky blackbird with a fascinating approach to raising its young. Females lay their eggs in the nests of other birds, which raise the cowbird chick, usually at the expense of its own. Once confined to the open grasslands of middle North America and associated with bison, cowbirds have surged in numbers and range as humans built towns and cleared woods. They have become a conservation problem for some native birds.

AT A GLANCE

Food
Brown-headed Cowbirds feed mostly on seeds from grasses and weeds, with some crop grains. Insects make up about a quarter of their diet. Females eat snail shells and sometimes eggs taken from nests. This helps provide the calcium needed for so much egg production.

Nesting
Cowbirds lay eggs in the nests of over 140 host species, from tiny kinglets to meadowlarks. Cowbirds prefer the nests of larger species. Common hosts include the Yellow Warbler, Song and Chipping sparrows, Red-eyed Vireo, Eastern and Spotted towhees, and Red-winged Blackbird.

Habitat
Brown-headed Cowbirds live in many open habitats, such as fields, pastures, meadows, forest edges, and lawns. When not displaying or feeding on the ground, they often perch high on prominent tree branches.

RANGE MAP

Breeding
Nonbreeding
Year-round

KEYS TO IDENTIFICATION

MALE

MEASUREMENTS (Both sexes)

Length	Wingspan	Weight
7.5–8.7 in	14.2 in	1.5–1.8 oz
19–22 cm	36 cm	42–50 g

SIZE & SHAPE. Brown-headed Cowbirds are smallish blackbirds, with a shorter tail and thicker head than most other blackbirds. The bill has a distinctive shape: it's shorter and thicker-based than other blackbirds', almost finchlike at first glance. In flight, look for the shorter tail.

COLOR PATTERN. Male Brown-headed Cowbirds have glossy black plumage and a rich brown head that often looks black in poor lighting or at distance. Female Brown-headed Cowbirds are plain grayish-brown birds, lightest on the head and underparts, with fine streaking on the belly.

BEHAVIOR. Brown-headed Cowbirds feed on the ground in mixed-species flocks of blackbirds and starlings. Males gather on lawns to strut and display; females prowl woodlands and edges in search of nests. Brown-headed Cowbirds are noisy, making a multitude of clicks, whistles, and chatterlike calls in addition to a gurgling song.

Cool Facts

A female cowbird spends no energy raising her young each year, so she pours everything into creating eggs—sometimes three dozen in a single summer.

Backyard Tips

This species often comes to backyards, eating sunflower seeds, corn, and other foods from tube and hopper feeders, as well as from the ground.

Flashing brilliant orange and black, Hooded Orioles light up open woodlands and parks as they pluck insects or sip nectar from flowers. These birds weave hanging nests, often "sewing" them onto the undersides of palm leaves, leading to the nickname "palm-leaf oriole." They also visit hummingbird feeders despite their size, awkwardly bending to get at the sweet water.

AT A GLANCE

Food
Hooded Orioles search the undersides of leaves for spiders and insects such as ants, beetles, grasshoppers, larvae, and caterpillars. They also eat fruit and take nectar from flowering plants and hummingbird feeders.

Nesting
Like other orioles, the Hooded Oriole weaves grass and plant fibers together to form a hanging basket. The female uses her bill to stitch the nest to the undersides of palm, sycamore, or eucalyptus leaves about 20 feet above ground.

Habitat
Hooded Orioles live in open woodlands with scattered trees, including cottonwoods, willows, sycamores, and especially palm trees. Hooded Orioles expanded their range northward after people began planting ornamental palm trees around their homes.

RANGE MAP

- ▇ Breeding
- ▇ Migration
- ▇ Nonbreeding
- ▇ Year-round

KEYS TO IDENTIFICATION

MALE

MEASUREMENTS (Both sexes)

Length	Wingspan	Weight
7.1–7.9 in	9–11 in	0.8 oz
18–20 cm	23–28 cm	24 g

SIZE & SHAPE. Hooded Orioles are medium-sized songbirds with longer and more delicate bodies than other orioles. They have long rounded tails and longish necks. Their bills are slightly curved, more so than other orioles'.

COLOR PATTERN. Adult males are brilliant black and orange. They have black throats, wings, and tails, with orange to yellow hoods, bellies, and rumps. Adult males flash white wingbars. Females are olive-yellow overall with grayer backs and thin white wingbars.

BEHAVIOR. Hooded Orioles make direct flights between trees with strong wingbeats. They are acrobatic foragers and often hang upside down while they grab their prey.

Cool Facts

Hooded Orioles sometimes include the songs of other species in their songs. In Arizona they sometimes mimic Gila Woodpeckers and Ash-throated Flycatchers.

Backyard Tips

To attract Hooded Orioles to your backyard, put out orange halves, hang up an extra hummingbird feeder, or plant flowering shrubs.

Nimble canopy dwellers of open woodlands, Bullock's Orioles dangle upside down from branches to catch insects, or while weaving their hanging nests. Adult males are flame-orange with a neat line through the eye and a white wing patch; females are washed in gray and yellow-orange. Listen for their whistling, chuckling song in tall trees along rivers and streams.

AT A GLANCE

Food

Bullock's Orioles eat insects and other arthropods, as well as fruit and nectar. They have a special method for eating juicy items: thrusting the closed bill into the flesh of either a fruit or a caterpillar, then prying the bill open to lap up the pooling juices with a brushy tongue.

Nesting

The female weaves the gourd-shaped nest from soft, pliable fibers in an isolated tree or at the edge of a woodland, commonly near water. The nest is usually suspended from the ends of flexible branches to discourage predators.

Habitat

Look for Bullock's Orioles in open woodland along streams, particularly among cottonwoods. It also occurs in orchards, parks, and oak or mesquite woodlands.

RANGE MAP

- Breeding
- Migration
- Nonbreeding
- Year-round

KEYS TO IDENTIFICATION

MALE

MEASUREMENTS (Both sexes)

Length	Wingspan	Weight
6.7–7.5 in	12.2 in	1–1.5 oz
17–19 cm	31 cm	29–43 g

SIZE & SHAPE. Bullock's Orioles are medium-sized songbirds with slim but sturdy bodies and medium-long tails. Orioles are related to blackbirds and share their long, thick-based, sharply pointed bills.

COLOR PATTERN. Adult males are bright orange with a black back and throat, large white wing patch, and orange face with a black line through it. Females and immatures have a yellowish-orange head and tail, a grayish back, and white edges to the wing feathers. Immature males have a black throat patch.

BEHAVIOR. Bullock's Orioles feed in the slender branches of trees and shrubs, catching caterpillars and also feeding on nectar or fruit. They are agile and active when searching for prey. Both sexes give a harsh chattering call.

Cool Facts

Both male and female Bullock's Orioles sing—the male more sweetly, the female often more prolifically.

Backyard Tips

Bullock's Orioles can be attracted to a half-and-half mixture of water and grape jelly, blended into a syrupy nectar and set out in a small, shallow container.

The House Finch is a recent arrival to much of North America (and Hawaii)—it originally hails from the southwestern U.S. This now-common bird has received a warmer reception than other arrivals such as the European Starling and House Sparrow. That's partly due to the cheerful red head and breast of males, and to the bird's long, twittering song, which can be heard in most of the neighborhoods of the continent.

AT A GLANCE

Food

House Finches eat seeds, buds, and fruits—cultivated and wild—and very few insects or other animal foods. At feeders they prefer black oil sunflower over the larger, striped sunflower seeds.

Nesting

House Finches nest in trees, cactus, and rock ledges, and also in or on buildings, lights, ivy, and hanging planters. The nest is a cup made of fine stems, leaves, rootlets, thin twigs, string, wool, and feathers, with similar, but finer materials for the lining. The inner cup is 1–3 inches across and up to 2 inches deep.

Habitat

House Finches frequent city parks, backyards, urban centers, farms, and forest edges across the continent. In the western U.S., you'll also find them in their native habitats of deserts, grassland, chaparral, and open woods.

RANGE MAP

Year-round

KEYS TO IDENTIFICATION

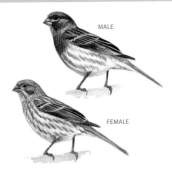

MALE

FEMALE

MEASUREMENTS (Both sexes)

Length	Wingspan	Weight
5.1–5.5 in	7.9–9.8 in	0.6–1 oz
13–14 cm	20–25 cm	16–27 g

SIZE & SHAPE. House Finches are small-bodied finches with fairly large beaks and somewhat long, flat heads. The wings are short, making the tail seem long by comparison. Many finches have distinctly notched tails, but the House Finch has a relatively shallow notch in its tail.

COLOR PATTERN. Adult males are rosy red around the face and upper breast, with streaky brown back, belly, and tail. In flight, the red rump is conspicuous. Adult females aren't red; they are plain grayish-brown with thick, blurry streaks.

BEHAVIOR. House Finches are gregarious birds that collect at feeders or perch high in nearby trees. When they're not at feeders, they eat on the ground, on weed stalks, or in trees. They move fairly slowly and sit still as they shell seeds by crushing them with rapid bites. Their flight is bouncy, like that of many finches.

Cool Facts

The male's red coloration comes from pigments in its food during the time it molts. The more pigment in the food, the redder the male. Females choose the brightest male available.

Backyard Tips

Fill your backyard feeders with black oil sunflower seed, which House Finches prefer over the thicker striped sunflower. They sometimes visit feeders in flocks of 50 or more.

The Purple Finch was famously described by Roger Tory Peterson as a "sparrow dipped in raspberry juice." In much of the U.S., it's an irregular winter visitor to feeders. Separating it from the more widespread House Finch requires a careful look, but the reward is a delicately colored, cleaner version of that red finch. In spring, the male sings his rich warbling song from the highest parts of trees, especially conifers.

AT A GLANCE

Food Purple Finches eat seeds from coniferous and deciduous trees and ground plants. They also take soft buds, nectar (extracted by biting the bases off flowers), berries, fruits, and some insects.

Nesting Purple Finches nest far out on a limb of a tree (usually coniferous), shrub, or vine tangle. Nests are often built under an overhanging branch for shelter, and made from twigs, sticks, and roots, lined with fine grasses and animal hair. The nests are about 7 inches wide and 4 inches tall.

Habitat Purple Finches breed mainly in coniferous forests or mixed deciduous and coniferous woods. During winter you can find them in a wider variety of habitats, including shrublands, old fields, forest edges, and backyards.

RANGE MAP

- ■ Breeding
- ■ Breeding (scarce)
- ■ Migration
- ■ Nonbreeding
- ■ Nonbreeding (scarce)
- ■ Year-round

KEYS TO IDENTIFICATION

MALE

FEMALE

MEASUREMENTS (Both sexes)

Length	Wingspan	Weight
4.7–6.3 in	8.7–10.2 in	0.6–1.1 oz
12–16 cm	22–26 cm	18–32 g

SIZE & SHAPE. Purple Finches are larger and chunkier than the chickadees, kinglets, and nuthatches they live near. Their powerful, conical beak is larger than a sparrow's. The tail seems short and is clearly notched at the tip.

COLOR PATTERN. Male Purple Finches have a pink-red head and breast blending with brown on the face, head, and back. Females are crisply streaked brown and white, with a neat white eyebrow stripe on a brown face. In both sexes, the chest streaks give way to a whitish belly.

BEHAVIOR. In forests in spring, Purple Finches can be noisy but hard to see as they forage high in trees. In winter they may descend to eat seeds from plants and stalks in weedy fields and at feeders. Their flight is undulating.

Cool Facts

The Purple Finch uses its thick bill and muscular tongue to crush shells and fruits to extract the seed within, or to get at nectar without eating the whole flower.

Backyard Tips

Purple Finches prefer black oil sunflower seeds, selecting thinner over wider ones. Coniferous trees in your backyard may encourage them to visit and discover your feeders.

CASSIN'S FINCH (Haemorhous cassinii)

Slightly less well known than its lookalikes (House Finch and Purple Finch), the Cassin's Finch is the characteristic rosy-tinged finch of the mountains of western North America. Small flocks twitter and forage in the tall evergreen forests and in groves of quaking aspen. Along with range and habitat, a good way to sort them out is to learn the Cassin's Finch's peaked head shape and thick, straight-edged bill.

AT A GLANCE

Food Cassin's Finches eat mostly seeds, as well as some insects. They pull seeds out of ponderosa pine cones or collect seeds from the ground. In summer Cassin's Finches eat moth larvae, particularly Douglas-fir tussock moths. In spring they eat large amounts of buds including quaking aspen, cottonwood, and manzanita.

Nesting Female Cassin's Finches build loose, frail nests of fine twigs, rootlets, and lichens. The nest is usually near the top of a conifer tree or on a side branch away from the trunk, 15 feet or more above the ground.

Habitat Cassin's Finches often live in mature forests of lodgepole pine and ponderosa pine, but are also found in other types of pines, spruce, fir, and quaking aspen forests, as well as sagebrush shrublands. They breed mostly between 3,000 and 10,000 feet elevation. They winter at lower elevations throughout their range.

RANGE MAP

■ Breeding
■ Nonbreeding
■ Year-round

KEYS TO IDENTIFICATION

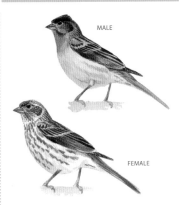

MALE

FEMALE

MEASUREMENTS (Both sexes)

Length	Wingspan	Weight
6.3 in	9.8–10.6 in	0.8–1.2 oz
16 cm	25–27 cm	24–34 g

SIZE & SHAPE. Cassin's Finches are small songbirds with peaked heads and long, notched tails. Their heavy bills are fairly long and straight. When perched, the tips of their wings extend farther down the tail than in other finches.

COLOR PATTERN. Adult males are rosy pink overall with a brighter red crown. Female and immature Cassin's Finches are brown and white with crisp, dark streaks on the chest and underparts. All forms have streaks under the tail.

BEHAVIOR. Cassin's Finches fly with an undulating pattern, rising when they flap and dipping when they glide. After breeding, they join foraging groups of Red Crossbills, Evening Grosbeaks, Pine Siskins, and other finches.

Cool Facts

The Cassin's Finch is an accomplished mimic, often adding the calls of other species into its own songs.

Backyard Tips

Cassin's Finches may come to sunflower seed feeders during winter. They also eat berries from fruiting shrubs, so consider planting native berry-producing species.

Huge flocks of tiny Pine Siskins may monopolize your thistle feeder one winter and be entirely absent the next. These nomadic finches wander widely and erratically across the continent in response to seed crops. Adapted to clinging to branch tips rather than hopping along the ground, these brown-streaked acrobats flash yellow wing markings as they flutter while feeding or as they explode into flight.

AT A GLANCE

Food Pine Siskins eat seeds of conifers and deciduous trees, soft buds of willows, emerging seedlings of many small plants, and tiny seeds of grasses, dandelions, etc. They also take some insects or feed at sap wells drilled by sapsuckers.

Nesting The small cup nest, composed of twigs, grasses, leaves, weed stems, rootlets, bark strips, and lichens, lined by softer fibers, is loosely attached toward the end of a horizontal branch in the middle heights of a conifer. Neighboring nests can be just a few trees away.

Habitat Pine Siskins prefer coniferous or mixed coniferous and deciduous forests with open canopies, but are opportunistic and adaptable. They forage in weedy fields, scrubby thickets, and backyards. They flock around feeders in woodlands and suburbs.

RANGE MAP

- ■ Breeding
- ■ Nonbreeding
- ■ Nonbreeding (scarce)
- ■ Year-round

KEYS TO IDENTIFICATION

MEASUREMENTS (Both sexes)

Length	Wingspan	Weight
4.3–5.5 in	7.1–8.7 in	0.4–0.6 oz
11–14 cm	18–22 cm	12–18 g

SIZE & SHAPE. Pine Siskins are very small songbirds with sharp, pointed bills and short, notched tails. Their conical bill is more slender than most finches' bills. In flight, look for their sharply notched tail and pointed wingtips.

COLOR PATTERN. Pine siskins are brown and very streaky finches with subtle yellow edgings on wings and tails. Flashes of yellow can erupt as they take flight, flutter at branch tips, or display during mating.

BEHAVIOR. Pine Siskins visit feeders in winter (particularly for nyjer seed) and cling to branch tips of pines and other conifers, sometimes hanging upside down to pick at seeds below them. They forage in tight flocks and twitter incessantly, even during their undulating flight.

Cool Facts

Pine Siskins can store seeds totaling as much as 10% of their body mass in a part of their esophagus called the crop, sustaining them for 5–6 nighttime hours of subzero temperatures.

Backyard Tips

Pine Siskins flock to feeders and the ground below for nyjer, millet, and black oil sunflower seeds. If your yard has plants or weeds with hardy seed heads, such as dandelion, these may also attract siskins.

Jabbering clouds of yellow, olive, and black Lesser Goldfinches gather in scrubby oak, cottonwood, and willow habitats or visit suburban yards for seeds and water. These finches primarily eat seeds of plants in the sunflower family, and they occur all the way south to the Peruvian Andes. Listen closely to their wheezy songs, which often include snippets of other birds' songs.

AT A GLANCE

Food The Lesser Goldfinch eats mainly seeds from the sunflower family, although they also eat coffeeberry, elderberry, and madrone fruits, as well as buds of cottonwoods, alders, sycamores, willows, and oaks. To eat seeds, the Lesser Goldfinch uses its bill to pry open the outer covering, shakes its head to loosen the husk, then swallows the seed.

Nesting Female Lesser Goldfinches weave together leaves, bark, catkins, and spiderwebs into a cup-shaped nest about 3 inches wide. She typically builds the nest in cottonwoods or willows 4–8 feet above the ground on slender twigs.

Habitat The Lesser Goldfinch makes its home in patchy open habitats of many kinds. From the western U.S. to South America, this songbird frequents thickets, weedy fields, woodlands, forest clearings, scrublands, farmlands, gardens, and even desert oases.

RANGE MAP

- Breeding
- Winter
- Year-round

KEYS TO IDENTIFICATION

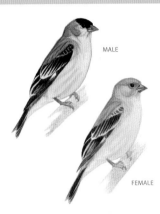

MALE

FEMALE

MEASUREMENTS (Both sexes)

Length	Wingspan	Weight
3.5–4.5 in	6–8 in	0.3–0.4 oz
9–11 cm	15–20 cm	8–11.5 g

SIZE & SHAPE. Lesser Goldfinches are tiny, stub-billed songbirds with long, pointed wings, and short, notched tails.

COLOR PATTERN. Males are bright yellow below with a glossy black cap and white patches in the wings; their backs can be black or dull green. They have a black tail with large white corners. Females and immatures have olive backs, dull yellow underparts, and gray-black wings with whitish wingbars.

BEHAVIOR. Lesser Goldfinches feed in busy flocks. They cling to dried flower heads or hang upside down to reach seeds. On the wing, they have the same dipping, bouncy flight as the American Goldfinch.

Cool Facts

Male Lesser Goldfinches in the eastern part of their range have black backs. Along the West Coast, their backs are green, with only a black cap.

Backyard Tips

Lesser Goldfinches readily come to feeders. These small finches eat many kinds of seeds from the sunflower family, including black oil sunflower and nyjer (thistle).

This handsome little finch, the state bird of New Jersey, Iowa, and Washington, is welcome and common at feeders where it takes primarily sunflower and nyjer seeds. Goldfinches often flock with Pine Siskins and Common Redpolls. Spring males are brilliant yellow and shiny black with a bit of white. Females and all winter birds are duller but identifiable by their conical bill, dark wings, wingbars, and lack of streaking.

AT A GLANCE

Food Goldfinches eat seeds almost exclusively, especially seeds from composite plants (in the family Asteraceae: sunflowers, thistle, asters, etc.), grasses, and trees such as alder, birch, western red cedar, and elm. At feeders they prefer nyjer (thistle) and sunflower seeds.

Nesting The female builds the nest, an open cup of rootlets and plant fibers lined with plant down, usually in a shrub or sapling in open habitat. The nest, often woven so tightly that it can hold water, is about 3 inches across and 2–4.5 inches high.

Habitat The goldfinch's main natural habitats are weedy fields and floodplains where thistles and asters are common. They're also found in cultivated areas, roadsides, orchards, and backyards. They visit feeders any time of year, but most abundantly during winter.

RANGE MAP

- Breeding
- Year-round
- Nonbreeding

KEYS TO IDENTIFICATION

BREEDING MALE

NONBREEDING MALE

MEASUREMENTS (Both sexes)

Length	Wingspan	Weight
4.3–5.1 in	7.5–8.7 in	0.4–0.7 oz
11–13 cm	19–22 cm	11–20 g

SIZE & SHAPE. This is a tiny finch with a short, conical bill, a small head, long wings, and a short, notched tail.

COLOR PATTERN. Adult males in spring and summer are brilliant yellow with a black forehead, black wings with white markings, and white patches above and beneath the tail. Adult females are dull yellow beneath, olive above. Winter birds are unstreaked brownish, with dark wings and two pale wingbars.

BEHAVIOR. American Goldfinches are active and acrobatic little finches that cling to weeds and seed socks, and sometimes mill about in large numbers at feeders or on the ground beneath them. They fly with a bouncy, undulating pattern and often call in flight, drawing attention to themselves.

Cool Facts

Goldfinches are among the strictest vegetarians in the bird world. They are even known to feed their baby chicks regurgitated seeds rather than insects.

Backyard Tips

Native thistles and milkweed attract goldfinches. At feeders they prefer nyjer and sunflower. They often eat on the ground in areas where there's little leaf litter.

EVENING GROSBEAK (Coccothraustes vespertinus)

A heavyset finch of northern evergreen forests, the Evening Grosbeak adds a splash of color to winter bird feeders every few years, when large flocks depart their northern breeding grounds en masse to seek food to the south. The yellow-bodied, dusky-headed male has an imposing air thanks to his massive bill and fierce eyebrow stripe.

AT A GLANCE

Food
In summer Evening Grosbeaks eat mostly invertebrates such as spruce budworm and other larvae. They also eat seeds including maple, box elder, ash, pine, and bindweed; also small fruits such as cherries, crabapples, snowberries, and hawthorn.

Nesting
Female Evening Grosbeaks build flimsy, saucer-shaped nests of small twigs and roots lined with grasses, lichens, or pine needles. They nest high in trees or large shrubs.

Habitat
Evening Grosbeaks breed in mature and regenerating evergreen forests, including spruce-fir, pine-oak, and pinyon-juniper. They also occur in aspen stands. In winter Evening Grosbeaks live in evergreen and deciduous forests as well as in urban and suburban areas. When wintering in towns they are most abundant in small woodlots near bird feeders.

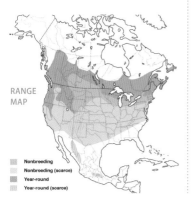

RANGE MAP

- Nonbreeding
- Nonbreeding (scarce)
- Year-round
- Year-round (scarce)

KEYS TO IDENTIFICATION

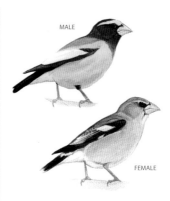

MALE

FEMALE

MEASUREMENTS (Both sexes)

Length	Wingspan	Weight
6.3–7.1 in	11.8–14.2 in	1.9–2.6 oz
16–18 cm	30–36 cm	53–74 g

SIZE & SHAPE. Evening Grosbeaks are large, heavyset finches with very thick, powerful, conical bills. They have a thick neck, full chest, and relatively short tail.

COLOR PATTERN. Male Evening Grosbeaks are yellow and black with a prominent white wing patch. They have dark heads with a bright-yellow stripe over the eye. Females and immatures are mostly gray, with white-and-black wings and a greenish-yellow tinge to the neck and flanks.

BEHAVIOR. Evening Grosbeaks make erratic movements southward in some winters, when they can be common at feeders. They forage in flocks in winter and break off into small groups or pairs during the breeding season.

Cool Facts

The Evening Grosbeak does not seem to use a complex song to attract a mate or defend its territory. It has a small repertoire of simple calls, including sweet, piercing notes and burry chirps.

Backyard Tips

Evening Grosbeaks show up irregularly at feeders during the winter to eat sunflower seeds. Participants in Project FeederWatch have helped scientists learn about their population trends.

Along with two other introduced species, the European Starling and the Rock Pigeon, House Sparrows are some of our most abundant birds. Their constant presence outside our doors makes them easy to take for granted, and their tendency to displace native birds from nest boxes makes their large numbers a genuine problem. But House Sparrows, with their capacity to live so intimately with humans, are just beneficiaries of our own species' success.

AT A GLANCE

Food House Sparrows eat grains and seeds, livestock feed, and discarded food. In summer, they catch insects by pouncing on them, following lawnmowers, picking them out of car grilles, or plucking them from lights at dusk.

Nesting House Sparrows nest in holes of buildings, streetlights, signs, etc., or in vines climbing the walls of buildings. They displace bluebirds and Tree Swallows from nest boxes. They make bulky nests using coarse materials that often fill the entire hole, adding finer material for the lining.

Habitat House Sparrows have lived around humans for millennia. Look for them in urban, suburban, and rural areas, from big cities to farms and pastures. They're absent from undisturbed forests and natural grasslands.

RANGE MAP

■ Year-round
■ Year-round (scarce)

KEYS TO IDENTIFICATION

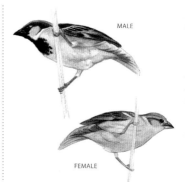

MALE

FEMALE

MEASUREMENTS (Both sexes)

Length	Wingspan	Weight
5.9–6.7 in	7.5–9.8 in	1.0–1.1 oz
15–17 cm	19–25 cm	27–30 g

SIZE & SHAPE. Compared to most native American sparrows, House Sparrows are chunkier, fuller in the chest, with a larger, rounded head, shorter tail, and stouter bill.

COLOR PATTERN. Male House Sparrows are brightly colored with a gray head, whitish cheeks, black bib, and rufous neck. Females are buffy-brown with dingy underparts. The backs of both are striped with buff, black, and brown.

BEHAVIOR. House Sparrows flutter from eaves and fence rows, fly in and out of nest holes hidden behind shop signs or in traffic lights, and hang around parking lots and outdoor cafés waiting for crumbs. Their noisy, sociable *cheep cheep* calls are familiar wherever they are found.

Cool Facts

House Sparrows take frequent dust baths, throwing loose soil and dust over their feathers as if bathing with water. Each one may defend a good dust-bathing spot against other sparrows.

Backyard Tips

House Sparrows are not native and can be a problem when they take over the nest sites of native species. They are frequent visitors to backyard feeders, where they eat most kinds of birdseed.

The Cornell Lab of Ornithology is a world leader in advancing the understanding and protection of birds. Every day, the Cornell Lab shares the joy and science of birds—bringing people of all walks of life together to learn about birds and contribute to scientific discovery and conservation.

SCIENCE. In the quest to understand nature, scientists and students at the Cornell Lab reveal new insights about birds, wildlife, and the ecosystems we all depend on for a healthy planet.

LIFELONG LEARNING. The Cornell Lab inspires people of all ages to explore the world of birds—and trains the next generation of conservation leaders. Tell a teacher about the BirdSleuth K–12 curriculum, delve into the online Cornell Lab Bird Academy, or become a field biologist in your own living room with live Bird Cams.

CITIZEN SCIENCE. More than 400,000 citizen-science participants help the Cornell Lab illuminate where birds are, how they migrate, and how birds are faring through time across the globe.

TECHNOLOGY. The Lab's engineers, computer scientists, and biologists invent new ways to use digital technologies to study the natural world—whether to forecast bird migrations, reveal the movements of birds across the hemisphere, or listen to night skies filled with the sounds of birds.

CONSERVATION. Communities, nonprofits, industries, and governments trust the Cornell Lab to provide the best scientific information for conservation decisions and action.

If you love birds and want to help, join more than 100,000 people who support the nonprofit Cornell Lab of Ornithology. As a member, you'll receive the Lab's beautiful and insightful quarterly magazine, *Living Bird*. Visit *birds.cornell.edu.*

EDITORS

Hugh Powell is the senior science editor at the Cornell Lab of Ornithology, where he writes and edits for *Living Bird* magazine and the Lab's All About Birds website and species guide. He has written about ecology, evolution, conservation, and ocean science in Hawaii, Peru, Iceland, Australia, and Antarctica for outlets including Smithsonian, Slate, and the Woods Hole Oceanographic Institution. For many years he was a field researcher in Georgia, Idaho, Montana, and Panama. Hugh lives in Williamstown, Massachusetts.

Brian Scott Sockin has authored eight books, including the Cornell Lab Publishing Group's children's picture book *Am I Like You?* and the Storytelling World Awards honor book, *C.A.R.E. Treasury of Children's Folklore*. Brian has a B.A. in psychology from Binghamton University and an M.B.A. from the Wharton School of Business. He is CEO of the Cornell Lab Publishing Group, which has afforded him a rare opportunity to pair his passion for nature and writing with his business career. Brian has worked intimately with the Cornell Lab of Ornithology for many years on numerous education and publishing initiatives, including the *wildbirdclub.com* family website. Brian is a native of upstate New York and now lives in Cary, North Carolina, with his family.

Laura Erickson has been a scientist, teacher, writer, wildlife rehabilitator, blogger, public speaker, photographer, and science editor at the Cornell Lab of Ornithology. She has written eight books about birds, including the Cornell Lab Publishing Group's children's picture book *Am I Like You?*, *The Bird Watching Answer Book*, and the *National Geographic Pocket Guide to Birds of North America*. Laura is a National Outdoor Book Award winner and a columnist and contributing editor for *BirdWatching* magazine. In 2014, she was awarded the prestigious Roger Tory Peterson Award for lifetime achievement in promoting the cause of birding by the American Birding Association. Laura also writes and produces a daily radio segment about birds. Laura lives in Duluth, Minnesota.

ILLUSTRATOR

Pedro Fernandes is a freelance wildlife illustrator. Born in Lisbon, Portugal, Pedro earned a degree in earth sciences and later studied science illustration at the University of California, Santa Cruz, and at the Cornell Lab of Ornithology, where he was a

Bartels Science Illustration Intern. As a child, Pedro wanted to be a condor when he grew up. Having failed at that, he settled for becoming a wildlife illustrator. He loves watching birds, drawing birds, and going places to see birds—his pretext to explore the natural world and an endless source of amazement and discovery. Pedro lives in Morocco.

DESIGNER

Patricia Mitter is the creative director of the Cornell Lab Publishing Group. After earning her graphic design degree in Caracas, Venezuela, she moved to the United States with her husband. She then began a new career path in the world of editorial design and soon learned that her passion for nature and animals was a perfect fit. Patricia is also a photographer and lives in Durham, North Carolina.

ASSISTANT EDITORS

Kathi Borgmann, Diane Tessaglia-Hymes, and Francesca Chu.

WRITERS

Gustave Axelson, Ben Barkley, Jessie Barry, Kathi Borgmann, Martha Brown, Alice Cascorbi, Victoria Campbell, Miyoko Chu, Laura Erickson, Rusten Hogness, Andrew Johnson, Tom Johnson, Roberta Kwok, Pat Leonard, Tony Leukering, Abby McBride, Kevin McGowan, Hugh Powell, Matt Savoca, Carolyn Sedgwick, Sarah Rabkin, Marie Read, Erik Vance, and Nathaniel Young.

ACKNOWLEDGMENTS

We owe our gratitude to the photographers who generously granted permission to include their photos in this book, including members of the Cornell Lab of Ornithology's Birdshare Flickr site. Special thanks to B. N. Singh, Brian Kushner, and Ken Phenicie, Jr., for their numerous selections and/or cover shots. Many thanks to all of the photographers (see pages 192–193).

We thank the Cornell Lab of Ornithology's Birds of North America team for the use of maps in this book, as well as the content at *birdsna.org*, which provided much of the information presented on each species.

The Cornell Lab's Macaulay Library provided sounds that you can hear using the Bird QR companion app for this book.

We thank Jessie Barry, Miyoko Chu, and Mary Guthrie for their guidance throughout the preparation of this book. Special thanks to Jill Leichter and Dan Otis for their editorial help, and Bartels Science Illustration Intern Virginia Greene for the illustrations on pages 44–45.

Development of the All About Birds website was supported by the National Science Foundation under grants DRL-9618945 and DRL-0087760. The opinions expressed on the site are those of the authors and do not necessarily reflect the views of the National Science Foundation.

Red-tailed Hawk

WEBSITES

All About Birds
AllAboutBirds.org

Bird Academy
Academy.AllAboutBirds.org

Birds of North America
Birdsna.org

eBird
eBird.org

Great Backyard Bird Count
BirdCount.org

Project FeederWatch
FeederWatch.org

NestWatch
NestWatch.org

Celebrate Urban Birds
CelebrateUrbanBirds.org

Habitat Network
www.Habitat.Network

Merlin Bird ID App
Merlin.AllAboutBirds.org

A

Accipiter
  cooperii 82
  striatus 81
Agelaius phoeniceus 171
Aix sponsa 69
Anas platyrhynchos 70
Aphelocoma woodhouseii 115
Archilochus alexandri 96
Ardea
  alba 78
  herodias 77

B

Baeolophus inornatus 127
Blackbird
  Brewer's 174
  Red-winged 171
  Yellow-headed 173
Bluebird
  Mountain 140
  Western 139
Bombycilla cedrorum 147
Branta canadensis 68
Bubo virginianus 94
Bunting, Lazuli 170
Bushtit 128
Buteo
  jamaicensis 84
  lineatus 83

C

Callipepla
  californica 71
  gambelii 72
Calypte anna 97
Campylorhynchus brunneicapillus 136
Cardellina pusilla 153
Cardinal, Northern 167
Cardinalis cardinalis 167
Cathartes aura 79
Catharus guttatus 142
Certhia americana 132
Chamaea fasciata 138
Charadrius vociferus 86
Chickadee
  Black-capped 124
  Chestnut-backed 126
  Mountain 125
Chordeiles minor 95
Circus cyaneus 80
Coccothraustes vespertinus 186
Colaptes auratus 106
Collared-Dove, Eurasian 91
Columba livia 89
Contopus sordidulus 108

Coot, American 85
Cormorant, Double-crested 76
Corvus brachyrhynchos 117
Corvus corax 118
Cowbird, Brown-headed 177
Creeper, Brown 132
Crow, American 117
Cyanocitta stelleri 114

D

Dove
  Mourning 93
  White-winged 92
Duck, Wood 69

E

Egret, Great 78
Eremophila alpestris 119
Euphagus cyanocephalus 174

F

Falco sparverius 107
Finch
  Cassin's 182
  House 180
  Purple 181
Flicker, Northern 106
Flycatcher, Ash-throated 111
Fulica americana 85

G

Geothlypis trichas 149
Goldfinch
  American 185
  Lesser 184
Goose, Canada 68
Grackle
  Common 175
  Great-tailed 176
Grebe, Pied-billed 75
Grosbeak
  Black-headed 168
  Blue 169
  Evening 186
Gull
  California 88
  Ring-billed 87

H

Haemorhous
  cassinii 182
  mexicanus 180
  purpureus 181
Harrier, Northern 80
Hawk
  Cooper's 82

Red-shouldered 83
Red-tailed 84
Sharp-shinned 81
Heron, Great Blue 77
Hirundo rustica 123
Hummingbird
Anna's 97
Black-chinned 96
Broad-tailed 98
Rufous 99

I

Ixoreus naevius 144
Icterus
bullockii 179
cucullatus 178

J

Jay
Gray 113
Steller's 114
Junco, Dark-eyed 165
Junco hyemalis 165

K

Kestrel, American 107
Killdeer 86
Kingbird, Western 112
Kingfisher, Belted 100
Kinglet, Ruby-crowned 137

L

Lark, Horned 119
Larus
californicus 88
delawarensis 87

M

Magpie, Black-billed 116
Mallard 70
Meadowlark, Western 172
Megaceryle alcyon 100
Melanerpes formicivorus 101
Meleagris gallopavo 74
Melospiza
lincolnii 161
melodia 160
Melozone
crissalis 156
fusca 155
Mimus polyglottos 145
Mockingbird, Northern 145
Molothrus ater 177
Myadestes townsendi 141
Myiarchus cinerascens 111

N

Nighthawk, Common 95
Nuthatch
Pygmy 131
Red-breasted 129
White-breasted 130

O

Oriole
Bullock's 179
Hooded 178
Oreothlypis celata 148
Owl, Great Horned 94

P

Passer domesticus 187
Passerculus sandwichensis 158
Passerella iliaca 159
Passerina
amoena 170
caerulea 169
Patagioenas fasciata 90
Perisoreus canadensis 113
Petrochelidon pyrrhonota 122
Phalacrocorax auritus 76
Phasianus colchicus 73
Pheasant, Ring-necked 73
Pheucticus melanocephalus 168
Phoebe
Black 109
Say's 110
Pica hudsonia 116
Picoides
nuttallii 103
pubescens 104
villosus 105
Pigeon
Band-tailed 90
Rock 89
Pipilo maculatus 154
Piranga ludoviciana 166
Podilymbus podiceps 75
Poecile
atricapillus 124
gambeli 125
rufescens 126
Psaltriparus minimus 128

Q

Quail,
California 71
Gambel's 72
Quiscalus
mexicanus 176
quiscula 175

R
Raven, Common 118
Robin, American 143
Regulus calendula 137

S
Sapsucker, Red-naped 102
Sayornis
  nigricans 109
  saya 110
Scrub-Jay, Woodhouse's 115
Selasphorus
  platycercus 98
  rufus 99
Setophaga
  coronata 151
  petechia 150
  townsendi 152
Sialia
  currucoides 140
  mexicana 139
Sitta
  canadensis 129
  carolinensis 130
  pygmaea 131
Siskin, Pine 183
Solitaire, Townsend's 141
Sparrow
  Chipping 157
  Fox 159
  Golden-crowned 164
  Harris's 162
  House 187
  Lincoln's 161
  Savannah 158
  Song 160
  White-crowned 163
Sphyrapicus nuchalis 102
Spinus
  pinus 183
  psaltria 184
  tristis 185
Spizella passerina 157
Starling, European 146
Streptopelia decaocto 91
Sturnella neglecta 172
Sturnus vulgaris 146
Swallow
  Barn 123
  Cliff 122
  Tree 120
  Violet-green 121

T
Tachycineta
  bicolor 120

  thalassina 121
Tanager, Western 166
Thrush
  Hermit 142
  Varied 144
Thryomanes bewickii 135
Titmouse, Oak 127
Towhee
  California 156
  Canyon 155
  Spotted 154
Troglodytes
  aedon 133
  pacificus 134
Turkey, Wild 74
Turdus migratorius 143
Tyrannus verticalis 112

V
Vulture, Turkey 79

W
Waxwing, Cedar 147
Warbler
  Orange-crowned 148
  Townsend's 152
  Wilson's 153
  Yellow 150
  Yellow-rumped 151
Woodpecker
  Acorn 101
  Downy 104
  Hairy 105
  Nuttall's 103
Wood-pewee, Western 108
Wren
  Bewick's 135
  Cactus 136
  House 133
  Pacific 134
Wrentit 138

X
Xanthocephalus xanthocephalus 173

Y
Yellowthroat, Common 149

Z
Zenaida
  asiatica 92
  macroura 93
Zonotrichia
  atricapilla 164
  leucophrys 163
  querula 162